Judges
The Perils of Possession

Pardes | פרדס
Institute of Jewish Studies

מגיד
MAGGID

Michael Hattin

Judges

The Perils of Possession

Pardes Institute of Jewish Studies
Maggid Books

Judges
The Perils of Possession

First Edition, 2020

Maggid Books
An imprint of Koren Publishers Jerusalem Ltd.

POB 8531, New Milford, CT 06776-8531, USA
& POB 4044, Jerusalem 9104001, Israel
www.maggidbooks.com

The publication of this book was made possible
through the generous support of *The Jewish Book Trust*.

ISBN 978-1-59264-523-7, *hardcover*

A CIP catalogue record for this title is
available from the British Library

Printed and bound in the United States

In loving memory of Irving and Beatrice Stone,
who dedicated their lives to the
advancement of Jewish education.
We are proud and honored to continue in their legacy.

Their Children, Grandchildren, and Great-Grandchildren
Jerusalem, Israel
Cleveland, Ohio USA

In honor of Faygie and Phil Schwartz
whose love of learning sets the bar
for their children, grandchildren, and great-grandchildren

Contents

Preface

The book of Judges is an integral part of our story as a people. It describes the struggles of the tribes of Israel to overcome their external enemies as well as their internal differences as they are forged into the nation of Israel in its land. It highlights their formidable transition from a nomadic, shepherding life to one settled and agrarian. It introduces us to the tribes' colossal challenge of how to respond to pervasive moral and cultural values, incompatible with our mission as a people. As such, it is a book of great relevance.

Like many of our other biblical texts that have been adopted by more than half of the world as inspiration for their own teachings, the book of Judges is known to most of us only in outline and only in translation. It is a tragic irony of our long and tumultuous history that the majority of the "people of the Book" have never read it. In order to remedy the situation, we would need to delve deeply into the original Hebrew text along with its three thousand years of accumulated commentary. Most of us, given the exigencies of the hour, are not likely to do so.

This volume is an attempt to introduce readers to the contents of the book of Judges without sacrificing breadth or depth. The touchstone of our biblical text tradition is *careful* reading, which is unlike other reading. Other reading tends to be information-driven, with the text simply a medium for conveying the information. Having attained the data, we can discard the text. In Jewish text study, however, the words themselves and even their very letters have intrinsic value. Every word is precious and every turn of phrase laden. Some of us refer to this phenomenon as the "divinity of the text" – the idea that the text of the Tanakh was inspired by God.

This approach regards the text of the Tanakh reverentially. Rather than a cursory reading to extract the information, the text of the Tanakh deserves profound study in order to ascertain the deeper meaning. On a practical level, this means that we are concerned not only with the basic message of the story, but also with the actual words and syntax of the text. Vocabulary, grammar, and literary structure are critical areas of investigation; themes, historical context, and realia are essential topics of enquiry. In Jewish text study, it is never enough just to get the general idea; one has to master the material. In Jewish text study, a single reading is insufficient; with each additional reading we gain more insights. In Jewish text study, a difficult passage is never denigrated or dismissed; it is studied again and again with the hope that we might yet understand it.

Considered from this perspective, studying the Tanakh might seem an overwhelming undertaking, and it is. Fortunately, though, we are not the first ones to read the Tanakh or to contemplate our own story within it. We are only a small part of a much longer continuum that extends back thousands of years. While we are called upon to extract fresh relevance and insight from the timeless words, we do not labor alone. We have at our disposal the vast accumulation of interpretive material that spans much of recorded history and much of the globe. This is both humbling and exhilarating.

I have been blessed to teach at the Pardes Institute of Jewish Studies in Jerusalem for almost twenty years. During that time, I have had the opportunity to learn the book of Judges with my students on a number of occasions. Each study has raised many perceptive questions and spurred much reflection. I am indebted to my students for their enquiries, their insights, and their never-ending demand to understand the text more deeply.

Much of the preliminary material for this study was prepared for an online course of Yeshivat Har Etzion's Israel Koschitzky Virtual Beit Midrash. The Yeshiva has always held a special place in my heart for its rigorous as well as thoughtful approach to the study of Jewish texts, whether Talmud, Halakha, or Tanakh. The VBM is an innovative institution that has pioneered serious online learning without forfeiting complexity and nuance. My initial course for the VBM on the book of Judges was never finished. I am pleased to finally present the completed study and am grateful to the VBM for their magnanimity of spirit in allowing me to publish the material in book form. I would also like to thank the many readers over the years who have been patiently waiting to find out what happened to Samson!

The dedicated team at Maggid Books are paragons of professionalism and skill; many thanks to Rachelle Emanuel, Carolyn Budow Ben-David, Ita Olesker, Tani Bayer, and Yehudit Singer-Freud. Rabbi Reuven Ziegler has been especially helpful during the course of this project. Special thanks are due to Mr. Matthew Miller, of Koren Publishers, for his foresight and for his unswerving dedication to the monumental project of making the Hebrew Bible and its interpretation available to intelligent and devoted English-speaking readers.

Finally, my profoundest thanks to my dear family – my wife Rivka, and my children Elchanan and Shvut, Akiva, Hillel, Leeba, and Miriam. Without your encouragement and patience, I would not have been able to complete this project. You are my source of strength and my safe harbor.

I would like to dedicate this work in memory of my dear parents Cecille and Bernard Hattin, שרה בת שמואל לייב and בעשא דב בן ר' אהרן, who were always supportive of my endeavors and proud of my accomplishments. As well, I remember fondly my dear sister Lisa, לאה בת בעשא דב ושרה, whose untimely passing cut short a life of kindness, generosity, and dedication to family, community, and Torah observance. May all their souls be secure in the bond of life.

כי אין מלה בלשוני הן ה' ידעת כלה

Michael Hattin
Alon Shevut
2020

❦ ❦ ❦

The author gratefully acknowledges the following people, whose generosity helped make this project possible:

In fond memory of Rav Daniel Beller, z"l, our dear and much-missed teacher, friend, and rabbi, who showed us through his midot and his teaching, the true meaning of the love of Torah.

Andrew and Ilana Album, Raanana, Israel

With gratitude to Rabbi Michael Hattin, our teacher and role model of derech Hashem, as we dedicate this book in loving memory to our parents and grandparents as aliyot for their neshamot:

Sybil bat Avrum   *Asher ben Yaacov*
Bella bat Aaron   *Shmuel ben Max*
Sarah bat Louis   *Avrum ben Isidor*
Rochel bat Yisroel Yehudah   *Aaron ben Dov Laib*

Michael and Carol Dean

Introduction

The book of Judges follows the book of Joshua seamlessly. In Joshua, the people of Israel traversed the Jordan River, entered the land, and began the process of conquering it. This involved major battles against coalitions of Canaanite kings, each of whom ruled over a petty city-state. First, the southern hill country was conquered, followed by the northern part of the country. Only then, did the settlement of the land begin in earnest.

While the actual warfare in the book of Joshua lasted for a relatively short time, settling the land took centuries. Only the initial stages are described in the book of Joshua – the allotment of territory to the tribes of Israel and their first halting steps in clearing the land and cultivating its slopes. Joshua died with much of the task incomplete.

The book of Judges begins where the book of Joshua ends. With the aged leader no more, the tribes of Israel naturally turn inwards, more concerned with their own fate than with a larger vision of the people as a whole. Each tribe must fend for itself; some are more successful in wresting their territory from the grip of the Canaanites, and some less. Joshua may have smashed the Canaanite military coalitions, but the Canaanite people and their culture remained largely intact. When the tribes of Israel fall prey to Canaanite idolatry and its associated values, retribution is swift and harsh. It takes the form of non-Israelite oppressors, regional despots, who overrun one or more tribes and impose tyranny.

It is against this backdrop that the book of Judges begins. While the book describes a series of tribal leaders that arise to lead the tribes to victory over their oppressors, it is unclear whether the events are recorded in exact chronological order. Did one judge follow another in quick succession, or could some of them have ruled concurrently in different regions of the country, with others appearing only after a lapse of time? Does the book of Judges offer us a comprehensive record of *every* judge who was active during this pivotal period of Israelite history, or only of the predominant ones? Might there have been others whose story is not told in our book?

The medieval commentaries, basing themselves mainly on earlier rabbinic traditions, were generally of the opinion that the judges followed one after another in quick succession and never overlapped. The straightforward reading of the text supports this view. Thus, for example, we read that Otniel brought stability for forty years and afterwards died. The text then says, "The people of Israel continued to do evil in God's eyes" (3:12), implying that their regression took place after the death of Otniel. This is even more explicit after the death of Ehud, where the verse reports, "The people of Israel continued to do evil in God's eyes, and Ehud was dead" (4:1). After Abimelech's demise, the verse states, "After Abimelech, Tola son of Pua arose to save Israel" (10:1), and so too concerning Ya'ir who followed Tola (10:3), Ibzan who followed Yiftah (12:8), Elon who followed Ibzan (12:11), and Abdon who followed Elon (12:13). These verses certainly indicate a sequence of judges who did not overlap, but it is still possible that some time elapsed between the death of one and the ascent of another. Tola, for instance, was the judge who arose after Abimelech, but perhaps some time passed between Abimelech's demise and Tola's becoming judge.

In contrast to the above judges, Deborah's death is never reported, and although forty years of stability are mentioned, this is followed by a non-committal formulation: "The people of Israel did evil in God's eyes" (6:1). Might this imply that the said evil was perpetrated while Deborah was still alive, perhaps in another region of the country? Samson's birth is introduced against the backdrop of Philistine oppression that extended for forty years after Abdon's death (13:1), so he certainly did not follow Abdon immediately. Nor is it clear that there was no substantial time lapse between Abdon's death and the beginning of the Philistine tyranny. Most glaringly, the verse states that Deborah arose when the people of Israel did evil after the death of Ehud (4:1) and after the forty years of stability that he bestowed (3:30). This would imply that there was no time for another judge between Ehud and Deborah. However, between those two verses the text states, "After him was Shamgar son of Anat... he too saved Israel" (3:31)! Perhaps we should conclude that while many judges did immediately follow on the heels of the judge who preceded them, this was not always the case. What is clear from the text is that the events of the book unfold over the course of approximately three to four centuries. This is in contrast to the book of Joshua that covers a relatively short time span of a few decades.

Structurally, the book of Judges can be divided into three sections. The first, comprising the opening two chapters, offers us an introduction to the story. We are reminded of Joshua's demise (already reported at the end of his book) and told about the challenges facing the tribes of Israel: Much of the land remains unconquered and many of the tribes demonstrate little will to claim their territory. We are then introduced to the pattern of Israelite history during this period – the story of the judges plays itself out as a series of repetitive cycles. In each cycle, the tribes stray from God by failing to uproot Canaanite settlement and consequently embracing Canaanite idolatry, they suffer oppression and then cry out to God for rescue. God relents and inspires a charismatic character, the judge, who rises from obscurity to lead the tribes of Israel in battle against their foes. This judge triumphs, restores some semblance of stability, and leads the people for a number of years. After the judge's demise, however, his hard-won accomplishments are forgotten, and once again the people stray from God. The cycle then repeats itself.

The second section of the book is the actual story of the judges and stretches from chapter 3 until the end of chapter 16. In this section, we encounter thirteen named leaders who are designated as judges, but not all of them receive equal treatment in the text. The exploits of some are described at length, while for others, only a brief mention is provided. Almost all of them do perform what might be expected from a judge – to save the tribes of Israel from harm. However, at least one of them does no such thing. Abimelech son of Gideon, who leads for a period of only three years, is entirely occupied with imposing his ruthless rule over the people that he is charged with saving. He is the only leader who seizes power after his father's death, thus introducing the pitfalls of hereditary rule. During his short tenure, there are no foreign oppressors that he defeats. In fact, *he* is the oppressor. His bloody career is so at odds with every other leader in the book that it is best to view him as an anti-judge. That being the case, it is more accurate to speak of twelve judges and one anti-judge.

Working with a total of twelve functional judges, we can immediately recognize the implications. In the Tanakh, numbers have significance, not only in an esoteric and mystical sense, but also as literary cues. For example, the number three, especially a duration of three days, highlights introspection and anticipation. The number seven symbolizes perfection and wholeness, such as in the days of creation or the branches of the Menora. The number ten represents a complete unit, as it does for us to this day. There are ten utterances at Sinai, not because God has no more to say, but rather because the list provides a full set of basic guiding principles. The number twelve is not about the months of the year (after all, in the lunar-solar calendar of Jewish tradition, sometimes there are thirteen months in a year), but about the twelve tribes of Israel. The eponymous twelve tribes are first introduced in Genesis 30; from then on, the people of Israel are typically enumerated or described as the Twelve Tribes.[1]

The reason why there are twelve judges, and no more or less, is precisely because there are twelve tribes. While most, but not all, of the tribes are represented by at least one judge, the point is not to be comprehensive in terms of their tribal identity but rather to indicate to the reader that this is a book about the tribes, not about the *nation* of Israel. In other words, during the period of the judges, tribalism reigns. Its effects are acutely felt at every point in the book. When a tribe is oppressed, they will usually have to deal with the threat on their own. Rarely do other tribes come to the aid of their compatriots, unless they themselves are also threatened. Rarely does a judge exercise any authority over, or rescue, any tribe but his own. This naturally leads to

---

1. As in, for instance, Genesis 49:28.

an important conclusion about the judges in the book – unlike Moses or Joshua, they are regional, rather than national leaders.

With this startling insight, it is now possible to appreciate why some judges are treated at length, while others receive only a few lines of text. We are familiar with the names Ehud, Deborah, Gideon, Yiftah, and Samson because the book tells us about them in a fair amount of detail. But how many of us recognize by name Otniel, Shamgar, Tola, Ya'ir, Ibzan, Elon or Abdon? How many of us remember significant details of their exploits? This is in spite of the fact that these seven "minor" judges actually outnumber the main five mentioned above. From this we may deduce that the point of the narrative is not to comprehensively relate the story of all of Israel's leaders over the course of three hundred or four hundred years, but rather to indicate that there were twelve of them, neither more nor less, because their story is the story of the tribes. In other words, it may very well be the case that many of these minor judges are included not because their exploits were pivotal or their lives memorable, but rather because we need a total of exactly twelve judges in order to construct a framework that is intended to highlight the theme of tribalism! While all twelve, without a doubt, were active during the period of Israelite history under discussion, the literary decision to include them all as part of a unified story is an artifice.

What follows from this premise is that we can probably assume that there were other judges during this period of Israelite history, perhaps many more than twelve. A case in point is the mysterious Bedan (I Sam. 12:11), whom Samuel mentions in his list of saviors of Israel. Surveying the period of the judges that preceded him, Samuel recalls the great oppressor Sisera, the menacing Philistines, and the aggressive Moabites. When the people cried out to God and pledged their renewed allegiance to Him, He sent "Yerubaal and Bedan, Yiftah and Samuel, and He saved you from your enemies round about, and you dwelt in security." While Yerubaal and Yiftah are familiar figures from the book of Judges, Bedan is not. Although rabbinic tradition and classical commentaries identify Bedan as Samson who hailed from the tribe of Dan (interpreting the name Bedan as "a son of the tribe of Dan"), it is much easier to assume that Bedan was a judge active sometime between Gideon and Yiftah, who is nowhere mentioned in the book of Judges and about whom we know nothing else.[2] To summarize, the point of our book is not to list all of the judges that ever lived, but rather to describe what the era of the judges was like: It was a tumultuous period, when the people of Israel were divided, discordant and factious. They were not united as a nation; they were not bonded as a polis. Every tribe and every clan within a tribe put its interests first. This is the essence of the "twelve judges" motif.

The third and final section of the book, comprising chapters 17–21, is the most disturbing. In this unit, no judge is mentioned. The two episodes in this final section present a leaderless Israel, racked by division and at the nadir of its moral decline. It is here that we confront the heart of darkness in the form of idolatry, rape, and murder. By the time the book concludes, we wonder how it was that the people of Israel reached such a low point. Our only consolation at the end is the anticipation of what follows the book of Judges – the book of Samuel with its cast of more positive and redeeming *national* leaders: Samuel, Saul, and David.

While the final chapters clearly end on a dismal note, we may be surprised to discover that the entire trajectory of the book actually anticipates this ending. This is because the middle section that tells the story of the twelve (or thirteen) judges does not simply describe them as undifferentiated, amorphous, and formulaic protagonists, but makes clear to the careful reader that their individual careers follow a declining arc. That is to say, the earlier judges are of a higher caliber than the later ones. Otniel, Ehud, and Deborah are leaders above reproach, who betray no obvious character defects or lapses of faith in God. They are successful on the battlefield and continue to lead nobly once they have left it. When the time comes for them to pass on, they do so gracefully. Gideon is less than an ideal judge – he is wracked both by self-doubt as well as doubts concerning God's support. In the end, he unwittingly writes for himself an infamous epitaph of Baal worship. When he is followed by his unscrupulous son Abimelech, we already know what to

---

2. The name Bedan also occurs in I Chronicles 7:17, where he is identified as an obscure descendant of Menashe. While there is no suggestion that the Bedan of Samuel is the Bedan of Chronicles, the point is that the name need not be explained as a wordplay indicating his tribe of origin.

expect. The final cohort of judges, represented by Yiftah and Samson, are deeply flawed leaders who save their tribes, but also unleash great destruction in their wake.

We may therefore divide the middle section of the book, chapters 3–16, into three smaller units: chapters 3–5 – Ehud and Deborah, chapters 6–10 – Gideon (and Abimelech), and chapters 11–16 – Yiftah and Samson. It should be readily apparent that the minor judges in the book can be understood to serve as "tribal fillers" for these others. The tripartite subdivision of the middle section is marked by a refrain, with variations, occurring as the introduction to each part in turn. Its general formula is:

> God said to Israel, "I took you out of Egypt, brought you to this land and defeated your enemies for you. I enjoined upon you not to worship the idols of these peoples or adopt their gods, but you did not listen to My voice!" (see Judges 2:1, 6:8–10, 10:11–14)

A fundamental truth about the judges and their epoch emerges from this analysis: Any particular judge is only as good as the people that he leads. He rarely offers a full-scale corrective, but only a temporary reprieve until the next cycle. He is the mirror image of his supporters. As the book progresses and the people of Israel descend deeper and deeper into idolatry and immorality, their decline is reflected in the leader that emerges to save them. For this reason, at the very end, *no* leader will emerge. The ancient rabbis expressed this most acerbically when they said:

> Yiftah in his generation is to be regarded as Samuel in his generation. This comes to teach you that even the most insubstantial of men who is appointed as a leader of the people must be regarded as the greatest of leaders. (Rosh HaShana 25b)

The above discussion is summarized in outline form on the following pages. The numbers in the left margin, from 1–21, correspond to the chapters of the book. A line of three asterisks indicates the basic breakdown of the book into three main sections. A Roman numeral introduces each judge in turn, who is followed by his tribal affiliation if indicated by the text. Next, the oppressor whom the judge must defeat is mentioned, and within the square brackets after the tyrant's name are two numbers. The first of these numbers refers to the number of years that the tribe suffers at the hands of the foe before the appearance of the judge. The second number indicates the total number of years that the judge leads the people. A question mark in place of a number means that the text does not report the data. (It is not entirely clear whether the years of oppression should be counted as part of the total career of the judge or not.) Finally, judges with an asterisk before their name are to be regarded as "major" judges, whose exploits are given in detail. Judges without an asterisk are "minor" judges whose entire careers are spelled out in one to three verses. The section of the judges is further broken down into three smaller units, as we have pointed out, with each one introduced by a verse of infamy.

OUTLINE OF THE BOOK OF JUDGES

1. Israelite tribes war with Canaanites: some successes and many failures.

   A messenger of God ascended from Gilgal to those that wept. He said, "I took you out of Egypt and brought you to the land that I swore to give to your ancestors. I said, 'I will never abrogate My covenant with you. As for you, make no covenants with the inhabitants of this land – break down their altars!' But you did not listen to Me. What have you done?" (2:1–2)

2. The cycle: idolatry → oppression → outcry → saving judge → stability/ death of judge → idolatry…

*   *   *

First Cycle – Judges above Reproach

3. (I) **Otniel ben Kenaz of Judah** vs. Kushan Rishatayim of Aram Naharayim [8/40]

(II) *Ehud ben Gera of Benjamin vs. Eglon king of Moab [18/80]

(III) Shamgar ben Anat of ? vs. Philistines [?/?]

4–5. (IV) *Deborah wife of Lapidot of Ephraim (?) and Barak ben Abinoam of Naphtali vs. Yavin king of Canaan and Sisera [20/40]

God sent a prophet to Israel. He said to them: "Thus says God the Lord of Israel, 'I took you out of Egypt and brought you forth from the house of bondage. I saved you from the clutches of Egypt and from the clutches of all of your oppressors. I drove them out from before you and I gave you their land. I said to you: "I am God your Lord; do not revere the gods of the Amorites in whose land you dwell." But you did not listen to Me!'" (6:8–10)

Second Cycle – Judges of Little Faith

6–8. (V) *Gideon ben Yoash of Menashe vs. Midian, Amalek, Bnei Kedem [7/40]

9. (Va) Abimelech ben Gideon [3]

10. (VI) Tola ben Pua ben Dodo of Issachar [23]

(VII) Ya'ir HaGiladi of Menashe [22]

God said to Israel, "Did I not save you from Egypt and from the Amorites, from the Ammonites, and from the Philistines? The Sidonites, Amalek, and Maon oppressed you, and you cried out to Me and I saved you from their clutches. But you have abandoned Me and served other gods. Therefore, I will save you no more. Go and cry out to the gods whom you have chosen – let them save you in your time of travail!" (10:11–14)

Final Cycle – Judges of Disrepute

11–12. (VIII) *Yiftah HaGiladi of Menashe vs. King of Ammon (and Ephraim) [18/6]

(IX) Ibzan of Beit Lehem (Zebulun?) [7]

(X) Elon of Zebulun [10]

(XI) Abdon ben Hillel of Piraton (Ephraim) [8]

13–16. (XII) *Samson ben Manoah of Dan vs. Philistines [40/20]

* * *

17–18. Idol of Micah

19–21. Concubine at Giva

This modest study assumes only a basic familiarity with the book of Judges. The reader who would like to get maximum benefit is highly advised to read the primary material of the book of Judges in tandem with this volume. I have supplemented the text with many informative footnotes that substantially expand on the discussion and offer the reader additional sources to ponder. I recommend consulting the footnotes for more information and analysis. Except when otherwise noted, all translations of verses and commentaries that appear in this book are mine alone.

Judges 1:1–36

Israel's Tragic Lethargy

> It came to pass after the death of Joshua, that the people of
> Israel enquired of God saying, "Who shall go up for us first to
> do battle against the Canaanites?" God said, "Judah shall go up,
> for behold I have given the land into his hands." Judah said to
> Simeon his brother, "Go up with me to secure my lot and we will
> fight [together] against the Canaanites, and then I will go with
> you to secure your lot." So Simeon accompanied him. (1:1–3)

Thus begins the book of Judges, with a description of the battles of the
tribe of Judah. The opening phrase of the book is reminiscent of the
beginning of the book of Joshua: "It came to pass after the death of
Moses the servant of God, that God said to Joshua son of Nun, Moses's
loyal servant..." (Josh. 1:1). We will have many occasions to compare
and contrast the book of Judges with the book of Joshua, and we will
discover that while the two books have much in common and sometimes overlap, they are fundamentally different in theme and outlook.

JOSHUA'S ACCOMPLISHMENTS

The book of Joshua described the Israelites' entry into the land of Canaan.
Some forty years after the exodus from Egypt, the people traversed the
Jordan River under the able leadership of Joshua. Moses the lawgiver,

who had taken them out of Egypt, brought them to Sinai to receive the Torah, and guided them during the entire period of their sojourn in the wilderness, died at the plains of Moab on the Jordan's eastern banks. Before his demise, at God's behest, he appointed a successor to lead the people into the new land, a capable teacher and gifted warrior by the name of Joshua. And Joshua was successful. Under his rule, the tribes of Israel united to battle the Canaanite confederacies, and they achieved impressive results. By the time Joshua died, the major military alliances of the Canaanites had been defeated and the land had been allocated to the Israelite tribes.

However, the defeat of the armies of the chief Canaanite city-states and the distribution of their lands did not signify the end of the conflict. The land was still largely unsettled, and Israel had yet to set down deep and durable roots. Obviously, it was not sufficient to defeat the Canaanites on the battlefield, a process that did not take more than a few years. In order to claim the land as their own, the people of Israel had to make it theirs by clearing its forests, terracing and cultivating its rocky slopes, and building their towns and cities, all the while avoiding the pervasive charms of Canaanite polytheism. The task of settlement required a much more ambitious timeframe than was available to Joshua, lasting many decades if not centuries. The associated mandate of extirpating all indigenous traces of idolatry could not possibly be completed overnight. Clearly then, the colossal undertaking could not be accomplished during Joshua's lifetime, lengthy though it was. God had indicated as much toward the end of Joshua's life: "Joshua was old, he had lived many days, and God said to him, 'You are now old and have lived many days, and so much of the land still remains to be possessed'" (Josh. 13:1). In fact, the matter had been spelled out many decades earlier in the Torah itself, when God addressed the people of Israel as they stood at Mount Sinai in the immediate aftermath of the revelation:

> I shall send My dread before you to rout all of the nations that you shall encounter, and all of your enemies shall turn their backs [in flight] from you. I shall send before you the hornet to drive out the Hivite, Canaanite, and Hittite from before you. *But I will not drive them out before you in a single year, for then*

the land will become desolate and the beasts of the field will mul-
tiply against you. Rather, I will drive them out very slowly, until
you increase and inherit the land. I shall establish your borders
from the Sea of Reeds until the Sea of the Philistines, and from
the wilderness until the river [Euphrates], for I shall give into
your hand the inhabitants of the land, and I shall drive them
out from before you. You shall not establish a covenant with
them or with their gods. Let them not dwell in your land, lest
they cause you to transgress against Me, for if you serve their
gods you shall become ensnared. (Ex. 23:27–31)

UNDERSTANDING THE NATURE OF MILITARY VICTORY

Thus, when the book of Judges begins, the land still remains "unconquered." The defeat of the Canaanite confederacies and their combined
armies in the time of Joshua may have removed the immediate existential
threat from the tribes of Israel, but the tribes still had to take possession
of their territories, and the local military menaces still had to be overcome. It is the story of that possession, its short-lived triumphs, and its
lengthy setbacks that constitutes the bulk of our book.

We may illustrate the distinction between military victory versus
effective and permanent possession with a modern, if somewhat imper-
fect, example. In the Six Day War of June 1967, the beleaguered and out-
gunned State of Israel achieved a crushing victory over its powerful Arab
foes, who had initiated the conflict with the express goal of destroying
it. Even as Egypt massed its forces in the Sinai Peninsula and closed the
Straits of Tiran to Israeli shipping, a *causus belli* by any objective definition, Israel waited for clarifications from the superpowers. As the drums
of war beat ever more feverishly in Arab capitals, Israel launched a surprise attack on the enemy airfields and destroyed their jets on the ground.
Syrian forces were repelled from the Golan Heights and the Jordanian
legions were forced to relinquish the ancient city of Jerusalem. By the
end of the war, Israel had not only defeated the military alliance consisting of Egypt, Jordan, Syria, and their allies, but had also succeeded in
conquering large tracts of enemy territory that had not been assigned
to it according to the Partition Plan of 1947. In the aftermath of the war,
the Arab world convened at Khartoum to unequivocally reject Israeli

overtures to return the conquered territories in exchange for peace,[1] and so the land remained in Israeli hands. However, the State of Israel hesitated to formally annex it, and so that acquisition of land was never followed up by a determined program of possession, and hence was never completed. As a result, decades after that conflict, the State of Israel still finds itself in the precarious and unenviable position of attempting to secure its borders, with no foreseeable end in sight. While we may continue to debate the merits of that war and its consequences, for our purposes one point is clear: Even an astounding military victory is not sufficient to guarantee possession of territory unless victories on the battlefield are resolutely followed by settlement.

TRIBES VS. A NATION

Because the conflicts recounted in the book of Judges are so very different from the battles waged in the book of Joshua – the latter consisting of a short series of intense battles, the former the much longer process of possession – the makeup of the respective fighting forces are also markedly different. Joshua's battles were undertaken as a national enterprise by all of the tribes together. Even the tribes that dwelt east of the Jordan had sent their complement of troops to serve under his command (see Josh. 1:12–18). In contrast, the battles in the book of Judges are primarily regional in scope and are waged by each tribe on its own to secure its land.

The opening of our book, therefore, while stylistically recalling the introductory phrases of the book of Joshua, highlights the glaring distinctions by focusing on the tribes of Judah and Simeon. For now there is no national leader, no national mission, and no corresponding national vision. Each tribe must act on its own to take possession of its portion. While a group of tribes sometimes collaborates, as do Judah and Simeon in our chapter, they more often labor alone. Perhaps this explains the inclusion of verses 9–15 that describe the conquest of the southern hill country in the environs of Hebron by Otniel son of Kenaz, kinsman of Caleb. The passage is almost an exact repetition of Joshua 15:13–19, and chronologically it belongs there since the conquest of Kiryat

---

1. See Michael B. Oren, *Six Days of War* (New York: Oxford University Press, 2002) for a complete account.

Sefer took place while Joshua was still alive. However, it is repeated here in a different tone. Whereas the passage in the book of Joshua spoke of Caleb and Otniel fulfilling their part of the national mission under the watchful gaze of the national leader, our section recasts those events in much more tribal terms. The accomplishments of Caleb and Otniel are understood here as belonging exclusively to the tribe of Judah rather than to the people of Israel as a whole. Tribal securing of territory, with its inescapable corollary of narrower, more sectarian concerns, engenders the book's greatest challenges and yields very unsatisfactory results.

CLOSENESS VS. DISTANCE

Another important difference between the opening lines of the two books is that the book of Joshua immediately introduced us to God's involvement in the story: "It came to pass after the death of Moses the servant of God, that God said to Joshua son of Nun, Moses's loyal servant...." While it is true that God's involvement became less overt as the book of Joshua progressed, our book already begins from a point of divine obscurity. Here, there is no prophet who directly communicates God's word to the people. God has not appointed an individual who is inspired to speak on His behalf. Instead, the people must "enquire" of Him, an expression that indicates consultation using the stones of the golden breastplate of the high priest. According to the provisions of the book of Numbers 27:15–23, when Joshua succeeds his mentor Moses as leader, he is to secure God's response to matters of national significance through the *urim* and *tumim* – mysterious names of God placed within the folds of the breastplate and its gemstones. The Torah states:

> He shall stand before Elazar the priest who shall ask for him before God by the law of the *urim*. In accordance with it they shall go out [to battle] and in accordance with it they shall come in [from battle], he and all of the people of Israel with him and all of the congregation. (Num. 27:21)

These twelve stones were engraved with the names of the tribes of Israel, and talmudic tradition relates that in response to the enquiry of a national leader, some of the letters would light up or otherwise stand

5

out. The high priest would then connect the highlighted letters into coherent words through divine inspiration.[2]

While Joshua surely made use of this method or something like it (see, for instance, Josh. 7:14–18), it was not the exclusive mode of communication between him and the deity. On many occasions, God spoke to Joshua directly, in a manner that did not seem categorically different from His conversations with Moses. While it is true that as the book of Joshua unfolded, God's involvement became less manifest,[3] this never implied His indifference. On the contrary, it pointed to the positive potential inherent in human decision-making that can only come to the fore when God recedes. God's immediacy was palpable for as long as Joshua and the elders that succeeded him served as the people's leaders, and nothing in the book suggested otherwise.

In contrast, as the book of Judges opens, God's response is secured exclusively through the *urim* and *tumim*, and this now points to more ominous prospects. The people enquire and the deity responds, but without the assurance of a prophet who could have unequivocally conveyed God's message to the people. This implies that the distance between God and the people has increased, and therefore their lines of communication are less direct. The unfolding narratives bear this out, forcefully describing the extent of the increasing estrangement.

JUDAH'S SUCCESS VS. THE OTHER TRIBES

As far as the mandate to take hold of the land is concerned, however, the conduct of the tribe of Judah is certainly above reproach. They do not hesitate to take possession of their portion of territory, dislodging the king of Bezek and his hordes (1:5), the inhabitants of Jerusalem (1:8), the Canaanites who dwelt in the Negev and the coastal lowlands (1:9), as well as the people of Hebron in the hill country (1:10). While some of the battles recorded in our chapter are out of place chronologically and properly belong to the chapters which describe the conquest in the book of Joshua,[4]

---

2. See Yoma 73a–b for a more detailed description of the mechanism of enquiry.
3. See Michael Hattin, *Joshua: The Challenge of the Promised Land* (Jerusalem: Maggid Books, 2014), 159–64, for an exhaustive treatment of this point.
4. See Radak on Joshua 1:8.

they are recorded here in order to emphasize Judah's efforts and the extent of the tribe's successes. Significantly, Judah's conquests conclude with a statement of divine approval, namely that "God was with Judah, and they possessed the hill country, but they were not able to possess the dwellers of the valley for they had chariots of iron" (1:19). Whatever lands Judah was capable of conquering and settling, they did so. Only the more heavily populated valleys, where the Canaanites had menacing chariots of iron that Judah could not defeat in battle, remained beyond their reach.

The picture was more complicated for the other tribes. Ambitious Joseph, composed of the fraternal tribes of Ephraim and Menashe and constituting, along with Judah, the nation's political, military, and cultural core, also showed initiative and enjoyed God's assistance in their conquest of Beit El (1:22), but many important parts of his territory remained in Canaanite hands. As for most of the other tribes, they were lax in their drive to settle the land:

> Menashe did not possess Beit She'an and its towns, Ta'anakh and its towns... so that the Canaanites still desired to live in those lands. Though Israel waxed strong and placed tribute upon them, they did not dispossess them.... Ephraim did not drive out the Canaanites who dwelt in Gezer, so that the Canaanites in Gezer dwelt in their midst. Zebulun did not drive out the inhabitants of Kitron and Nahalol, so that the Canaanites dwelt in their midst and paid tribute. Asher did not drive out the inhabitants of Akko... so that the tribe of Asher dwelt among the Canaanites who inhabited the land, for they did not dispossess them. Naphtali did not drive out the inhabitants of Beit Shemesh.... The Amorites forced the tribe of Dan into the hill country, for they did not allow them to descend into the valley. (1:27–34)

As the above text makes abundantly clear, the majority of the tribes did not oust the Canaanites and were content to allow them to remain. For some of the tribes, the situation was more dire. The tribe of Asher, for example, assigned the prosperous and densely settled region of the Phoenician coast, was unable to overcome the indigenous peoples at all, and in the end dwelt among *them*. The tribe of Dan was prevented from achieving any foothold in the valleys of the Sharon plain, and instead had to stake out new territories in the hill country. Most of the tribes, then, were quickly exhausted by the struggle to drive out the Canaanites and to settle their land, and opted instead for the more slothful approach of "containment." The Canaanites could be subjugated and forced to pay tribute. Was it really necessary to entirely dislodge them? But in failing to drive out the Canaanites, the tribes of Israel unleashed a dynamic that was to have far-reaching and destructive consequences.

ALLOWING THE CANAANITES AND THEIR MORAL SYSTEM TO REMAIN

The Torah, especially in the book of Deuteronomy, speaks repeatedly of the necessity to drive out the Canaanites. The confrontation with the Canaanite threat was not perceived by the Torah to be a clash of race, ethnicity, or historical narrative, but rather of values. The polytheistic Canaanites, like other peoples of the ancient Near East, championed a pantheon of gods that were shallow, hedonistic, and often cruel. Those gods fostered a corresponding morality that was relativistic in the extreme. It is no coincidence that the Canaanite culture, although materially much more advanced than Israel's, did not bequeath to posterity a single document that could be unequivocally regarded as a significant statement of moral or ethical import. With genuine alarm, then, the Torah regarded a continued Canaanite presence among the tribes of Israel as a corrosive influence. Their beliefs and practices could effectively spell the demise of the people of Israel by undermining the unique creed of ethical monotheism that Israel was to champion.

In its ongoing polemic against the Canaanites, the Torah repeatedly emphasizes that it was their moral values that were incompatible with Israel's mission. A single quote, harshly worded but not exceptional or exaggerated, illustrates the point:

> When God your Lord cuts off the nations [from the land] that you are going to inherit, and you drive them out and inhabit their land, then be careful lest you become ensnared by them after they have been destroyed from before you, and lest you enquire after their gods saying, "How did these nations serve their gods? I will do so as well." Do not do so to God your Lord, for all the abominations

that God hates they perform for their gods; they even burn their sons and daughters in the fire to their gods! [Rather] you shall observe all of the things that I command you; do not add to it nor subtract from it. (Deut. 12:29–13:1)

Most early rabbinic and medieval interpretations maintain that the acceptance by the Canaanites of the so-called Seven Noahide Principles would have been sufficient to guarantee their well-being and continued presence in the land. While a comprehensive discussion of these principles is beyond the scope of this study,[5] it can safely be said that they frame an absolute morality that is predicated upon the acceptance of a higher authority. The principles include (1) the rejection of idolatry, prohibitions concerning (2) blasphemy, (3) murder, (4) adultery, (5) theft, (6) consuming a limb torn from a living animal, as well as (7) an obligation to maintain a judicial system. God's directive to drive out, or else reform, the Canaanites was the only way to protect Israel's exceptional ethical patrimony, a precious and fragile possession in an ancient world awash in warfare, cruelty, and moral neglect.[6]

SOUNDING THE ALARM

The opening verses of the book of Judges are therefore disquieting in the extreme. The proverbial alarm bells were sounding shrilly, but Israel remained indifferent:

Menashe *did not possess* Beit She'an and its towns…. Ephraim *did not drive out* the Canaanites who dwelt in Gezer…. Zebulun *did not drive* out the inhabitants of Kitron and Nahalol…. Asher *did not drive out* the inhabitants of Akko…. Naphtali *did not drive out* the inhabitants of Beit Shemesh…. The Amorites forced the tribe of Dan into the hill country, for they did not allow them to descend into the valley. (1:27–34)

---

5. See Sanhedrin 59b and associated commentaries for an analysis of the principles.
6. See Hattin, *Joshua: The Challenge of the Promised Land*, 165–83 for an exhaustive treatment of the subject.

Leaderless, and no longer certain of their mission, the people of Israel instead settled down, content to farm their fertile plots, raise their flocks and families, and leave the process of possession incomplete. The Canaanites continued to dwell among them, with their religious and moral systems intact, and the siren call of their gods soon took effect. What is this opening chapter, then, if not a veiled accusation against Israel's serene and self-satisfied smugness, a subtle critique of their lack of national vision, and a restrained indictment of their misguided priorities? "History will vindicate me," the disappointed and dispirited narrator seems to be saying, "for today's indifference will undermine tomorrow's security. As long as the Canaanite worldview has not been rejected, even though Joshua may have long ago vanquished their armies on the battlefield, they will continue to represent an existential threat to Israel's calling."

And so it was. The remainder of the book of Judges, while revolving around a series of inspired regional leaders, really traces the story of Israel's tragic lethargy. Sure enough, it was not possible for the people to suffer an unrepentant Canaanite population in their midst while remaining aloof from their cultural and moral values. The repeated warnings of the Torah, addressed to the people from the moment they left the land of Egypt until the very eve of their entry into the land forty years later, must have sounded at the time like over-anxious preoccupation. But the leaders among them, like inspired leaders in every generation, could see the writing on the wall:

> Observe carefully all that I command you this day. Behold I will drive out from before you the Amorite, Canaanite, Hittite, Perizite, Hivite, and Jebusite. Guard yourselves from establishing a covenant with the inhabitants of the land that you will enter, lest they be a snare in your midst. Rather, you shall break down their altars, smash their idolatrous pillars, and cut down their shrine trees. You shall not bow down to another god, because God is zealous, He is a zealous God. For if you establish a covenant with the inhabitants of the land, then they shall stray after their gods and sacrifice to them, and they shall invite you to partake of their sacrifices. Then you will take their daughters for your sons, and their daughters shall stray after their gods and cause your sons to stray after their gods. You shall not make any molten images. (Ex. 34:11–17)

Judges 2:1–3:6

The Pernicious Cycle

The second chapter of the book of Judges opens with an enigmatic event: "A messenger of God ascended from Gilgal to those that wept (*habokhim*)."

The identity of the messenger is not divulged, nor is the historical period or even the location of the event. However, what is crystal clear is the message that the anonymous figure conveys in the name of God:

> He said: "I took you out of Egypt and brought you to the land that I swore to give to your ancestors. I said, 'I will never abrogate My covenant with you. As for you, establish no covenants with the inhabitants of this land – break down their altars!' But you did not listen to Me. What have you done? I therefore said that I will not drive them out from before you, but they will be like thorns to you and their gods will ensnare you." As the messenger of God said these things to all of Israel, the people lifted up their voices and wept. They therefore called that place Bokhim [literally: "those that weep"], and there they offered sacrifices to God. (2:1–5)

GILGAL AND BOKHIM – PATHETIC
ECHOES OF THE BOOK OF JOSHUA

Presumably, "those that wept" refers to the people of Israel who bemoaned their lack of success in settling the new land and in uprooting the Canaanite cults. But why does the passage divulge neither the identity of the messenger nor any other pertinent information about the assembly? When studying the book of Judges there is a natural tendency to compare and contrast it with the preceding book of Joshua. This is justifiable on chronological as well as on thematic grounds. Chronologically, the book of Judges is the continuation of the book of Joshua with its opening events immediately following Joshua's death. While it is true that the time span of the former is much greater (circa 350 years) than that of the latter (circa 50 years), the two nevertheless constitute a single continuum in time. Thematically, the two are also intertwined, for while the book of Joshua chronicled the beginning of the conquest and settlement of Canaan, the book of Judges details the unfolding of that process, telling the sorry tale of its dismal failures.

We can therefore best appreciate the sudden appearance of this messenger from Gilgal against the backdrop of the book of Joshua. Gilgal, located just west of the Jordan River somewhere on the outskirts of the town of Jericho, was the location of the Israelites' first encampment after they traversed the swollen streambed during the springtime of Joshua's leadership. There, they cast off the infamy of the wilderness wanderings by performing mass circumcision and celebrating their first Passover as a nation in their land (Josh. 5:2–12). There too Joshua was unexpectedly visited by the angelic "captain of God's armies," who brandished his menacing sword in the direction of Jericho and brought the Israelite leader an encouraging message of divine support on the eve of engaging the Canaanites in battle. In other words, Gilgal is not only a geographical location, but it is a place associated with anticipation and triumph.

In our passage, however, the messenger[1] ascends from Gilgal bearing ominous tidings of defeat and setback. The people, far from

---

1. In the original Hebrew, the messenger is referred to as *malakh Hashem*. The term broadly means "messenger" but is often used in the more narrow sense of angel. The

being in a celebratory mood, cry out because he informs them that the Canaanite menace will not be neutralized. Thus, rather than constituting a festive assembly similar to Joshua's Passover at Gilgal, the meeting at Bokhim underscores the unraveling of Israel's destiny in the new land. By echoing events associated with Joshua, our book emphasizes the terrible divergence that is now unfolding: This time the messenger's mission to the people is about reversal and defeat, for he bears no sword symbolizing victory, but only painful words of divine rebuke. In rabbinic literature, some views associate the mysterious messenger with the zealous Pinhas,[2] grandson of Aaron the high priest and long-lived scion of the priesthood. Perhaps we should adopt this view only if we also embrace its midrashic corollary: That one of the messengers sent by Joshua to spy out Jericho on the eve of the conquest was none other than this same Pinhas![3] Those spies returned with a report of imminent success in conquering the land, and the contrast with our passage is therefore glaring in the extreme.

THE RECURRING CYCLE OF THE BOOK

The matter is underscored in the text by the flashback that follows. In verses 6–10 we are told that Joshua had sent the people forth to settle the land. As long as Joshua and the elders were alive, as long as the generation of the conquest remembered, the fidelity of Israel to God and to His commands was assured. But then a "different generation arose that knew not God nor the acts that He had wrought for Israel" (v. 10).

What follows next is crucial, for the verses now describe the spiritual malaise that will pervade the entire era of the judges:

---

exegetical question therefore is: Was this a human prophet or a divine envoy? While the commentaries and the translators entertain both possibilities, it is the second option that provides us with a stronger parallel to the episode in the book of Joshua.

2. See Leviticus Rabba 1:1 for this tradition. As is often the case in situations such as these, the literal reading of the midrash is much less significant than its thematic implications – identifying the messenger with Pinhas is the ancient rabbis' way of inviting us to contrast this messenger and his message with the parallel events in the book of Joshua and to draw the necessary conclusions.

3. See Joshua 2:4, and Rashi and Radak ad loc.

The people of Israel did evil in God's eyes and they served the *baa-lim*. They abandoned God the Lord of their ancestors who had taken them out of the land of Egypt, and instead followed other gods from the gods of the nations that were round about them.... God became angry with Israel and gave them over to maraud-ers who attacked them...until it became unbearable for them.... God established judges who saved them from the hands of their attackers.... But when the judge died, they would return to corrupt their ways...to follow other gods...for they would not abandon their deeds and their grievous ways. God became angry with Israel and He said: "Because this nation has transgressed My covenant that I commanded their ancestors and did not listen to Me, I in turn will not continue to drive out even one man from the nations that Joshua left when he died. They will instead serve as a test for Israel to ascertain whether they will observe the way of God to follow them [the commands] as their ancestors did, or not." So God granted a reprieve to these nations and did not drive them out quickly, and He did not turn them over to Joshua. (2:11–23)

The recurring cycle is defined by a series of sequential steps: (1) The people stray from God by adopting the practices and values of their Canaanite neighbors; (2) a corrective comes in the form of oppression at the hands of some regional enemy; (3) the people cry out at their insufferable situation; (4) God responds by designating a "judge" who saves the people from the hands of their oppressor and restores stabil-ity; (5) the people's tenuous loyalty to God dissipates with the death of the judge and they soon return to their recidivistic ways, thus setting the cycle in motion once again. While chapter 1 of the book focused upon the failure of the people to drive out the Canaanites and to uproot their pagan culture, chapter 2 introduces the monumental consequences of that decision: Israel adopts the ways of their neighbors and becomes estranged from God, and harsh retribution follows. This two-stage process – failure to effect physical dispossession followed by adoption of religious and cultural norms – generates the downward spiral.

What is most striking in the cycle is the irony of the divine response. While Israel actively seeks appeasement with its Canaanite neighbors, preferring spiritually corrosive coexistence to stark self-definition, God consistently foils any possibility of rapprochement and relationship by introducing an underlying hostility against Israel that fuels their oppression. In a scene first staged here but replayed many times throughout history, the people of Israel painfully discover that, try as they might, they cannot abandon their unique mission in the world, neither by passive detachment nor by active divestment.

THE CANAANITE FETISHES

While the general thrust of the above passage is clear, there are a number of specific terms that require definition. First, we must understand the objects of the people's misplaced affections, the so-called *baalim* (v. 11, singular *baal*) and *ashtarot* (v. 13, singular *ashtoret*) that were staples of Canaanite pagan belief and the focus of their ceremonial and ritual lives. The medieval commentaries, living some 1500–2000 years after Canaanite polytheism had been extirpated, could only guess at the identity and nature of these pagan gods. Radak (Rabbi David Kimchi), for instance, correctly surmised that the *baalim* were regarded as masters by their worshippers. He was less accurate when he claimed that *ashtoret* idols typically came in the shape of female sheep (commentary on 2:13). What guided him in arriving at both definitions were the only tools at his disposal: the linguistic and cross-referential data provided by the Hebrew Bible itself. Thus, *baalim* is the plural form of *baal* that in many other non-cultic contexts means "master or owner" (see, for instance, Ex. 21:28). *Ashtarot*, never precisely defined in the Scriptures, occasionally occurs in the context of sheep, as in Deuteronomy 7:12: "He will love you, bless you, and multiply you. He will bless the fruit of your womb and the fruit of your earth, your grain, wine, and oil, the calves of your cattle, and the lambs [*ashtarot*] of your sheep upon the land that He swore to give to your ancestors." Radak therefore concluded that *baalim* must be masters while an *ashtoret* must look like sheep.

Thanks to archaeological discoveries, we now know that Baal was in fact the most important member of the Canaanite pantheon. He was avidly worshipped throughout the land as the god of storms, wind, and rainfall; his weapon of choice was the thunderbolt. Baal's consort was

Ashtoret,[4] who was often represented as a well-endowed female and revered as the goddess of fertility.[5] This fertility theme was preserved by the text of Deuteronomy quoted above – "the lambs (*ashtarot*) of your sheep" – even as the idolatrous implications of the name were neutralized. We must appreciate that Canaan, a land that was dry and arid for much of the year, lacked any large rivers or lakes, and its hot valleys and terraced slopes depended in ancient times exclusively upon rainfall for their bounty. This guaranteed that worship of the *baalim* and *ashtarot* was widespread and taken seriously. But that worship frequently included unsavory rituals, sometimes with the active participation of temple prostitutes as well as various animals – all in the name of invoking the gods' favor for rain and bounty. Canaanite cultic practices were therefore synergies of exuberant ceremony and unbridled debauchery.

Of course, Baal and Ashtoret could easily tolerate the inclusion of other gods in the pantheon, even the God of Israel. In polytheism, there is always room for more gods. But the converse was not possible: Since God is an absolute and transcendent being, neither dependent upon the whims of fate nor subject to its limits, the worship of any other forces – even when these could be understood as being ultimately subject to His authority – is intolerable. But while the exclusivity of the deity is demanded by the Torah, what tended to develop in ancient Israel, under the pervasive influence of Canaanite culture, was the combining of His worship with the worship of the Canaanite gods, in a process known as syncretism. Thus, Israel worshipped God (often as a national divinity) while incorporating the worst of Canaanite belief and practice into their worldview. Accordingly, oppressed Israel could capriciously abandon

---

4. Ashtoret, or Astarte, was widely venerated, and is the forerunner of the Greek Aphrodite and the Roman Venus.

5. One of the great contributions of modern scholarship to the study of the Tanakh has been the illumination of obscure and long-forgotten aspects of ancient life. These insights have been afforded through excavation of archaeological remains. Our sages and bible commentators did not have this material at their disposal and therefore had to speculate about the identity or significance of pagan gods. In spite of these limitations, they were often able to arrive at reasonable conclusions by carefully comparing other biblical contexts that referred to the gods in question. However, since the Tanakh in general does not share its knowledge of pagan mythology with the reader, this aspect was often poorly understood.

their Canaanite fetishes and embrace God for relief, and then just as quickly perform an about-face and discard His exclusive worship for the spiritual intoxication provided by the *baalim* and the *ashtarot*.

THE ROLE OF THE JUDGE

The other term that must be more precisely defined at this point is the title and eponym of our book: Judges. What exactly was the role of these *shoftim* as they are called in the original Hebrew? The primary connotation of the word, especially as it is used in post-biblical rabbinic literature, is an adjudicator, an exclusively legal definition that is too narrow for our context. No doubt, the judges often did judge the people and adjudicate their disputes as evidenced by the example of Deborah (4:4). However, this was not their main function. The judges in our book utilized their leadership skills to rally the people in casting off the oppressive enemy yoke through the taking up of arms. Ehud (3:15) and Gideon (7:16) were gifted fighters and Yiftah a born statesman and strategist (11:1). These judges of ancient Israel were more akin to talented, charismatic generals who retired to more prosaic political and judicial pursuits after the enemy had been vanquished. A few of the judges (such as Deborah, or Gideon early in his career [see 6:25–32]) also provided religious and spiritual guidance and are remembered by posterity for their devotion to God.

A judge, then, in the context of our book is a combination of an inspired leader, military strategist, and religious figure, who is defined primarily by his or her accomplishments on the battlefield. Thus it is that Samson, who neither provided leadership nor set any vaunted spiritual example, is nevertheless characterized as a judge (16:31). It should be noted that in ancient Israel, the roles of civic leader, judicial authority, and military strategist tended to overlap; the strict separation of powers that is such a prominent feature of our modern western democracies was unknown in the ancient world. It should therefore not surprise us that when our book speaks of the "judges," the term indicates much more than a magistrate.

Judges 3:7–11

The Dynamics of Oppression

With the death of Joshua and the elders that succeeded him, Israel's resolve in pursuing the wars of conquest began to diminish. Content to allow the Canaanites to remain with their pagan cults intact, Israel eventually began to stray from God by adopting the natives' corrupt beliefs and practices. God, in turn, did not provide any more assistance for the task of driving out the remaining Canaanites, so that Israel's fidelity to Him and His Torah might be tested by their continued presence:

> These are the nations that God allowed to remain in order to test Israel: All those who knew not of the Canaanite wars [of conquest] .... The five Philistine governors, all of the Canaanites and Sidonites and Hivites who dwelt at Mount Lebanon, from the mount of Baal Hermon until the approach of Hamat. (3:1–3)

THE GEOGRAPHICAL FRAMEWORK

Geographically, the remaining nations were associated with the coastal plain of the Mediterranean Sea, from Gaza in the south until the Lebanon mountain range and beyond in the north. The Philistines, who were invaders from afar (probably from the island of Crete),[1] dwelt in cities along the coast and were organized into a federation of five powerful city-states. At the time of the judges, their presence was just beginning to be felt in the land, but due to their superior technology and more extensive military experience, the pressure that they exerted upon the towns and cities of the interior steadily increased until, by the dawn of Israelite monarchy, it was intolerable. The Philistines remained a potent and much-feared force until they were finally overpowered by David centuries after the events of our book.

As for the Canaanites, Sidonites, and Hivites who dwelt at Mount Lebanon, these were all powerful merchant peoples who controlled the sea trade in the eastern Mediterranean basin. "Canaanite" is therefore perhaps used here in its more generic sense of "merchant."[2] The Sidonites were Phoenicians located around the present-day coastal town of Sidon, about forty kilometers north of the contemporary Lebanese border, while the Hivites dwelt at the foot of majestic Mount Hermon that straddles that same border area. All the above suggests that the area of successful settlement by the Israelite tribes was mostly confined to the rocky central hill country, while the coastal plain and its associated fertile valleys and, farther north, its naturally protected harbors, remained almost entirely in the hands of the indigenous peoples.[3]

THE SCOURGE OF INTERMARRIAGE AND ITS CAUSES

The people of Israel, however, rather than continuing their struggle to possess the land and build the nation predicated upon the principles of ethical monotheism, "dwelt in the midst of the Canaanites.... They took their daughters for wives and gave their own daughters to their sons, and they served their gods" (3:5-6). This was the essence of the

---

1. The emergence of the Philistines is an ongoing discussion in academic circles, but an Aegean Sea origin seems most plausible.
2. See Proverbs 31:24: "She fashioned a mantle and *sold it*, and gave a belt to *the Canaanite*."
3. Parenthetically, it should be pointed out that more than any other biblical books, a thorough knowledge of local geography is necessary for the study and appreciation of the books of Joshua and Judges. Blessed with the existence of the State of Israel, we are in the unique position of being able to access the knowledge that was unavailable to earlier generations.

problem: Allowing the Canaanites to maintain their cultural presence in the land constituted an invitation to intermarry with them, for they were the dominant culture. Intermarriage, in turn, necessarily led to the Israelites adopting the easier way of life – that of idolatry.

Who could fail to appreciate the parallels between the struggles of the ancient tribes of Israel in their new land and the challenges that face contemporary Jewry today? As we all know, in a confrontation between two cultural worldviews, the one accepted by the majority is at a decided advantage before the clash is even joined. Its norms and conventions, its laws and customs, have already won over adherents who are frequently more settled, more respected and more powerful. The onus is therefore on the minority culture to prove its worth, a task made even more daunting when its own followers are not entirely committed to the cause. Of course, the difficulty is greatly amplified when the norms of the minority culture demand moral or ritual restraints that are not enjoined by the majority view. No wonder that ancient Israel rarely succeeded in prevailing for any length of time against the cultural dominance of the Canaanites and the surrounding peoples any more than modern-day Jewry prevails in its struggle to maintain a serious and dedicated cultural identity in the lands of its dispersion![4]

The commercial character of the aforementioned Canaanites, Sidonites, and Hivites is also significant, for it suggests that commercial ties are frequently the impetus for the social and cultural ties that must necessarily follow, and that themselves eventually culminate in intermarriage. It is not possible for most people to develop serious business ties with their peers while eschewing the development of some sort of social relationship. As the social ties become deeper, they are naturally perceived to be less threatening. They then tend to grow in intensity, especially when they are driven by a conscious desire to identify with the dominant and less restrictive culture. Intermarriage, at least insofar as cultural or moral values are concerned, rarely yields a balanced outcome.

---

4. Clearly, there is a universal dimension to the discussion: Any minority group that seeks to preserve cultural values that demand a more restrictive lifestyle will struggle to do so in the presence of a dominant culture that presents the allure of greater freedoms and fewer responsibilities.

Though perhaps "love conquers all" with respect to the spousal relationship, for the children that are raised in the shadow of intermarriage, only one worldview will most likely prevail, and that is not necessarily the view that is argued most eloquently or persuasively but rather the view that demands less. And ancient idolatry, like its present-day descendants of relativism, hedonism, and materialism, demanded far less than what is enjoined by the absolute God of Israel: moral restraint, spiritual growth, and devotion to a higher meaning.

KUSHAN RISHATAYIM AND REGIONAL SUBJUGATION

So it was that ancient Israel served the Baal and the *ashera*, the latter denoting some sort of sacred tree and its local shrine that served as the focal point for idolatrous (and invariably lascivious) rites. "God's anger was kindled" (3:8), and retribution came in the form of oppression by Kushan Rishatayim, king of Aram Naharayim. The area of Aram Naharayim (literally: "Aram between the two rivers") is well known to us from a myriad of other biblical references, beginning with the story of our own forebears Abraham and Sarah (see Gen. 24:10). It is situated at the conjunction of northeast present-day Syria and northern Iraq, namely the lands delineated by the headwaters of the great Euphrates and Tigris rivers. Kushan Rishatayim is otherwise unknown, but the surname must be a sobriquet, for the transliteration literally means a "double measure of wickedness."[5] Perhaps he was thus dubbed by his Israelite vassals in the wake of the eight years of harsh subjugation that he imposed upon them.

However, Israel was saved from the oppression by Otniel, a descendant of Kenaz, Caleb's younger brother. This Caleb was none other than Caleb son of Yefuneh, the tribal elder of Judah sent by Moses decades earlier to scout out the land of Canaan in the aborted mission of the spies (see Num. 13:6). Caleb and his contemporary, Joshua son of Nun from the tribe of Ephraim, were the only two spies to return

---

5. For a similar effect, see Genesis 14:2. The names of four of the five kings led by the king of Sodom in his battle against invaders, while clearly Canaanite, are intentionally transliterated into Hebrew in a way that highlights their villainy: Bera, from *ra* meaning evil; Birsha from *rasha* meaning wicked; Shinav, containing the word *sina* meaning hatred; Shemever, and Bela, whose name means "he swallowed up."

declaring that the new land could be conquered (Num. 13:27–14:10). As for Otniel, we met him at Devir in the environs of Hebron, for he had conquered the territory from the Canaanite giants that dwelt there and, in consequence, had won the hand of Caleb's daughter Akhsa in marriage (see 1:10–15; Josh. 15:15–19).

His emergence as Israel's first judge is therefore doubly significant. First, Otniel represents the final link with the generation of Joshua and the elders that succeeded him, a powerful memory of a more glorious past and perhaps the potential for its eventual reestablishment. In addition, as a champion of the settlement of the land who personally battled the Canaanites and prevailed, Otniel reminds us of another dimension of Joshua's inspired leadership: The absolute resolve to succeed. Taken together, Otniel represents the antithesis of Israelite apathy that had unleashed the dangerous dynamic of cultural compromise that now threatened to undo all of Joshua's efforts.

It is therefore not surprising that in the ancient rabbinic sources, Otniel is presented as a successor figure to Joshua himself:

> "Otniel son of Kenaz captured it [the town of Devir]" (Josh. 15:17). This is an example of the verse that states: "The sun rises and the sun sets" (Eccl. 1:5). Said R. Abba son of Kahana: Don't we already know that the sun rises and the sun sets? Rather, the verse indicates that before the Holy One blessed be He causes the sun of one righteous leader to set, He already causes the sun of his successor to rise…. Before Moses's sun set, Joshua's sun had risen; before Joshua's sun set, Otniel's sun had risen, as the verse states: "Otniel son of Kenaz captured it." (*Yalkut Shimoni* II:26)

THE EXAMPLE OF OTNIEL: OBJECTIVE HISTORICAL REALITY VS. THE MORE EXALTED IDEAL

However, Otniel's successful tenure also points to a popular misconception concerning the political situation during the period of the judges. Unlike his predecessor Joshua, Otniel is most certainly a regional leader. There is no indication whatsoever that he exercises any sort of national rule, and everything that we know about him and his exploits places him within the southern region of the tribe of Judah. In other words, as the first of the judges, Otniel introduces us to a new period in Israelite history, an era during which the tribes act independently and are the objects of external threats that tend to be confined to particular areas of the land. Rarely did any judge transcend his tribal affiliation to achieve more widespread rule, certainly not for sustained periods much beyond the immediate exigencies of the hour of battle. Though the text invariably speaks of Israel straying from God and of oppressors harshly ruling over Israel, the dynamics at play were local. Israel did not stray from God as a consequence of some sort of widespread movement decided upon in a national plebiscite, but rather because in every region of the land there were Canaanites whose cults attracted the surrounding, local Israelites to their way of life. Therefore, to be more accurate if less dramatic, it was tribes of Israel that strayed from God. Kushan Rishatayim and the other oppressors that followed him did not subjugate Israel as a nation, but only a tribe or two that were the focus of their oppressive campaign.

The text presents us with a more widespread reading of Israelite infidelity not because it has revised the objective, historical truth, but rather because insofar as spiritual matters are concerned, it is the correct reading. One of the most unique features of the biblical mindset is that it tends to view life's experiences through the prism of the community or nation. No Israelite stands alone, neither insofar as his mission is concerned, nor with respect to his fate. All Israelites are bound together, a lesson driven home in the most startling fashion by the example of Achan and the ban placed upon the booty of Jericho (Josh. 7). After the miraculous defeat of Jericho, the first Canaanite town to be conquered, Joshua imposed a ban upon the taking of any spoils, to drive home the lesson that victory was exclusively due to God's intervention. But Achan of the tribe of Judah succumbed to temptation and took some items for himself. What followed was his untimely extirpation, but not before the entire fate of the nation was placed in the balance: "Israel has transgressed and abrogated My covenant that I have commanded them!" God thundered (7:11), indicating that nationhood implies a critical corollary: co-responsibility.

What historical reality did not furnish, the Tanakh deliberately fosters in its narrative. A particular tribe is oppressed, but all of Israel must (if only vicariously) experience their suffering. A judge arises to liberate his tribal region, and all of Israel breathes a collective sigh of relief. While such national identification was almost always absent from the landscape, the text nevertheless invokes it as a statement of what ought to be, rather than what was. Do we not, even to this day, trumpet the call for universal Jewish unity during a historical period that, in light of our widespread dispersion and its effects, is not unlike the age of tribalism associated with the period of the judges? Doesn't reality paint a much more sober picture of Jewish divisiveness and division, factionalism and narrow, partisan concerns, both in the modern State of Israel as well as in the Diaspora? Is our call for solidarity a cruel mockery of the historical truth, or is it instead the preservation of an ancient ideal (hammered into our consciousness by the very text of the book of Judges) that we hope will one day be realized, and which will only be realized if we continue to dream of it?

Judges 3:12–31

Ehud and Shamgar

Forty years of calm follow the ascent of Otniel son of Kenaz to the position of judge. While Otniel's victory over Kushan Rishatayim ushered in a long period of stability, the situation quickly deteriorates after Otniel's death. "The people of Israel continued to do evil in God's sight" (3:12), and Otniel is no longer alive to restrain or to guide them. As is so often the case in the book, the demise of the judge is the invitation for the people of Israel to stray from God, a dynamic that always unleashes the same harsh corrective: externally imposed oppression.

> God strengthened Eglon the king of Moab over Israel, for they had done evil in God's sight. He [Eglon] gathered the people of Ammon and Amalek to his side, went and struck down Israel and possessed the town of date palms." (3:12–13)

THE GEOGRAPHICAL CONTEXT

In this brief description of the oppressor and his cohorts, there is a wealth of geographical information. The petty kingdom of Moab, whose people descended from Lot the nephew of Abraham and were thus distant if hostile kin (see Gen. 19:30–38), was located along the eastern shores of the Dead Sea in modern-day Jordan. Frequently, Moab was allied with its northern neighbor and ethnic relative Ammon, whose small realm was centered around the city of Rabbah, located about thirty kilometers northeast of the Dead Sea on the border of the desert near the sources of the Yabbok Stream. In biblical times, the Ammonite capital was known as Rabbat Bnei Ammon (Rabbah of the people of Ammon), a name that has been preserved in that of present-day Jordan's capital, Amman, located near its ruins. Sometimes, the Moabites and Ammonites would join forces with their southern kin Edom, who inhabited the territory to the south of the Dead Sea, but the participation of the Edomites is absent from Eglon's coalition recorded in our chapter.

As for the Amalekites, they were a nomadic tribe who wandered with their flocks in the arid regions of the northern Sinai and Negev, and were frequently implicated in the reprehensible activities of marauding and pillage. By pedigree, the Amalekites were descendants of Esau (see Gen. 36:12), and thus shared a cultural connection with their more settled Edomite kin. The tribes of Israel had first made their unsavory acquaintance decades earlier, as they journeyed forth from Egypt, wearily pausing at Refidim. There, Amalek had unexpectedly attacked, concentrating their assault upon the weak and weary who straggled at the rear of the Israelite column (see Ex. 17:8–16). Throughout the biblical narratives, Amalek is consistently portrayed as a mercenary opportunist, swooping in from the wilderness to prey upon the settled areas whenever hardship strikes or the prospect of gain shows itself. It is no wonder that early on, the Torah had singled out their heartless and venal conduct for special censure (see Deut. 25:17–19).[1]

Eglon concentrates his attack against the "town of date palms," elsewhere identified as the city of Jericho.[2] The valley of Jericho, located in the hot plain of the Jordan River, is well watered by underground springs and to this day provides an excellent climate for the cultivation of the date palm. Jericho is located on the Jordan's western banks and Eglon's campaign against the region indicates that he and his cronies forded the Jordan River, penetrated into the territory of the tribe of

---

1. For a more complete sketch of Amalek and their nefarious lifestyle, see Numbers 14:40–45 and especially I Samuel 30:1–6.
2. See Deuteronomy 34:3.

Benjamin west of the river,[3] and established a Moabite presence. This would imply not only a seizure of Benjamin's lands but also the overrunning of the Israelite tribes of Reuben and Gad who dwelt east of the Jordan, for Eglon could not have reached the river without traversing their territory. The tribe of Benjamin shared a border to their north with the tribe of Ephraim, and the Israelites of that tribe were surely anxious about the developments unfolding at their doorstep.

EHUD'S HEROIC EXPLOITS

Ehud son of Gera, a left-handed warrior from the tribe of Benjamin, now arises as the people's savior. This development reinforces our earlier observation: The rise of a judge is precipitated by the oppression of his tribe. He does not emerge as a savior of Israel but rather as a deliverer of his own kin. Eglon's oppression is felt most acutely in Benjamin, and Ehud appears out of Benjamin's ranks.

The narrative provides us with a gripping account of Ehud's bravery, for he seems to initiate the revolt against Moabite rule singlehandedly. While the textual details are scant, they are sufficient to recreate a fuller account. The wily Benjamite leads a delegation of his compatriots bearing tribute for the king, but he also carries a concealed miniature double-edged dagger on his thigh. After lulling the vigilance of his hosts with the lavish presentation of the gifts, Ehud sends the other Benjamite emissaries homewards and then urgently requests an exclusive audience with the obese monarch. This appeal intrigues the king and his entourage, who are convinced that loyal Ehud's private message contains important news of an impending Israelite plot. Certainly, no one entertains the thought that groveling Ehud will dare to attack the king unarmed, especially after his preceding show of obeisance! But as Ehud enters the king's private chambers, the attending ministers fail to notice his small and honed weapon, for being left-handed he unexpectedly wears it on his right side. Claiming to bear a message from God, Ehud brings the rotund ruler to his feet, and as Eglon struggles to rise from his throne (an act that required the use of both of his hands),

---

3. See Joshua 18:11–28 for the delineation of the tribal territory of Benjamin and the mention of Jericho.

Ehud plunges the knife into his swollen and vulnerable belly and messily dispatches him. Stealing away and locking the chambers after him, Ehud takes his leave.

Note that all of the details provided by the text are necessary for understanding the story. The text reports that Ehud is left-handed (v. 15) because he will use this to fool the sentries who expect him to carry arms on his left side and not his right. Ehud's weapon – a short double-edged dagger – is carefully described (v. 16) only because it highlights its lethality while explaining how he succeeded in sneaking past the guards while wearing it. Eglon's corpulence is mentioned (v. 17) because it will make him particularly vulnerable as he attempts to rise in order to receive the "word of the Lord." Ehud's decision to leave the dagger in Eglon's belly is vividly presented (v. 22) because it will clarify how he calmly exits without bloodstains and without arousing suspicions. We might generalize by saying that the Tanakh tends to provide details only as needed for understanding the narrative at hand. In the case of Ehud, every piece of data, especially the gory details, sheds light on his achievement and has no other literary significance. In contrast to other ancient literature that regarded bloody exploits as entertaining, it is rare for the Hebrew Bible to describe weaponry at length or else report how a killing took place.[4]

By the time the Moabite princes realize the fate of their king, Ehud is already well on his way. Breathlessly arriving in the hill country of Ephraim, Ehud sounds the rallying cry with the shofar and then leads the people (who presumably are awaiting his return) into battle. Ehud employs a clever strategy, for he first seizes the fords of the river east of Jericho and thus prevents the fleeing Moabites from escaping across the Jordan River to regroup. About ten thousand Moabites are killed in the ensuing battle and the threat of their coalition is lifted. The passage concludes with the formulaic observation that "the land was peaceful for eighty years" (v. 30), but the verses shed no further light on Ehud's exploits, either as judge or as general, during that lengthy period.

---

4. I Samuel 17:4–7 and 48–51 provide a glaring exception where both Goliath's armor as well as his bloody demise at the hands of David and his sling are painstakingly described. The justification for the gruesome data is self-evident: David's victory over the well-armed giant highlights the critical theme that spiritual strength and not military power brings triumph, as he himself states in I Samuel 17:45.

THE BRIEF ASCENT OF SHAMGAR

There is, however, a brief postscript to the account, a single verse appended to the exploits of Ehud but clearly separated from them in the original Hebrew text by an open line:[5]

> After him, was Shamgar son of Anat who smote six hundred Philistines with an ox goad; he too saved Israel. (3:31)

This is all we know of Shamgar. He is obliquely mentioned later in the victory song of Deborah (ch. 5), where his leadership is described in the context of her report concerning the regional instability that formed the backdrop for her own miraculous triumph over the king of Hatzor:

> In the days of Shamgar son of Anat, in the days of Yael, the roads were deserted, and the wayfarers would take circuitous routes [to avoid the menacing Canaanites]. (5:6)

Thus, it seems from Deborah's mention that while Shamgar may have relieved the plight of the people by overpowering the Philistines, his exploits were insufficient to restore safety to the countryside. The oppressors still prowled, and Israel still cowered before them. Shamgar's unusual weapon, an ox goad, is a sharpened agricultural implement that was used to drive the oxen forward as they plow the fields. The implication is clear: The pastoral tribes of Israel, who, unlike the Philistines, did not hail from a martial or even an urban tradition, were lightly "armed" only

---

5. In the Hebrew Bible, there are no chapter breaks or numbered verses as we understand them today. Rather, the original text is broken up into smaller sections by either an "open" or a "closed" break. An open break means that the previous verse ends mid-line and the new section begins on the next line. A closed break is when the previous verse ends mid-line, a space is inserted, and the next section begins on the same line. Intuitively, an open break constitutes more of a pause in the flow of the narrative. The breakdown of the Hebrew Bible into chapters and the numbering of its verses are not the product of Jewish tradition. The process began with the early translations of the Hebrew Bible into Greek and Latin and only achieved its final and current form in the thirteenth century CE under the stewardship of Stephen Langton, the archbishop of Canterbury. Clearly, interpretation of any passage is impacted by how it is offset from the surrounding text.

with their farm tools, thus constituting easy prey for their more technically advanced neighbors. That Shamgar was able to prevail against six hundred of the Philistines while armed with nothing more than his ox goad was a triumph of singular dimensions but also an achievement of little lasting impact.

SHAMGAR'S OBSCURE TRIBAL AFFILIATION

Concerning Shamgar's tribal affiliation, the biblical text is uncharacteristically silent. R. Eliezer, in an unrelated talmudic discussion, insists that "that there wasn't a single tribe that did not provide at least one of the judges" (Sukka 27b). But even while he insists that every tribe supplied a judge, R. Eliezer does not provide us with a definitive list. Rashi, commenting upon R. Eliezer's vague remark, says:

> A judge is one who saves the people of Israel, one of those that led the people from the death of Joshua until Samuel anointed Saul as king over Israel. Joshua was from Ephraim, Ehud from Benjamin and Gideon from Menashe – these were the children of Rachel. Samson was from Dan, and Barak was from Kedesh Naphtali – these were the children of Bilha. Ibzan is synonymous with Boaz who was from Judah, Eli from Levi, Tola from Issachar, Elon from Zebulun. For all of these, their tribes are indicated explicitly. *Concerning Otniel, Yiftah (11:1), Shamgar, Ya'ir (10:3), and Abdon (12:13), I do not know the names of their tribes,* nor is there any explicit mention in the text of a judge arising from the tribes of Reuben, Simeon, Gad or Asher. (Rashi, Sukka 27b)

While Rashi is undoubtedly correct in declaring that concerning Otniel, Yiftah, Ya'ir and Abdon the text does not explicitly mention tribal affiliation, this is for the simple reason that the necessary information can be easily gleaned from other textual cues that are provided. Thus, Otniel is from the family of Caleb (3:9) who descended from Judah (Num. 13:6). Yiftah and Ya'ir are both described as "Gileadites," and thus are from that branch of the tribe of Menashe who much earlier had settled the Gilead east of the Jordan River and possessed it (Num. 32:39–42). Ya'ir is named after his forebear of the same name

(Num. 32:41), while the "Gilead" designation associated with Yiftah, originally a geographic appellation, was bestowed upon the entire clan of Makhir (a son of Menashe) when they first settled the highlands east of the Jordan River. As for Abdon, we are told by the text that he was "the son of Hillel from Piraton," a town located in the "land of Ephraim at the hill of the Amalekites" (12:13–15), thus making Abdon an Ephramite.

NO JUDGE FROM REUBEN, GAD, OR ASHER

At the same time, as Rashi asserted earlier, there is no textual evidence for a judge from Reuben, Gad, Simeon or Asher. It is entirely reasonable that no judge came from either Reuben or Gad. Both of these tribes were composed of semi-nomadic shepherding clans who dwelt on the eastern side of the Jordan River and were far removed, geographically and politically, from the fate of their brethren on the other side. Eastern Menashe managed to maintain its connection to events in the Land of Israel only because a large part of the tribe was settled on the western side of the river. As for Asher, only of this tribe did the book report that they "dwelt in the midst of the Canaanites who inhabited the land, for they did not drive them out" (1:32). In other words, in all probability Asher faded into obscurity and was lost to the national polity when it amalgamated into its Canaanite surroundings. Is it mere coincidence that when Deborah rebukes those tribes that were absent from the ranks at the battle of Mei Merom (5:15–17) she singles out Reuben, "Gilead," coastal Dan (but not its northern clans) and Asher?

The implication of all of the above is that every tribe that (a) was settled in the Land of Israel proper and (b) did not entirely merge into the surrounding Canaanite landscape, provided at least one judge. According to this line of reasoning, we should have expected to hear about a judge from the tribe of Simeon! Could it be (and we can only speculate) that Shamgar was that judge and that he hailed from the tribe of Simeon? If so, then this would locate his activities in close proximity to his nemeses, the Philistines, who settled the coast from Gaza in the south to Ekron about fifty kilometers northwards.

The Philistines were a sea people who migrated from the southern reaches of the Aegean Sea and arrived on Canaanite shores sometime in the thirteenth century BCE. Though they initially established their confederacy of city-states along the Mediterranean coast near their landing points, they soon sought to expand their power inland. This brought them into conflict with the tribe of Dan whose lands bordered them to the north (Josh. 19:40–48), as well as with Judah whose territory began in the foothills to the east of the Philistine towns. The tribe of Simeon never achieved territorial independence, and its people were instead settled among Judah's southwestern towns (compare Judges 1:1–3), particularly in the arid Negev region of Be'er Sheva (Josh. 19:1–9). If in fact Shamgar was from Simeon, geographically speaking, we can perfectly comprehend his conflict with the Philistines.

SHAMGAR OF SIMEON AND SAMSON OF DAN

If our identification is correct, we can draw an even more cohesive parallel, for the only two judges who are reported to have fought the Philistines are Shamgar and Samson, whose exploits are recounted later in the book. Samson hailed from Dan to the northwest of Simeon, whose inhabitants were directly under Philistine oppression, and he thus constituted the natural analogue to Shamgar from the south. Additionally, both men are credited with unusual feats of strength, performed not with sharpened weapons of war but rather with mundane and innocuous objects. Shamgar humbled them with an ox goad, while Samson famously employed the jawbone of an ass (15:15) or even his bare hands. Finally, both men are described as battling the Philistines without the support of their respective constituents. Nothing at all is reported about Shamgar rallying his tribe, and Samson's own people, cowed by Philistine oppression, were vehemently opposed to his forays and went so far as to turn him over to the enemy forces (15:11–13)!

But now emerges a most glaring contrast. The tale of Samson is the longest of any judge recorded in the book; it describes in detail not only the events leading up to his birth, but also his vigorous youth, his amorous adulthood, and finally his untimely and tragic demise. The account of Shamgar, on the other hand, is but a single verse in length! How may we account for the discrepancy?

Here we turn to the report of the *Yalkut Shimoni*, a wide-ranging repository of midrashic material arranged in Germany in the thirteenth century. It solemnly declares:

There arose judges and kings from all of the tribes, save for the tribe of Simeon that furnished neither a judge nor a king. This was on account of the transgression of Zimri their prince (see Num. 25:1–9), and indicates how grievous is the transgression of sexual immorality! (*Yalkut Shimoni* II:42)

R. ELIEZER VS. *YALKUT SHIMONI*

This tradition, otherwise unattested, conflicts with the opinion of R. Eliezer quoted earlier, who declared that "that there wasn't a single tribe that did not provide at least one of the judges" (Sukka 27b). For the *Yalkut*, there was one tribe that did not provide a judge: Simeon. It is impossible to reconcile both of these views – either the tribe of Simeon furnished a judge or it did not. It is, however, possible that both R. Eliezer and the *Yalkut Shimoni* agree on the *substance* of Simeon's exclusion from the story.

If we assume that Shamgar son of Anat was the judge from the tribe of Simeon, thus completing R. Eliezer's list, then we might argue that the narrative intentionally obscured his origins and lineage because of Zimri's indiscretion, as reported in *Yalkut Shimoni*! It will be recalled that Zimri was one of the tribal chieftains of Simeon. He had flagrantly opposed the leadership of Moses and the moral imperatives of God by engaging in a defiant act of immorality with one of the princesses of Midian whose idolatrous fetish he had adopted as his own god. His specific act had been precipitated by a more widespread phenomenon:

While Israel was encamped at Shitim, the people began to stray after the daughters of Moab. They had invited the people to participate in sacrifices to their gods and the people had eaten and bowed down to their gods. Israel thus became aligned to Baal Peor, and God became angry with Israel. (Num. 25:1–3)

All of this had occurred as the people were encamped on the Jordan's eastern shores in preparation for entering the land, and as a direct consequence the tribe of Simeon was decimated by plague.

SHAMGAR'S OBSCURITY

We can now appreciate why Shamgar's exploits were intentionally understated. As scion of Zimri, prince of the tribe of Simeon, Shamgar was guilty by association. The tribe and its prince had earlier been responsible for supporting intermarriage and idolatry, the very sins regarded by the book of Judges as the source of Israel's failure to secure itself in Canaan. We might argue that obscuring Shamgar's tribe was not meant to be a critique of his personal conduct that may have been above reproach, but was intended as a more general indictment of tribal practices that could only lead the people of Israel to ruin.[6]

The time horizon of the Tanakh, unlike our shortsighted perspective, spans centuries. Zimri and his consort may have long since died but the infamy of his act continued to bear noxious fruit. As intermarriage and idolatry again rear their ugly heads in Israel, the narratives of the book sound the alarm by obliquely recalling Zimri's infamy. The devastation earlier wrought on Israel at the plains of Moab is symbolically remembered by our story's omission of Shamgar's origins, thus reinforcing the primary equation: Intermarriage and idolatry can only spell national ruin and consignment to oblivion.

Much time had passed since those events, and Zimri's crime was forgotten, but the book of Judges remembered. Thus, even as Shamgar's heroic exploits were recounted, his more complete biography was stricken from the record in order to drive home the essential point: Israelite identity and the beliefs and values that are its foundation, are precious sources of strength and inspiration. We surrender our identity at our own peril as we seek an easier and more comfortable life. To stand for something constructive and meaningful necessarily requires us to declare our uniqueness. When we no longer subscribe to the national project of the people of Israel – the ethical monotheism that obligates us to God as well as to man – then we effectively write ourselves out of the story.

---

6. It must be significant in this respect that Shamgar is called "the son of Anat," the only judge whose genealogy is traced through his mother's line. The name Anat is known to us from extra-biblical sources as a fierce Canaanite goddess of warfare!

Judges 4:1–24

The Battle at the Kishon Stream

Chapter 4 of the book of Judges opens with a familiar refrain: After Ehud's death, Israel again strays from God, and a new tyrant arises to remind them of the consequences of their infidelity. The mighty Yavin king of Hatzor, whose chief of staff is the menacing Sisera of Haroshet Hagoyim, subjugates the people of Israel, and at his disposal are nine hundred chariots of iron! The text emphasizes, the only time in the book of Judges, that the oppressor imposes his rule with "ruthlessness" – *beḥozka* (4:3), indicating that Yavin is a particularly pitiless fellow.

Although we know nothing else of this Yavin, his city-state of Hatzor is well known to us from biblical as well as extra-biblical sources. In modern times, extensive excavations have turned the ancient tell of the town into the largest archaeological site in the State of Israel, and numerous strata of occupation have been exposed. First mentioned in the Tanakh among the cities captured by Joshua and the invading Israelites (Josh. 11), Hatzor is located in the upper Galilee region, about ten kilometers north of the Sea of Galilee. Overlooking an important section of a major trade route that extended along the length of the Mediterranean coast and then turned inland, from Egypt in the south to Damascus in the north (and, from there, on to Mesopotamia), the city was well positioned to take advantage of the commercial and military possibilities. To control Hatzor was to exert influence not only regionally, but also nationally and internationally. Not surprisingly, our passage refers four times to Yavin as the "king of Canaan" rather than as the king of Hatzor (vv. 2, 23–24).

By introducing Yavin as the next tyrant in the series, the text shifts our attention away from the southern tribes of Benjamin and Judah toward their northern brethren settled in the regions of the Galilee and along the Phoenician coast. This is to indicate that while the political challenges that arose during the period of the judges may have been regional – each tribe or group of tribes fighting for its own piece of territory and its own cultural survival – the religious and spiritual challenges of those conflicts were national in scope.

In the book of Joshua, some one hundred and fifty years before the events of our chapter, the city of Hatzor was also ruled by a certain Yavin, leading us to the conclusion that this name must be a dynastic or honorific title much like "Pharaoh" of Egypt or "Abimelech" of the Philistines.[1] At that time, the king of Hatzor crafted a coalition of four large northern Canaanite city-states, along with their innumerable allies, to oppose the Israelite onslaught under Joshua, but to no avail. Joshua unexpectedly engaged and then crushed them at Mei Merom, and Hatzor was captured and burnt to the ground. Mute testimony to the great conflagration can still be seen at the excavations of the site. Hatzor was not rebuilt until the time of Solomon some three centuries later when it became one of his most important administrative centers (I Kings 9:15). Solomonic Hatzor came to an abrupt end in the eighth century BCE when the northern kingdom of Israel was conquered by the Assyrians (II Kings 15:29).

YAVIN KING OF HATZOR?

Significantly, though, according to the most reasonable interpretation of the archaeological evidence currently available, Hatzor was

---

1. Abimelech appears in the Tanakh as the ruler of Philistine Gerar during the periods of Abraham (Gen. 20–21) and Isaac (Gen. 26). Many centuries later, David poetically refers to Akhish the king of Gat (a Philistine town) as Abimelech in Psalms 34:1.

no longer settled at the time of the judges! How then to explain the prologue to our chapter, that clearly seems to describe the oppressor and his city as very much in existence? The answer is to be found in a close reading of the passage in question, an exercise which provides us with an important lesson in how to approach historical or geographical references in the biblical text when these appear to be at odds with conventional (and well-supported) evidence. The second verse of the chapter states:

> God gave them [the people of Israel] over to Yavin the king of Canaan who had ruled (*asher malakh*) at Hatzor, and his chief of staff was Sisera, and he was dwelling at Haroshet Hagoyim. (4:2)

We have already suggested that the name Yavin, having occurred earlier in the context of the book of Joshua, was not to be understood as a proper name but rather as a dynastic title. The use of the past perfect tense in our verse to describe Yavin's reign ("who had ruled") must therefore be indicating that the ancestral dynasty had ruled Hatzor in the past but *no longer did so*. Instead, the rule of the king was centered at Haroshet Hagoyim, and it was from there that loyal Sisera was dispatched to plunder and pillage. In other words, the dynasty of Yavin that had ruled at Hatzor before its destruction was not extirpated entirely by Joshua but continued to play a prominent (albeit diminished) role after the battle of Mei Merom. While the immediate power base of Hatzor lay in smoldering ruins, the Yavin dynasty survived (although the king himself was killed in battle – see Josh. 11:10). It regrouped after its defeat at the hands of Joshua and eventually its rule was reconstituted in some form at Haroshet Hagoyim.

Therefore, when our verse says that "he was dwelling at Haroshet Hagoyim," it refers not to Sisera, the chief of staff, but rather to Yavin himself. The implication is that, eventually, a new Yavin came to the throne whose exploits recalled some of the dynasty's ancient glories when it had still reigned from Hatzor, and in a curious and ironic twist (of which the Tanakh is most fond), he reestablished his rule over his nemeses, the Israelites. Thus, Joshua's awesome legacy of triumph was undone.

It is Radak who alerts us to this reading. As he explains:

When the verse states that "he had ruled at Hatzor" it means before Joshua defeated them and burnt the city, also killing the king. Yavin was the king of Hatzor at that time, and remnants of that family went to Haroshet Hagoyim and reestablished themselves. Their king was also called Yavin after his forebear. (Radak on Judges 4:2)

As for Haroshet Hagoyim, the name may mean "forest of the nations,"[2] or perhaps "implements (of war?) of the nations,"[3] but its location has not been identified with certainty, nor has it ever been established whether the reference is to a region or to a particular place. What is clear, though, is that the inclusion of Haroshet Hagoyim in the verse is to indicate that Yavin's oppressive rule was centered there at that time for Hatzor, which had been the ancestral seat of his family's rule, was then in ashen ruins (and remained so until Solomon rebuilt it).

ARCHAEOLOGY VS. THE BIBLE

The reasonable solution of Radak raises an important methodological point. Often a conflict between a biblical verse and an archaeological finding is not the result of a corruption or lacuna that crept into the ancient text on the one hand or a faulty interpretation of the scientific data on the other, but rather is the product of a cursory and superficial reading of the passage in question. It is this lack of care that creates the conflict by supposing a difficulty even where none need exist. It is generally, and by some begrudgingly, agreed that the Tanakh is remarkably accurate in its portrayal of historical periods and in its presentation of historical facts and, as loyal students of the text, we must assume that its portrayals and presentations are reliable. But that does not absolve us from the responsibility to read the verses carefully. Quite the contrary. The text of the Tanakh uses an economy of words while conveying a wealth of information, and one must always proceed with reverence and exercise caution when engaged in its study. This is especially the case for those that believe Prophets and Writings (*Nakh*) to be the inspired word of God.

---

2. From the word *ḥoresh* – see, for example, Isaiah 17:9; Ezekiel 31:3.
3. From the word *ḥarash* – see, for example, I Samuel 13:19; II Samuel 5:1.

At the same time, however, it must be borne in mind that historical and geographical data are only peripheral to the Tanakh's more exalted agenda of correcting the human condition, by both nurturing our bond with God as well as by providing us with the moral and spiritual tools to develop our innate sense of goodness. And here we must part ways with the detached methods of the academics, for they consistently treat the text of the Tanakh as dry, historical literature that is devoid of any transcendent meaning, as no different in import than any other text that dates from the same historical period, and certainly no more deserving of our respect. Naturally with assumptions such as these, when confronted by a seeming contradiction between the verse and the archaeological record, their tendency is either to treat the biblical text as a careless distortion or else to accuse it of duplicity.

RECONSTRUCTING THE BATTLE

Although the location of Haroshet Hagoyim is shrouded in obscurity, the narrative provides us with more than sufficient information to reconstruct the epic battle in which Sisera is defeated and the iron rule of Yavin broken. The heroine of our story is the prophetess Deborah, the wife of Lapidot, who judges Israel from her seat of power in the hill country of Ephraim, between "the Rama and Beit El" (4:5), not more than about five kilometers east of the modern town of Ramallah. The provocations of Yavin and Sisera are centered quite a bit to the north, at the Jezreel Valley. This flat and fertile plain constituted in ancient times the most strategic pass in Canaan for those traveling along the Mediterranean coast toward Asia Minor or Mesopotamia, and its terrain was perfect for the staging of Sisera's nine hundred iron chariots that overawed the northern tribes of Zebulun and Naphtali then chafing under Yavin's yoke. By controlling the Jezreel Valley, Yavin effectively ruled over the entire northern region.

Deborah responds by summoning Barak son of Abinoam from Kedesh Naphtali, a town in the upper Galilee about twelve kilometers north of the ruins of Hatzor. Following Deborah's directives, he gathers ten thousand men and ascends with her to the summit of Mount Tavor (4:10). Mount Tavor, located at the confluence of the tribal boundaries of Zebulun, Naphtali, and Issachar (see Josh. 19:23, 34), rises approximately three hundred and fifty meters above the flat landscape like an inverted bowl. From its rounded peak, at the northeastern entrance to the Jezreel Valley, the entire plain is plainly visible. The enemy is effectively kept at bay for chariots cannot ascend the mountain's slopes. Thus, Barak's men secure a safe vantage point while they await further instructions from the prophetess.

The last geographical detail that provides the key to reconstructing the entire episode is the stream of Kishon (vv. 7, 13), a watercourse that begins its route near the foot of Mount Tavor and flows along the floor of the Jezreel Valley all the way to its exit at the base of the Carmel range by the Mediterranean Sea. While the final western ten-kilometer stretch of the watercourse until its discharge on the coast is a perennial stream, the rest is a *wadi* or dry streambed. This means that during the long summer months, it is dry and easily traversable, but during the rainy season it can suddenly fill with a torrent that may even overflow its banks and cause extensive flooding along the fertile valley floor.

The text states:

> She [Deborah] sent and summoned Barak son of Abinoam from Kedesh Naphtali, and she said to him: "Behold, God the Lord of Israel commands you to draw ten thousand men from the tribes of Naphtali and Zebulun to [the summit of] Mount Tavor. I will draw to you, to the stream of Kishon, Sisera the chief of staff of Yavin with his chariots and his multitude, and there I will deliver him into your hand!" (4:6–7)

Barak does as commanded and gathers his men to the heights of Tavor. Yavin, moving to counter the threat to his harsh and tyrannical rule, immediately dispatches his able and obedient general Sisera, with nine hundred iron chariots at his disposal, to overawe the irregular Israelite forces. Sisera and his charioteers, however, unable to ascend the steep slopes of Mount Tavor, wait instead in the valley along the banks of the Kishon Stream.

What happens next is not stated explicitly in the narrative of chapter 4 but is all but plainly spelled out in Deborah's epic song of triumph in chapter 5. Suddenly Barak and his men charge down the mountain at Deborah's signal to battle Sisera, just as an unexpected cloudburst darkens the sky. The sudden downpour quickly fills the Kishon and its overflowing torrent now turns the valley floor into a muddy trap.[4] Sisera's charioteers, who earlier brimmed with confidence because of their superior weaponry, are now stricken with fear as it becomes clear that their vaunted iron chariots will offer them no advantage and in fact have become a grave liability. Barak and his lightly armed militia of ten thousand fighters engage the enemy and overwhelm them, and Sisera himself dismounts from his chariot and flees the battlefield on foot!

IMPLICIT EVIDENCE FROM THE TEXT

Although the text of chapter 4 makes no mention of any unusual precipitation and is content to simply describe the victory as an intervention of God, a careful reading of the passage provides much evidence that the divine involvement took the form of a sudden storm and a resultant flash flood of the valley floor. The text states:

> They told Sisera that Barak son of Abinoam had ascended to Mount Tavor. Sisera sounded the alarm to gather all of his chariots – nine hundred chariots of iron – as well as all of the people that were with him, from Haroshet Hagoyim to the stream of Kishon. Deborah said to Barak, "Arise, because this is the day that God will deliver Sisera into your hand, does not God go forth before you?" Barak descended from Mount Tavor followed by ten thousand men. God discomfited Sisera and all of the chariots and the encampment by the sword before Barak, and Sisera dismounted the chariot and fled on foot. (4:12–15)

Our first line of evidence relates to the location. As pointed out above, the stream of Kishon is a watercourse that begins near the foot of Mount Tavor and flows along the floor of the Jezreel Valley until its exit at the

---

4. What is so remarkable about this phenomenon is that the actual cloudburst often takes place at some distance from the flash flood. The precipitation quickly drains into the streambed along its length and the floodwaters gather momentum as they flow downhill toward the sea. The consequence of the effect is that at the actual point of contact with the raging waters, the sky may be cloudless and clear, so that there is no warning of the impending doom.

base of the Carmel range by the Mediterranean Sea. The fact that the passage refers more than once (vv. 7, 13) to the Kishon as the site of the victory may refer to its occasional habit of suddenly filling with water and flooding the area.

AN UNUSUAL VERB FORM

A linguistic usage by Deborah herself, on the eve of the battle, reinforces the point. Summoning Barak, she instructs him to gather ten thousand men from the tribes of Zebulun and Naphtali. This gathering of forces is termed *umashkheta*, literally meaning "and you shall draw" (v. 6) and is Deborah's oblique indication to Barak that he may very well have to employ a certain amount of arm-twisting in order to raise the necessary forces from the midst of tribes that had been for so long terrorized by Yavin and his tyranny. But significantly, his "drawing" is to be matched by a divine response: "I will draw (*umashakhti*) to you, to the stream of Kishon, Sisera the chief of staff of Yavin with his chariots and his multitude, and there I will deliver him into your hand!" (v. 7).

While Deborah's intent is clearly to inspire Barak by informing him that his own efforts to raise a force will be rewarded by God's intervention, in accordance with the recurring Scriptural motif that human initiative invites divine assistance, the use of the verb form M-SH-KH is of more than passing interest. Though it broadly signifies "to draw close" (see Ex. 12:21; Song. 1:4), "to pull" (Gen. 37:28; Jer. 38:13), or "to be lengthened" (Ex. 19:13; Josh. 6:5), in rabbinic usage it is sometimes used in connection with water. Thus, for example, in the discussion of labor-intensive agricultural activities that are to be curtailed during the intermediate days of festivals (Ḥol HaMoed), R. Eliezer rules that "one may draw (*moshkhim*) the water from tree to tree, as long as one does not irrigate the entire field" (Mishna Moed Katan 1:3). In the discussion of watercourses that are fit for ritual immersion, the Mishna in Mikvaot 5:3 states that "a spring whose water is drawn (*mashukh*) into many small courses is still considered a spring if one added drawn water (*himshikhu*) to it in order to increase its volume."

In other words, the root M-SH-KH can be used in connection with water, presumably because it flows downhill and thus can be directed or drawn, and by extension can also draw other objects along with it. In our context of the book of Judges, the use of the term in Deborah's directive may therefore be a veiled and proleptic reference to the nature of the divine involvement that will transpire, stated (as prophecies typically are) in language whose full import can only be appreciated after the fact.[5]

EVIDENCE FROM THE TRIUMPHAL SONG OF DEBORAH

While the evidence adduced so far is predicated upon implication and is therefore indirect, much stronger support may be brought from the verses themselves. The narrative description of the fourth chapter is supplemented by the following chapter, namely the renowned song of triumph written by the prophetess in commemoration of the victory. Composed as lyrical poetry, Deborah's inspired words are counted among the most celebrated in the Hebrew Bible. The relevant passage relating to the actual moment of engagement followed by the astonishing victory states:

> Zebulun endangered itself unto death, and Naphtali ascended upon the heights. The kings came to do battle, then the kings of Canaan battled at Ta'anakh upon the waters of Megiddo, and they took no payment of money. From the heavens they fought; the stars in their courses fought against Sisera. The stream of Kishon swept them away, the ancient stream, the stream of Kishon, my soul treads with strength! Then the hooves of the horses galloped, the prancing, the prancing of the stallions. (5:18–22)

Here, the poem describes the heroic courage of ill-equipped Zebulun and Naphtali who trusted in God, answered Barak's call, and prepared to do battle with their powerful overlord. It then describes the opposing force, a coalition of Canaanite kings eager to reassert their hegemony

---

5. This assumes that rabbinic Hebrew (meaning the Hebrew employed at the time of the Mishna, circa first century BCE until third century CE) can shed light on biblical usages, an axiom that is well-known to any serious student of the Bible. For a striking illustration of this fact as well as of the unfamiliarity of even some of the third century scholars with unusual biblical terms, see Rosh HaShana 26b.

over the Israelite tribes, prepared to forego the enticing compensation pledged by Yavin to enlist local support for his punitive campaign.

But now the poem turns to the supernatural, for it claims that the stars themselves left their heavenly courses to do battle with Sisera! Might it be suggesting a spate of hailstones (quite common in the region during the course of heavy precipitation) that fell upon the discomfited foe, further adding to his despair?[6] Or is it a reference to the popular pagan belief that one's fate is determined by the stars, and in this case, they themselves had dictated that Sisera would perish? Could the reference be, perhaps, to a downpour so severe that it seemed as if the very heavens had become undone?

THE MOST PLAUSIBLE THEORY

While we cannot determine the meaning of the phrase with absolute confidence, adopting the imagery of thunderheads, lightning, and severe precipitation certainly furnishes a plausible reading, especially in light of the subsequent description of the Kishon streambed. Upon its banks, the poem suggests, the charioteers lost their sure footing and were "swept away" by the torrent, in contrast to the soul of the Israelite forces that "tread with strength" and did not slide (v. 21). The poem completes the picture of an utter rout by mentioning the remaining enemy forces that beat a hasty retreat upon their horses, thus leaving Sisera alone to face the Israelite onslaught. Of course, the initial reference to the "waters of Megiddo," describing the course of the Kishon as it winds its way through the Jezreel Valley and makes its way to the Mediterranean Sea, reinforces the flash flood theory. So too Deborah's poetic prologue in verse 4 that describes God's victorious march from "Seir and the fields of Edom" that caused the "earth to quake and the heavens to rain, the heavy clouds to drip with water." While it is possible to relate to all of these lyrical verses as nothing more than bold imagery, thereby minimizing their value as sources of empirical data, we may also read them as emphatic descriptions, couched in vivid poetic terms, of events that actually took place.

---

6. Compare to Joshua 10:11: "While they were fleeing the people of Israel, at the descent of Beit Horon, God cast upon them great stones from heaven all the way until Azeka. More died from the hailstones than had been dispatched by the people of Israel by the sword."

Perhaps the matter can be settled by historical evidence since the flooded Kishon streambed was instrumental in deciding battles during other periods as well. In the spring of 1799, the armies of Napoleon swept through Egypt and the Land of Israel, at times encountering stiff resistance from the Ottoman Turks and their local allies. In a pitched battle that took place in the strategic Jezreel Valley, always a sight of conflict and struggle, the Kishon Stream suddenly overflowed its banks. Many retreating Arab irregulars were swept away by the deluge that descended from Mount Tavor and that filled the usually dry tributaries of the Kishon with raging torrents.

If Sisera was overwhelmed by walls of raging water, then we have a perfect echo of another miraculous triumph over tyranny: The drowning of Pharaoh's cavalry and men, his "six hundred choicest chariots" (Ex. 14:7) at the Sea of Reeds, in the aftermath of the Israelites' exodus from Egypt. The link between the two events becomes undeniable when we recognize the set of similar circumstances that generated God's intervention in both. Suddenly we can appreciate the parallel of the weak and downtrodden Israelite tribes emerging triumphant over their mighty overlords much as their ancestors unexpectedly prevailed against Pharaoh and his minions. Both accounts paint a picture of abject Israelite weakness, overwhelming enemy strength, cruel and brutal oppression, and a caring God who will not countenance the injustice indefinitely. Both accounts speak of a heavily armed, overconfident foe bearing down on a desperate and frightened Israel, with the intense apprehension suddenly relieved by a wholly unexpected turn of events. Both portray fearless leaders who call down the divine intervention: Moses lifts his staff to part the waters, and Deborah gives the signal to Barak to charge down Mount Tavor just as the streambed begins to overflow. At the center of the congruence are the waters, violent waves that sweep away the enemy while Israel emerges unscathed to offer a song of praise. We will revisit this comparison and its implications later.

Judges 4:1–5:31

Deborah and Yael

The book of Judges preserves the names of a total of thirteen figures who acted as judges, during the troubling period associated with Israel's conquest and settlement of the land of Canaan. The challenges of the age were great but the stamina of the people was often weak, and no judge ever succeeded in restoring peace or securing serenity for very long. For some judges, the narratives describing their exploits are long; concerning others, the text tells us almost nothing. But of all of the judges whose lives are recorded in this short but remarkable book, only one has bequeathed to posterity a triumphal song of praise: Deborah.

Deborah is introduced to us rather abruptly. We are told nothing about her birth, upbringing, or family, only that she was the wife of the otherwise unknown Lapidot (4:4). We know naught about her home or village, her children or her friends. The only details we are given are that she was "a prophetess who judged Israel at that time," and that she dispensed her instruction and inspiration, "between the Rama and Beit El" under a sturdy date palm that had uncharacteristically taken root in the hill country of Mount Ephraim. (v. 5).

RABBINIC READINGS

Not surprisingly, the rabbis (their opinions preserved in the midrashic collection of *Yalkut Shimoni*) felt obliged to fill in some of the otherwise missing details. They tell us, for instance, in comments echoed by Rashi, that Lapidot, Hebrew for "torches," was so called because Deborah would fashion wicks to kindle the lights of the Menora, and these, in turn, would be dutifully delivered by her husband to the Tabernacle at Shilo. What is striking about such a statement is not that it tends to stress Deborah's spiritual disposition. What else to expect from a prophetess than for her to be busy fashioning wicks in her spare time, in order to spread the ethereal light emanating from the House of God! Rather, what is unusual about Rashi's formulation is that it has the pronounced effect of downplaying any independence that Deborah's husband may have had, for his personal name and identity is entirely overridden by the nature of his enabling but subservient role.

According to other fanciful traditions (quoted by Radak) that identify Lapidot with Barak based on the related meanings of their names (Barak means "brightness" or "lightning"), Deborah's central role in securing victory is highlighted even more. In this reading (that lacks any primary textual evidence), Barak, the Israelite general who led the troops to triumph, was also Deborah's husband. But in this phrase that introduces us to Deborah for the first time, Barak is memorialized in the text not as the military leader who prevailed against the chariots of Sisera, but rather as the devoted husband who conveyed Deborah's handiwork to the holy precincts!

Whatever the real truth about Deborah's background and family, it is clear that the rabbis extracted the cues that they did from the passage in order to emphasize Deborah's special and unusual role in the episode. In this, there can be no doubt that they were inspired by the biblical text itself. After all, in his response to Deborah's summons to don the mantle of fighting general, Barak exclaims, "I will go if you go with me. But if you do not go with me, then I will not go" (v. 8). Similarly, she informs him that God will bestow victory on the people of Israel "by the hand of a woman" (v. 9).

Some of the traditions preserved in the rabbinic writings concerning this matter betray a discomfort with a woman occupying so prominent a leadership role. R. Naḥman of the fourth century CE, for instance, detected in Deborah's name (the Hebrew word for a bee) an indication of her stinging arrogance (see Megilla 14b). R. Berakhya, also of the fourth century CE, saw intimations of ruin for a generation that could furnish no competent leader other than a woman! But more representative is the following statement that, notwithstanding its surprise at a woman leading the people, nevertheless recasts that surprise into a powerful argument for the primacy of personal merit and ability, irrespective of creed, gender, or economic status:

> What was it about Deborah's character that allowed her to be a prophetess over Israel and to judge them? After all, wasn't Pinhas son of Elazar (the well-known activist priest and leader) functioning at the time?[1] Calling heaven and earth as witness, I hereby testify that whether a person is a gentile or Jew, man or woman, slave or maidservant, the Holy Spirit rests upon him only in accordance with his deeds! (*Tanna Devei Eliyahu Rabba*, 9)[2]

THE ROLE OF YAEL

The decisive role played by women in the episode is not confined to Deborah. Though she is the driving force behind Barak's success in rallying the Israelite irregulars and then leading them into battle at her signal, the victory is not complete until Sisera the tyrant foe is captured and killed. And this final act is performed by Yael "the wife of Hever the Kenite" who woos the fleeing and frightened Sisera with reassurances of protection, plies him with sleep-inducing goat's milk, and then kills him by driving a tent peg through his skull (4:17–21). One may draw a direct textual parallel between Deborah and Yavin the king of Hatzor on the

---

1. The reference to Pinhas requires some elaboration. In the midrashic tradition, Pinhas the son of Elazar enjoyed a fantastically long life of several centuries. The anchor for these traditions is his appearance in the final narratives (Judges 20:28) with the assumption that the stories of the book of Judges, including its conclusion, are arranged chronologically. In any case, the effect of these midrashic traditions is to explicitly insert Pinhas at critical moments in the narrative, often for a didactic purpose.
2. *Tanna Devei Eliyahu Rabba* is a composite midrash whose final redaction took place in the tenth century CE.

one hand, and Yael and Sisera on the other. Just as the menacing king of Hatzor dispatches his loyal minion but does not himself participate in the battle, so too Deborah inspires and sends Barak to engage the foe while she remains uninvolved in the actual fighting. Just as Sisera symbolizes overreaching enemy power, so too Yael represents street smarts and simple resolve that she leverages to prevail.

Significantly, when proud Sisera enters the fray as a seasoned warrior aching for the kill, he is ably met, disarmed, and then defeated not by his natural nemesis Barak, but rather by the noble but otherwise obscure Yael. All of this casts Barak as the anomaly in the episode, a fact reinforced by his utter failure to capture and kill Sisera. Pursuing the runaway Canaanite, complete victory almost within his grasp, he is unexpectedly met by Yael who emerges from her tent and pronounces matter-of-factly: "Go, and I will show you the man whom you seek" (v. 21). She then proceeds to invite him into her dwelling where he finds Sisera lying down dead with the tent peg still lodged in his temple! Sisera was defeated far from the battlefield, and by a woman!

WOMEN SECURING THE VICTORY

What might be the significance of the fact that military triumph here is secured by women? On the simplest level, it is intended to highlight the extent of the achievement. In ancient times, women did not participate in warfare, and few and far between are the reports in Tanakh (or other contemporary sources) of women physically engaging enemies on the battlefield. The active participation of women in any aspect of warfare was so unusual that to be dispatched in battle by a woman was regarded as a particularly ignominious end. Take, for example, the incident of rapacious Abimelech son of Gideon, who succeeded his father as judge by viciously killing all other rivals including his own half-brothers, as reported in chapter 9 of our book. Abimelech established his rule over the people of Shekhem and its environs for a period of three years, but then a falling-out occurs between him and the town's nobles. He quickly amasses his troops and moves against the opposition, first besieging and reducing the town of Shekhem, and then attacking the adjacent town of Tevetz. However, before he is able to proclaim victory, the people of Tevetz and its nobles flee to the citadel and bolt the entrance. Abimelech approaches the tower in order to set it aflame but is abruptly felled by a millstone dropped by a woman on the roof. His skull fractures, he quickly calls his armor bearer and implores him to kill him, "lest they say about me: 'a woman killed him!'" (9:54). His loyal attendant fulfills his last wish and slays him.

Returning to our context, the defeat by a woman emphasizes the miraculous nature of the triumph. Not only was powerful Yavin and his threatening deputy Sisera, with nine hundred chariots of iron at his disposal, defeated by the poorly armed and untrained Israelites, but the victory was secured from beginning to end by female non-combatants who had no battle experience whatsoever!

A MOTHER AND A WIFE

There is more. In one particularly telling reference, Deborah refers to herself as "a mother in Israel." The people trembled before the Canaanite threat in the years leading up to the confrontation, and even the well-traveled routes were abandoned by wayfarers who feared being attacked:

> In the days of Shamgar son of Anat and in the days of Yael they ceased using the roads, and those that went on the way chose roundabout routes. Unwalled towns ceased in Israel, they ceased, until I, Deborah, arose, I arose like a mother in Israel." (5:6–7)

What did Deborah mean by declaring herself to be a mother in Israel? It could only have meant that she was intensely concerned for the people, pained by their anguish, and absolutely determined to change the dismal situation. Like a mother who cares for her children, Deborah the consummate leader cares for her "offspring," the nation of Israel, and this leads her to do everything within her power to improve their lot. And in this endeavor she is not alone. Yael, introduced as the "wife of Hever the Kenite," unexpectedly appears on the scene, just as menacing Sisera is fleeing the battlefield. But she cannot oppose him with weapons, the use of which is entirely beyond her skill. Instead, Yael invites the weary general with soft offers of protection, gives him satisfying sustenance, cradles him in her inviting arms and covers him with warm blankets, and then summarily executes him as he sleeps, her steady hands never becoming sullied with the handling of male weapons of war. The tent peg, a potent symbol of domesticity, is her weapon of choice and is especially effective in her small and delicate hands.

In essence, then, just as Deborah acts as a "mother" to save Israel, Yael employs a dramatic inversion of her wifehood, using its trademarks of loving concern and loyal empathy to ensnare the general. How else to understand the charged sexual metaphors that Deborah utilizes in her song to describe Yael's exploit (5:27: "Between her legs he bowed, fell and lay down."), if not as expressions of admiration for the simple shepherdess's resourcefulness in utilizing her womanly skills? Thus, the episode furnishes us with a mother and a wife securing victory for a ragtag army of irregulars in order to indicate that war is ignoble, killing is tragic, but freedom from enemy domination must nevertheless be achieved. "We did not ask to become warriors," the women in the episode seem to be saying, "nor are we enamored with the male cult of killing. The glory of the battlefield does not impress us. But we will nevertheless fight and prevail, precisely because our lives and the lives of our loved ones are at stake. The enemy is not inspired by our dreams for a secure and peaceful future for our children; his only desire is for domination and tribute. But we will not be subdued!"

THE MOTHER OF SISERA

This reading, which sees in the Israelite women's role a positive statement of core values and not simply a detached expression of remarkable triumph, is reinforced by Deborah herself in her unsympathetic portrayal of another mother, namely that of Sisera. Toward the end of her song, she paints a poignant image of the Canaanite general's mother who expectantly awaits his return, but in vain:

> By the window, Sisera's mother peers out, and she wails by the casement [saying], "Why does his chariot tarry in coming? Why is the sound of the hoof beats delayed?" Her wise attendants answer her, as she too tells herself: "Surely they have found many spoils and they divide them, a captive girl or two for each fighter, a spoil of colored cloths for Sisera, a spoil of embroidered colors, double embroidered colors for the necks of the spoil!" (5:28–30)

Our initial tendency is to pity Sisera's mother, for we can only too well understand her pain as her beloved son fails to return from battle, but Deborah quickly deflates our sympathies. For while she, as a "mother in Israel," and Yael, as a wife among the allied Kenites, decry bloodshed and take up the fight because they must, Sisera's mother is cut from different cloth. In her veins, Canaanite blood flows, and she cannot for a moment perceive the pain of Israelite mothers who also wait anxiously for the return of their own beloved sons from the battlefield. The worldview of Sisera and his mother is conditioned by Canaanite values, and her greatest comfort is to imagine her son engaged in the aftermath of bloody victory, taking captive fearful and defenseless Israelite girls[3] who are mockingly bedecked with spoils by the foe.

Thus, while the women of Israel proclaim life's inherent sanctity and celebrate its inviolate worth, leaving their proverbial tents to counter the threat but never reveling in the enemies' demise, Sisera's mother dreams of more bloodshed. How striking that Deborah's triumphal song, though commemorating God's triumph and Sisera's downfall in superlative terms, never once gloats over the enemies' defeat! Absent from its verses are any of the typical proclamations of victory songs, ancient and modern, that belittle the foe, demonize him, and unabashedly rejoice over his gory end. The real struggle, then, is not between Sisera and Barak but rather between the mother of Sisera and Deborah, between the obsequious attendants and Yael, between the amorality of the Canaanites and their culture of death and the ethical morality of the Torah.

---

3. Significantly, the term employed by Sisera's mother to describe these Israelite captive women, one or two for each warrior (v. 30), is *raḥam raḥamatim*. This word was understood by the medieval commentaries neutrally to mean "a woman or two" or "a maiden or two." In fact, however, the word is a pointed anatomical reference (i.e., the womb) and while its cognate forms can be employed sympathetically (*raḥamim* means "compassion," implying that this is a particularly maternal trait), here it is used as a coarse pejorative.

Judges 5:1–31

Deborah's Victory Song

With the completion of the fifth chapter of the book of Judges, we conclude the first division of the book. Let us briefly review what we have explored thus far. Recall that unlike the book of Joshua, our book offers a very unsympathetic portrayal of the people of Israel, charging them with repeated acts of treachery against God, and then starkly narrating the consequences of the divine displeasure which inevitably follow. The circumstances were undoubtedly difficult. The brief and bloody wars of conquest were long over while the great and extended task of settlement still loomed large before the people, challenging not only their physical fortitude but their moral and spiritual fiber as well. Slowly, the tribes cleared the sparsely settled hill country and established themselves in the more fertile and populated valleys, and everywhere they were continuously confronted with a daunting choice: To oppose their Canaanite nemeses and their relativistic ways tooth and nail, or to accommodate and even embrace them. Choosing the former invariably entailed armed conflict and physical danger while choosing the latter often provided social and commercial opportunity. Predictably, but with tragic consequences, many of the tribes chose the latter. By granting amnesty to the Canaanites and to their morally corrupt ways, in direct contravention to the Torah's shrilly repeated proscriptions, Israel courted disaster, defeat, and downfall.

Although the people strayed from God and were punished, they unfailingly cried out to Him for relief from their foes. and He responded to their pained entreaties. A tribal leader, introduced abruptly and with obscure origins, would arise to save them from oppression. Suffused with divine inspiration and military skill, the judge would initiate a counterattack, push back the enemy, and secure a brief respite of peace; but tribal unity was never achieved. No longer threatened, the people would again stray, and a new cycle of oppression by foes, return to God, and salvation by a judge would inevitably unfold.

THE FIRST FOUR JUDGES

The four judges introduced to us have been, without exception, positively portrayed. Otniel son of Kenaz (3:9), the kinsman of Caleb; Ehud son of Gera (3:15) of Benjamin; Shamgar son of Anat (3:31), the peasant warrior; and valiant Deborah the wife of Lapidot (4:4) all led the people faithfully, beat the oppressor admirably, and avoided controversy assiduously. There are no recorded instances in the text of any one of them betraying a lack of trust before battle or else of succumbing to self-aggrandizement in the afterglow of their victories. They commit no missteps as they selflessly secure liberation for their people and when their era of leadership is over, they pass from the scene honorably. Though the biblical text is often reticent with the details of a protagonist's biography, it is never silent on matters of his or her morality. The failure to mention any flaws concerning these four judges should therefore be taken as an endorsement of their reign.

Perhaps the matter can be highlighted by briefly contrasting our quartet with the career of the last of the judges, the potent Samson from the tribe of Dan. Though Samson single-handedly slew more Philistines than any of these four personally dispatched from the ranks of their respective enemies, he is not remembered fondly by the book. Repeatedly, his unwillingness or inability to control his passions is recounted, and always as an explanation for why he was ultimately ineffectual. The first four judges represent the ideal exercise of authority under the difficult national circumstances of the time. The other judges in the book present us with more questionable models of leadership. Their careers are often tainted by self-doubt, self-interest, and self-debasement.

THE VISUAL STRUCTURE OF THE TEXT

Chapter 5, the victory song of Deborah the prophetess, provides us with an exceptionally appropriate conclusion to this first section of the book. Its soaring and lyrical verses are unusually vivid and constitute one of the Tanakh's greatest epic songs. Even before considering its motifs, we note its curious graphical appearance, for in a scroll of the original Hebrew (and in good editions of the Tanakh) it stands out from the rest of its context as something that is visually unique. The rabbis of the Talmud referred to this graphic form in the following passage:

> R. Ḥanina bar Papa said: R. Sheila of Kefar Timrata expounded that all of the passages of biblical song are written as "half bricks arranged upon whole bricks" and "whole bricks arranged upon half bricks." The exceptions to the rule are the list of the rogue Haman's ten sons [Est. 9:6–9] and the list of the kings of Canaan [Josh. 12:9–24], for they are composed as half bricks arranged upon half bricks, and whole bricks upon whole bricks. What is the reason for the distinction? So that they should have no resurgence from their downfall. (Megilla 16b)

This means that each line of the song is divided into a stitch of text ("half brick") that is then separated by a blank space ("whole brick") from the concluding stitch of text, while the next line of song inverts the sequence, like this:

הַהוּא	בַּיּוֹם	בֶּן־אֲבִינֹעַם	וַתָּשַׁר דְּבוֹרָה וּבָרָק
בְּהִתְנַדֵּב	בִּפְרֹעַ פְּרָעוֹת בְּיִשְׂרָאֵל		לֵאמֹר:
שִׁמְעוּ מְלָכִים הַאֲזִינוּ			עַם בָּרְכוּ יְדֹוָד:
אֲזַמֵּר	אָנֹכִי לַידֹוָד אָנֹכִי אָשִׁירָה		רֹזְנִים
יְדֹוָד בְּצֵאתְךָ			לַידֹוָד אֱלֹהֵי יִשְׂרָאֵל:
אֶרֶץ	בְּצַעְדְּךָ מִשְּׂדֵה אֱדוֹם		מִשֵּׂעִיר
גַּם־עָבִים נָטְפוּ	רָעָשָׁה גַּם־שָׁמַיִם נָטְפוּ		
זֶה	הָרִים נָזְלוּ מִפְּנֵי יְדֹוָד		מָיִם:

> Deborah and Barak son of Abinoam sang on that day saying:
> When there was great strife in Israel, the people offered them-
> selves, praise God! Hear kings, listen princes for I will, to God,
> I will sing, making melody to God Lord of Israel... (beginning
> of the Song of Deborah from Judges ch. 5)

The overall effect of the technique is to create the appearance of stacked elements, with each line of text sitting solidly above a space and each space above a line. The commentaries understood the visual aspect of the form to suggest stability, like a section of a solidly constructed wall with alternating bricks in its successive courses. They interpreted the symbolism literally as an expression of the enduring permanence or truth of the song's message:[1] Israel's triumph is enduring and her enemies will perish.

There is only one other example of this phenomenon in the Tanakh,[2] and that is the song sung by Moses and the people of Israel after the great victory over the Egyptians at the Sea of Reeds, as recorded in Exodus, chapter 15.

THE SONG AT THE SEA – COMPARISONS AND CONTRASTS

The parallels between these two events are myriad as mentioned above: Both episodes introduce oppressive overlords armed with numerous chariots, both describe an Israelite people ill-equipped for battle and psychologically overawed, and in both situations miraculous and unexpected salvation is accomplished by torrents of water as the yoke of the tyrant is cast off forever. It is therefore quite natural for Deborah to have seen God's exploits at the stream of Kishon as mirroring Israel's experiences at the shores of the Sea of Reeds, and for the text to have emphasized that link by employing a similar graphic convention.

At the same time, however, there are also numerous differences. Chief among them is that the song of Moses and Israel, only about two

---

1. See Rashi on Megilla 16b for the implications of the format.
2. Concerning the graphic form of David's song of triumph in II Samuel 22, there is a lack of consensus in the early manuscripts. Those versions that incorporate the form of "half-bricks arranged upon whole bricks" imply the same idea: David's triumph is eternal and his foes' downfall is forever.

thirds the length of Deborah's epic, is a more narrowly focused composition that employs repetition for emphatic power. It describes God's might in winning the victory over Pharaoh and his host (Ex. 15:1–5) and then describes it again (vv. 6–12). It goes on to intimate in the Egyptian defeat the future downfall of all of Israel's foes (vv. 13–16), concluding with a prophetic vision of Israel achieving stability and permanence in their land and building the Temple to glorify God (vv. 16–17). Suffused with inspiration, the song's final note is decidedly eschatological in tone, proudly proclaiming for the entire world to hear: "God will reign forever and forever!" (v. 18).

SIMPLICITY VERSUS COMPLEXITY

There is, in effect, only one subject that is discussed in the song at the sea, and that is God's saving might, present and future: God overthrew the Egyptians, God foiled Pharaoh's nefarious plan, God will lead His people to Canaan and overwhelm the surrounding nations hostile to Israel's mission, and ultimately God will prevail. According to the song's central theme, Israel's role in securing its salvation is correspondingly small.

Deborah's hymn neither negates God's intervention nor downplays it, but at the same time it acknowledges the role of numerous human characters in securing the victory. While she gratefully sings of God's involvement (Judges 5:1–5), she also notes her own role (v. 7), her fighters' bravery (vv. 9–11), and especially Yael's selfless heroism (vv. 24–27). In one memorable couplet, Deborah even blurs the distinctions between them, crediting all of them with securing the triumph together: "Arise, arise Deborah; arise, arise and speak song, get up Barak and take your captives, son of Abinoam. Then a remnant ruled over the mighty among the nations, God gave me dominion over the powerful!" (vv. 12–13).

And unlike the song at the sea that portrays Israel united in receiving God's salvation, Deborah discusses the complex and divisive dynamic that was at work among the tribes of Israel. Some of them selflessly volunteered for what must have seemed like a lost cause, while others, who were geographically beyond the threat of Yavin and Sisera's tyranny, remained aloof and coolly unconcerned:

Why did you, [Reuben], sit among the sheepfolds to hear the bleating of the flocks? For the divisions of Reuben there was much soul-searching! Gilead dwelt on the other side of the Jordan; and Dan, why did he dwell with ships? Asher sat on the shores of the sea and dwelt securely in his harbors. But Zebulun was a people that delivered its life to die, as did Naphtali, upon the heights of the field. (5:16–18)

Paralleling these tribal divisions were communal and personal ones, for Deborah indicates that not everyone took part in the battle or in the routing of the foe that followed:

Cursed be [the people of] Meroz, says the messenger of God, may her inhabitants be utterly cursed, for they did not come to the assistance of God, to the assistance of God against the mighty. But among the women may Yael the wife of Hever the Kenite be blessed, among the women in the tents may she be blessed. (5:23–24)

THE SPIRIT OF THE AGE

With a few terse verses, Deborah admirably succeeds in expressing the spirit of the age, the political and religious tensions characterizing the turbulent times. God had brought Israel to the gates of Canaan and had subdued their Canaanite foes but had also delegated responsibility to them, making them the masters of their own fate. Israel was promised His assistance but also burdened with His demands. National triumph was not guaranteed, but was instead contingent upon the moral choices that the people would make.

At the same time, the tribes of Israel, recently and uneasily fused into a loose coalition, would have to desire unity in order to achieve it. Tribal divisions, narrow sectarian interests, partisan politics, and local and regional concerns would need to be overcome for the nation as a whole to prosper and for their mandate to succeed. But as Deborah poignantly describes it, these twin objectives of embracing responsibility while fostering peoplehood and national mission were, for now, beyond Israel's reach. Israel faltered and suffered setback, and everywhere disunity reigned. Judges such as herself stepped in to temporarily fill the breach, but more time and effort would be needed to effect meaningful and lasting change.

THE TENSION OF THE HUMAN CONDITION

That the song at the sea sounds simpler and more straightforward should not surprise us. Precisely because Israel had scarcely left Egypt when that triumph unfolded, the reality of the situation was so much starker and one-dimensional. At the Sea of Reeds, with cruel overlords bearing down with thoughts of bloody vengeance on their minds, the former slaves were psychologically paralyzed. Armed resistance was unthinkable, Pharaonic acceptance of their surrender implausible, flight impossible. There was nothing at all for the people of Israel to do save to entreat Moses for divine intervention. And while Israel did obey God's directive to enter the sea, the other choices placed before them were, to say the least, limited. Even their disunity could not serve as a detriment to their deliverance, for what other possible venues for preservation were available to them? They therefore entered the churning waters as one. Thus it was that the people of Israel, artificially united by the overwhelming circumstances, did little to secure their own salvation while God did all. How else to sing His praises, as the dead Egyptian host washed up upon the azure shores, than to ascribe the triumph exclusively to Him! How else to view that triumph, reflected as it was through a prism of divinely imposed parameters, as anything but messianic!

The events at the streambed of Kishon, celebrated in Deborah's epic poem, should be regarded as a more typical appraisal of the human condition. God grants us the gift of choice, which we freely exercise in accordance with our will, but then we must live by the consequences. God is never absent, His concern never distant, His involvement never lacking; but He has given us a role to play in the unfolding of our own destiny. Rarely do we stand at the shores of the sea confronted by utter and complete powerlessness to affect or to change our lives. At such a moment, indeed, there is nothing to be done except to plunge into the frigid waters and to hope for a miracle. But more often than not, there are real choices to be made, concrete initiatives to be seized, and opportunities to be realized.[3] God was present at Kishon and Deborah never begrudges Him (as we often do!) the verity of His involvement. But human beings such as Barak, Yael, the selfless tribes of Zebulun and Naphtali, and Deborah herself, heeded the call and were counted, thus securing for themselves a real and primary role in the triumph.

---

3. Note that Sisera's overthrow is determined by a human initiative that is divinely inspired: It is Deborah who signals to Barak when to charge down the slopes of Mount Tavor (4:14). Had he done so too soon, before Sisera's chariots were overcome by the waters, the Israelite irregulars would have been annihilated. Too late, and Sisera and his men would have fled the battlefield, to regroup and counterattack later. As is often the case in the Tanakh, divine miracles are veiled as "perfect timing," and it is inspired human agents who proclaim the moment that generates the fateful confluence. See Joshua 8:18–29 for another example.

Judges 6:1–32

The Appointment of Gideon

Sometime after the remarkable victory of Deborah and Barak over Yavin and his chief of staff Sisera, a triumph that ushered in a forty year period of relative calm and stability, the people of Israel were again confronted with a situation of grave difficulty. Having strayed once more from God, Israel was abandoned to its own devices, and foreign domination was quick to follow. This time, it was the Midianites that oppressed them, ably assisted by their enthusiastic allies Amalek and *bnei kedem*, the eastern peoples. For seven years, this triad of trouble descended upon the Israelites like a plague of locusts (6:5), consuming everything in their path:

> They would despoil all of the land's produce, until the outskirts of Gaza, leaving no sustenance in Israel, neither sheep, cattle, nor donkeys. For they and their flocks would come up with their tents … they and their camels were innumerable, and they would come to the land to despoil it. (6:4–5)

Israel cried out to God and He responded by dispatching a prophet to the people, but this messenger of God bore no tidings of hope:

Thus says God the Lord of Israel: "I took you out of Egypt and brought you forth from the house of bondage. I saved you from the clutches of Egypt and from the clutches of all of your oppressors. I drove them out from before you and I gave you their land. I said to you: 'I am God your Lord; do not revere the gods of the Amorites in whose land you dwell.' But you did not listen to Me!" (6:8–10)

RECALLING AN EARLIER PASSAGE

The anonymous prophet's words of rebuke, that squarely lay the blame for the people's predicament at their own doorstep, recall an earlier passage from chapter 2, also delivered under similar circumstances of failure and despondency:

A messenger of God ascended from Gilgal to those that wept (*habokhim*). He said: "I took you out of Egypt and brought you to the land that I swore to give to your ancestors. I said: 'I will never abrogate My covenant with you. As for you, make no covenants with the inhabitants of this land – break down their altars!' But you did not listen to Me. What have you done? I therefore said that I will not drive them out from before you, but they will be like thorns to you and their gods will ensnare you." As the messenger of God said these things to all of Israel, the people lifted up their voices and wept. They therefore called that place Bokhim [literally: "those that weep"], and there they offered sacrifice to God. (Judges 2:1–5)

In essence, the two pronouncements are the same. In both, the unnamed prophet remembers the people's exodus from Egypt, a defining act of divine kindness as well as the touchstone of Israel's unique sense of mission. In both, the messenger goes on to recall God's repeated caution: Do not adopt the polytheism of the Canaanites, their colorful cults of fertility and death, their licentious rites and moral relativism, their shrines that were to be found upon every high place and under every leafy tree. Finally, in both passages, the prophet concludes by declaring Israel's infidelity to God's teachings, a crime made all the more treacherous and tragic in light of God's gracious bestowal of the gift of the land.

BEGINNING A NEW ERA

The overall effect of the visit from the mysterious prophet is to recall the earlier passage and its message. But it is also to suggest, as the earlier passage did, that we are now embarking upon a new section of the book. Recall that the first chapter of the book was introductory, summarizing some of the tribes' early triumphs in dislodging the Canaanites while indicting the lethargy of the others. The second chapter introduced, with the visit of the mysterious divine messenger and the people's resultant tears, the recurring and wretched cycle of the book: disloyalty to God's Torah, foreign oppression, pained outcry, appointment of a saving judge, brief respite of stability, and disloyalty to God's Torah once again. With the third chapter, the saga of the judges began in earnest, and the stories of Otniel, Ehud, Shamgar (mentioned only in passing), and Deborah unfolded seamlessly. It was Deborah's triumphant hymn, recalling in theme, style and tone Israel's song at the sea some two centuries earlier, which fittingly concluded the book's first section. The era of these earlier judges was now officially over, and with their demise, the era of selfless, righteous, and inspirational leadership also came to a close.

With the appearance of the mysterious divine messenger in chapter 6 of our book, introducing the career of the judge Gideon, a new and more uncertain era begins. Henceforth, the moral caliber of the people's leaders will be noticeably less impressive than that of their forebears, exactly mirroring the declining moral spirit of the people of Israel themselves.

THE ADVERSARIES AND THEIR SITE OF ATTACK

All three of the oppressors in our story – Midianites, Amalekites and the easterners – are well known to us from other biblical contexts as marauding tribes that would regularly infiltrate settled areas. Inhabiting the extensive desert regions of the southern Negev and the Sinai and Arabian peninsulas, these shepherding tribes also participated in the profitable business of camel caravans, which would transport goods and people across the arid and inhospitable expanses that extended between the urban centers of Egypt and Mesopotamia. If famine forced their hand and reduced grazing for their flocks, then they would supplement their decreased income with proceeds from raids into inhabited lands. If those lands were reasonably fertile and weakly defended, then their incursions might be more frequent and last much longer. And so it was that the homesteading Israelites, subsistence farmers busily at work with a simple and rural economy of terrace farming, found themselves in the unenviable position of providing for their more numerous, more powerful, and wholly unwelcome distant kin.

Recall that the book of Judges as a whole unfolds against the backdrop of a tribal versus a national organization. The tribes of Israel, each one assigned its own specific territory by Joshua, often acted according to their own narrow self-interests, and rarely did they all come together to advance any sort of national agenda. The judges were therefore often no more than regional leaders, and their battles were never waged on behalf of the whole nation. Though the book often speaks of "Israel being oppressed," it is really only certain tribes that suffered the brunt of the enemy's tyranny, while other tribes remained entirely unaffected.

The geographical locus of our chapter is the more northern reaches of the country – the hills of Menashe, and the sloping lands of Asher, Zebulun and Naphtali (6:35) – all of them bordering the Jezreel Valley, Menashe to its south and the other three to its north. This valley, stretching arc-like all the way from the Mediterranean coast at the Carmel range until the foot of Mount Tavor some forty kilometers to the east, not only constitutes one of Canaan's most fertile plains, but also contains the land's most strategic and profitable international route. All commerce or armies passing from Egypt to Damascus and on to Mesopotamia, or in the opposite direction, traverse this valley or else must take routes that are much less direct and topographically more challenging. For this reason, every conflict in the book of Judges that involved the central or northern tribes ultimately resolved itself somewhere in the verdant Jezreel Valley. This time, it was the tribe of Menashe, nestled in the rugged but productive hill country, that was Midian's target of choice, and the trouble therefore came right to our protagonist's door.

GIDEON THRESHES THE WHEAT

The messenger of God, an ethereal being in the guise of a human body, suddenly appears in Ofra at the homestead of Yoash from the clan of Aviezer and plants himself under the shade of a terebinth, fixing his gaze upon young Gideon. The lad, his old father Yoash too bent from cares to attend to the threshing, is busy beating the wheat stalks by hand at the wine pit in order to conceal the small amounts of grain from the Midianites (6:11).

In those days, threshing of wheat typically took place out in the open for all to see. With the onset of summer, the stalks were spread upon flat and open ground. An ox or other beast of burden would then slowly draw a huge sledge, its undersurface embedded with sharp stones, over the grain. This detached the ears from the stalk while effectively breaking open the tough husks to release the kernels. Later, the kernels were separated from this chaff by the process of winnowing. In winnowing, the crushed grain was thrown heavenward, so that the wind blew away the lighter chaff while the heavier kernels fell to the ground to be later collected and ground. Clearly, it was most efficient to perform these tasks in a more exposed location, at an elevation if possible, so that the winds could do their work with greater efficiency.[1] However, here the passage indicates that Gideon beat the stalks with a stick, and did so at the *gat*, a depression dug into the bedrock for the collection of wine that ran off as the grapes were crushed. Unlike threshing, pressing the grapes was done in a sheltered area during the fall, with the collection pit dug at a lower elevation so that the resulting wine could be drawn downward by gravity. The overall effect of this curious introduction to Gideon's appointment is therefore to highlight the people's dire situation. The Israelites needed to be ever on guard in the face of the Midianite menace, and were therefore forced to thresh their grain only in small amounts and at secluded and improbable locations.

The visitor now turns to industrious Gideon and extends a brief greeting: "May God be with you, valiant one!" (6:12). In the context of biblical social intercourse, such a salutation is as innocent and innocuous as the statement "how are you?" is for us. In fact, in *Megillat Ruth*,[2] Boaz greets his busy reapers with the very same expression: "He said

---

1. See, for instance, II Samuel 24:18–25 for a reference to the elevated location of the "threshing floor of Ornan the Jebusite," later purchased by David to become the site of the Temple.
2. The events of *Megillat Ruth* unfold during the "rule of the judges" (Ruth 1:1).

to them, 'May God be with you!'" to which they politely and reflexively responded, "May God bless you!" (Ruth 2:4). In Judges, however, the messenger's remarks trigger a poignant and pained outburst from the young Gideon: "Please sir, if God is truly with us, then why has all of this befallen us? Where are all of His wonders that our ancestors would recount, saying that God took us out of Egypt? Now, God has abandoned us and given us over to the clutches of Midian!" (Judges 6:13).

GIDEON IS APPOINTED

The pathos of the moment is captured perfectly by an early midrash of the rabbis that is brought by Rashi claiming that the events of the chapter occurred around the time of Passover (Rashi, 6:13). Just a night earlier, the rabbis explain, Gideon had sat down to the Seder with his aged father and family, and his father had recounted the story of the exodus. That perennial tale of national renewal, predicated upon a conception of an absolute God that cares about human suffering and intervenes to save the oppressed from the oppressor, is still fresh in Gideon's mind when the mysterious visitor arrives and watches as he furtively beats the grain and then spirits it away from the prying eyes of the Midianites. The visitor offers a harmless greeting, but as often happens when the recipient is tormented by some inner crisis, the inoffensive words open a floodgate: "Where is He now?" cries Gideon, "Where has He been? Why doesn't He save us from our distress?"

God, however, is not angered by Gideon's audacity. Far from it. By railing against Him, Gideon actually demonstrates that he cares much about Him and especially about the fate of His people. By recounting Israel's plight in the midst of a demonstration of his own, Gideon ties his destiny to theirs. Turning toward him, the visitor locks his otherworldly eyes on Gideon's own, and a shiver goes down the young man's sturdy spine. Peering intensely into his soul, the messenger now reveals the true nature of his visit to the hamlet of Ofra and speaks the word of God: "Go with this strength and save Israel from the clutches of Midian. Behold, I have appointed you!" (6:14). Thus Gideon is designated to be Israel's liberator, in a modest epiphany that unexpectedly unfolds at the obscured site of his old father's wine pit. But God, who can forcefully speak to man from the midst of consuming fire, can also tenderly address him from the depths of his own broken heart. The nature of all revelation, however, is to demand from us a response: Gideon's verbalizations of concern for his people, if not matched by a genuine preparedness to assist in relieving their plight, would be a shallow exercise in self-righteousness.

Gideon, taken aback by the sudden turn in the conversation, faces his mysterious visitor and says: "Dear God, how shall I save Israel? Behold my clan is the smallest in Menashe and I am the youngest in my family!" (6:15). The tribe of Menashe, whose territory extended both west as well as east of the Jordan, was composed of six main clans, all of them descendants of Gilead, son of Makhir, son of Menashe: Aviezer, Helek, Asriel, Shekhem, Hefer, and Shemida (see Josh. 17:1–2). These clans all settled west of the Jordan, while other sons of mighty Makhir joined the eastern-dwelling tribes and carved out a huge swath of territory east of the Jordan River, known as the land of Gilead. Here, Gideon invokes both the relative insignificance of his clan Aviezer as well as his own lowly stature in the family in an attempt to evade the mission, but to no avail. "I will be with you," God gently responds, "for you shall strike down the Midianites as a single man!" (6:16). Unconvinced, the young Gideon requests a sign, and later requests two more.

RECALLING MOSES

In many respects, Gideon's conduct in this passage and God's response call to mind another liberating figure who sought mightily to dissuade God from choosing him and then had to be fortified with multiple signs: Moses. Summoned at the beginning of the book of Exodus by the burning bush that was not consumed, Moses removed his footgear at God's behest and stood in awe as the deity announced His intent to rescue the people from Egypt. But when God appointed him as His emissary to Pharaoh, he politely refused: "Who am I that I should go to Pharaoh and that I should take the people of Israel out of Egypt?" God then responded just as He did now to Gideon: "I will be with you." and then proceeded to arm the erstwhile shepherd with an arsenal of potent signs calculated to strengthen his hesitant spirit (Ex. 3–4).

But while Moses may have doubted his suitability for the mission, he never was in doubt that it was God Himself who communicated to him from the midst of the burning bush. Gideon, on the other hand, though he responds to the visitor's appointment with the dawning realization that perhaps the latter has been sent by God Himself (6:15), remains uncertain that his visitor is in fact a divine emissary. Presenting an offering of goat meat, matzot,[3] and stew, Gideon expects the visitor to partake of the meal but is instead instructed to place it upon a rock after spilling the stew upon it. The visitor then lifts his staff and touches the food with its tip, and suddenly it is entirely incinerated. In the meantime the visitor, actually an angel in disguise, ascends heavenward with the flames.[4] Gideon then realizes that God's angel has indeed addressed him.

FATEFUL ENCOUNTERS

The motif of the "disguised angel," always anonymous but bearing critical tidings while in human form, occurs elsewhere in Tanakh. Abraham's three visitors, who came to announce the pregnancy of Sarah and birth of Isaac and then proceeded to Sodom, arrived at his tent in the guise of men. Only later during their visit did it became apparent to Abraham that they were in fact divine angels who supped at his home (see Gen. 18). The ruse was reenacted when the visitors came to the house of Lot in Sodom posing as tired travelers, only later revealing their true nature when the house was surrounded (see Gen. 19). Jacob, who had fled eastwards from his brother Esau's wrath only expecting to reencounter it some twenty years later upon his return to Canaan, crossed the path of a mysterious man of the night who was subsequently revealed to be a divine being (see Gen. 32:25–31). As Joshua stood at the outskirts of Jericho, the people of Israel having just crossed the Jordan and entered the land, a man appeared before him bearing a drawn sword. Joshua was initially unsure about the identity and loyalties of the man but it soon became apparent that the apparition was in fact an angelic "captain of God's hosts" who had arrived to fortify Joshua on the eve of the battle. Realizing the true identity of the nighttime visitor, Joshua fell to the ground before

---

3. Matzot (unleavened bread) is a biblical favorite of quick-thinking hosts with unexpected guests, since they can be prepared quickly. See Genesis 18:6 and 19:3.
4. Actually, the text reports only that "the angel of God disappeared from his sight." In the parallel scene from the story of Samson, the matter is explicit "the angel of God ascended in the flame of the altar" (Judges 13:20).

him (see Josh. 5:13–15). Finally, in our own book, Manoah and his wife, the parents of mighty Samson, initially mistook their guest for a man, only later realizing that they had been visited by an angel of God (ch. 13). The recurring motif impresses upon us the preciousness of the encounter as well as its awesome potential. How often do we interact with random people during the course of our lives; how little do we realize at the time that some of those encounters will in fact turn out to be fateful. God's messengers constantly cross our path; most of the time they are of the non-ethereal variety, but they are His messengers nonetheless. When our biblical protagonists rendezvous with God's heralds disguised as men, destiny beckons. What appeared initially to Gideon as a polite meeting of little significance, as the curious man sat down near him, watched him thresh diligently and then courteously greeted him with encouraging words, was revealed to be life-transforming. And every person in his or her own life, when sensitive to the presence of God that is never far away, realizes that in mundane moments of encounter destiny is sometimes engaged.

DEEDS OF TRUST

That very night, God says to Gideon:

> Take your father's ox as well as the second seven-year-old ox, destroy the altar of the Baal that is your father's, and cut down the sacred tree that overhangs it. Build instead an altar to God your Lord upon the summit of this stronghold at the level place, and then take the second ox and offer it up as a wholly burnt sacrifice using wood from the sacred tree that you shall cut down. (6:25–26)

Gideon's unexpected appointment as leader of the people of Israel, as their designated savior from the Midianites, is not extended gratis. He will have to prove his suitability by demonstrating fortitude and faith, by publicly proclaiming his opposition to the corrupt values and corrosive belief system current among his own compatriots. In effect, before embarking on his mission to destroy the Midianites, Gideon must first demonstrate his resolve to destroy a more pernicious enemy much closer at hand: The Baal worship pervading Israelite culture and undermining the ethical absolutes of the God of Israel.

By this time in biblical history, the people of Israel had whole-heartedly adopted the idolatrous practices of their Canaanite neighbors. Worship of the storm god Baal, chief of the Canaanite pantheon, was widespread. Canaanite idolatry, like Canaanite politics and Canaanite commerce, was ever a local affair, with household or village shrines covering the hilltops and dotting the countryside the length and breadth of the land. These shrines were often adorned with sacred trees, *asherot*, that were regarded as potent expressions of vitality and regeneration. The trees, sometimes planted singularly and often arranged in groves, provided welcome shade as well as cultic meaning for the performance of the lascivious rites that characterized Baal worship.

Now, God calls upon Gideon to destroy the altar of the Baal, to cut down its sacred tree, and to execute retribution by using its very wood to offer a sacrifice to God, a sacrifice consisting of a consecrated ox raised for seven years to the glory of the storm god himself! In short, Gideon is to utterly destroy the local shrine and replace it with a testament to his steadfast trust in God, emphasizing to the people that their long-term salvation from oppression cannot be won without a fundamental shift in their worldview and moral system. He is to demonstrate in a concrete way what had always constituted the Torah's message on the matter: Reject idolatry and its values and prosper; embrace them and perish. But while Gideon does not oppose or evade the divine demand, well-founded fear overcomes him. It is only under cover of darkness that he musters ten of his servants to assist him in carrying out the deed, for he knows that the townspeople will not take well to the eradication of their temple (6:27). This lack of confidence in God and in himself, while completely understandable under the circumstances, is nevertheless indicative of the weaker mettle of Israel's judges during this time. If Deborah ever doubted, we heard nothing of it. If Ehud ever hesitated, the text did not report it. But doubt and hesitation will be the hallmarks of Gideon's conduct throughout his career.

THE RESPONSE OF THE PEOPLE

On the morrow, the villagers of Ofra arise to discover the outrage carried out against their god and its shrine, and the evidence quickly points to Gideon as the perpetrator. The enraged people, in a stunning and ironic reversal of the Torah's pronouncement that those that embrace idolatry have committed a capital crime (see Deut. 17:2–7), now demand that Gideon be put to death, but his father's quick thinking saves the day. In a stroke of genius, Yoash presents himself as an ardent supporter of Baal while simultaneously undermining the efficacy of worshipping the storm god. Rather than surrendering his son to the mob, he instead suggests that Baal be allowed to fight his own battles: "Will you then fight for Baal or save it (from harm)? Let he who strives with Baal be put to death by morning, for if he is a god then he will strive with him for throwing down his altar!" (6:31).

It is in the aftermath of this pivotal episode that Gideon takes on the new name of Yerubaal, or "the one who strives with Baal," for his mission will be not only to relieve Israel's political plight but to address their spiritual challenges as well. How astounding indeed that the inhabitants of Ofra, Israelites all, have become champions of Baal and his protectors, while the God of Israel is either brazenly ignored by them or else admitted only grudgingly to their idolatrous pantheon! The showdown at Ofra is the first time in the Hebrew Bible that people of Israel pronounce their willingness to kill opponents of idolatry and the new development does not bode well.

Judges 6:33–7:25

The Attack against Midian

Having passed the trial of trust,[1] and buoyed by his new nom de guerre, Yerubaal sounds the shofar and rallies a fighting force against the Midianite multitudes then encamped at the Jezreel Valley. But the tribal and sectarian spirit of the age is indicated by the fact that his own clansmen from the tribe of Menashe are supplemented by irregular fighters from Asher, Zebulun, and Naphtali, all of whom settled in areas directly menaced by the Midianite incursion. The other tribes who were not oppressed by the Midianites absented themselves from the battle preparations. Nevertheless, Gideon does not proceed until he once again secures signs from God – not one but two! In the first, a clump of wool

---

1. The events associated with Gideon's assumption of leadership – breaking ranks with his father, destroying idolatry under cover of darkness, facing down his townspeople's rage, being preserved from harm by a logical retort to the mob, and acquiring a new name – all echo a famous midrash in Genesis Rabba 38 that describes the coming of age of the patriarch Abraham. In that tale, Terah the father of Abraham leaves his shop of idols in the care of Abraham who proceeds to smash the contents while his father is away. When Terah returns, he presents the young lad to the tyrant Nimrod who unsuccessfully engages Abraham in logical debate about the nature of the gods and then attempts to kill him. Abraham is miraculously saved by divine intervention. It should be borne in mind that many midrashic tales are clever and didactic reworkings of earlier biblical texts.

is dew-soaked while the threshing floor remains dry, while in the second, the wool is dry and the threshing floor becomes damp (6:37–40).

In both signs, two opposites face off. The wool is an animal product from which textiles are spun; the threshing floor is the site of grain, the quintessential yield of agriculture. One became soaked while the other remained dry and then the sign was inverted. In all probability, the warring opposites symbolized in Gideon's mind the conflict between two opposing ways of life that could not be reconciled in the rugged and fertile highlands of Menashe. On the one hand, the marauding Midianites and their flocks (the wool) had infiltrated from the arid eastern lands and tightened their hold upon the terraced hills, while on the other, the industrious Israelite farmers wringing subsistence from the soil (the grain) dreamt of liberation. God responds to Gideon's entreaties and the signs are granted in accordance with his request. The preparations for battle can now commence, with the protagonist having inflicted a stinging defeat upon idolatrous Baal even while showing a penchant for the methods of Baal's adherents, who put their trust in signs, portents, and prognostications.

"REFINING" THE FIGHTING FORCE

> Yerubaal, being Gideon, awoke the next morning with all of the people that were with him and encamped at the spring of Harod, while the camp of the Midianites was to the north of the hill of Moreh in the valley. (7:1)

The fighting force that Gideon assembles at the spring of Harod on the northern slopes of Mount Gilboa is impressively large, numbering some thirty-two thousand irregulars, but God suddenly tells the warrior to pare the numbers! "There are too many people with you for Me to surrender Midian to you, for then Israel may be arrogant against Me and say, 'My own power has delivered me'" (v. 2). Astoundingly, God informs Gideon that it is not victory against Midian that is the objective, but rather victory against idolatry, syncretism, and their corollaries of overbearing pride and spiritual self-delusion. If Israel were to prevail against Midian by sheer force of their numbers, they would fail to recognize God's pivotal role in either their oppression or their deliverance, ascribing the whole sorry interlude and its happy ending to the vagaries of human history. However, if Israel prevails against the Midianite hordes, even with a tiny force of three hundred souls, then God's involvement will be well-nigh undeniable. Thus it is that twenty-two thousand returned home for (understandably!) feeling fearful (v. 3), while the remaining ten thousand are further reduced by the ordeal at the waters that follows.

In this curious test of distinguishing between those who would fight and those who would return from the front, God tells Gideon to allow the men to drink from the spring waters of Harod. Whoever bends to the surface and hurriedly scoops dribs and drabs of the water up to his mouth is to be selected for the battle; all those who prostrate themselves and drink while in a bowing posture are to be rejected. While the modern commentaries offer intriguing explanations, ascribing, for instance, the precious commodity of initiative to the scoopers and assuming sloth for the bowers, the medievals read the context more realistically, for the subject here (as it is throughout the narrative) is the polemic against Baal. Rashi therefore explains that those who prostrated themselves in order to drink did what was natural for them, for the practice among the worshippers of Baal was to genuflect and to bow in its presence. The scoopers, on the other hand, avoided (or at least were unfamiliar with) that particular position, indicating that they were loyal to the God of Israel.[2]

THE DREAM

In the end, only three hundred fighters remain, a mere remnant of the thirty-two thousand who answered Gideon's initial call. No wonder the hapless warrior now needs a further divine sign to lift his flagging spirits on the eve of the battle:

> That night, God said to Gideon, "Arise and descend to attack the [enemy] camp, for I have given it into your hand! But if you are fearful to go down, then go descend with your servant Pura to the camp. You shall hear what they say, and then your hands will be strengthened and you shall descend to attack the camp." (7:9–11)

---

2. It is intriguing to note that in the traditional worship of the synagogue to this very day, bowing to the ground is uncommon, and can only be performed within strict parameters (see *Shulḥan Arukh, Oraḥ Ḥayim* 131:8 with commentaries).

Gideon and Pura go down toward the edge of the Midianite encampment and overhear the conversation just as one fellow tells his compatriot of his dream. The man relates that in his dream he saw a round, flat[3] barley bread rolling through the encampment, eventually striking and overturning the tent. The compatriot is immediately certain as to the import of the vision: "It is none other than the sword of Gideon son of Yoash, the man of Israel. God has given Midian and the entire camp into his hand!" (v. 14).

Gideon's ongoing need for reassurance, as well as God's willingness to indulge it, are both striking features of the episode. The tally of miraculous signs so far provided to Gideon to inspire his confidence now stands at four (6:17, 37, 39, 7:9)! While earlier judges had to contend with challenges at least as great as those of Gideon (such as Deborah facing the menace of Sisera and his nine hundred chariots of iron [4:3]), none merited quite the same degree of divine hand-holding that the Menashite has thus far received. This fact highlights not only the enormity of the trial that Gideon must overcome but also his own limited spiritual resources. God must therefore intervene repeatedly to save Gideon from losing faith not only in Him but also in himself.

While we tend to focus our exclusive attention on the leader's foibles and shortcomings, we must also bear in mind the more serious implications: The judge and leader of the people is a moral and spiritual reflection of those that he or she leads. Seldom, if ever, do we find any of the judges *shaping* the character of the people; invariably, they are portrayed as products of their age, now more successful and now less, but always arising out of obscurity as a *response* to the contingencies of the hour, and never altering the destiny of their tribes for long. Thus, if the caliber of the judges decreases as the book progresses, then that is more than a statement about mediocre governance; it is an indictment of the spiritual state of the people of Israel.

Returning to the specifics of the episode, we are struck by the compatriot's response. How many of us would have proclaimed to our confused and sleepy fellow, with no hesitation whatsoever, that the

---

3. Radak understands the word *tzalil* to mean "roasted" – a barley bread roasted on the coals not unlike our pita.

significance of such a curious dream was that "it is none other than the sword of Gideon son of Yoash, the man of Israel. God has given Midian and the entire camp into his hand!"? Surely, the strange vision could have been interpreted differently. The irony of the scene is obvious: While Gideon frets and fusses and fears the worst, the vastly more powerful Midianites, whose fighters and flocks fill the valley like "locusts in number" (7:12), regard him with alarm as being fortified for victory while they are destined for defeat!

As for the significance of the barley bread and the tent, here again we have intimations of Israelite versus Midianite pursuits. The Israelites engage in farming and agriculture (the barley bread), the Midianites in nomadic shepherding (the tent). Seeing that the barley bread rolls into the camp, strikes the tent, and overturns it, the friend assumes that it refers to current concerns. News of Gideon's massive and spirited troop rally had no doubt reached the Midianites, while reports of the sobering reduction in the number of fighters by divine selection perhaps had not. So the Midianites are anticipating a massive onslaught, an attempt by the Israelite agriculturists to exact vengeance for so many years of pillage and plunder at the hands of the easterners' innumerable flocks. The cryptic dream is therefore eminently intelligible.

THE ISRAELITE ONSLAUGHT

In the end, Gideon prevails, not by the brute strength of his force but by employing the divinely inspired element of surprise, always a favorite expression in Tanakh of God's involvement in the arena of human history. The Midianites are hardly anticipating a nighttime attack – surely a force rumored to number in the tens of thousands could not successfully conceal their movements and mount an offensive under cover of darkness! But it is precisely because Gideon has scarcely three hundred fighters under his command – the very antithesis of overwhelming force – that a sneak preemptive attack is possible. Arming his men with shofars and with clay jars containing lighted torches (7:16), dividing his force into three groups with each attacking from a different direction (vv. 16, 21), and choosing the precise and confusion-filled moment of the late night changing of the guard (v. 19), Gideon succeeds in throwing the Midianite camp into disarray.

In an instant, the silent and comforting night, crowned by an ink-black vault ornamented with innumerable points of light, is shattered. Confounded by the noise of the smashing jars, the shofar blasts, and the outcry of the Israelite force; dazzled by the burning torches that suddenly appear out of the darkness to threaten the tents with conflagration, bewildered by the enemy forces that attack from three directions simultaneously, and utterly convinced that the wily and ruthless Israelite has a colossal army at his disposal, the Midianites begin to flee. Panic seizes the camp and, as often happens when vast crowds are suddenly startled, the dread takes on a destructive dynamic of its own – "God caused the sword of each one to be against his own fellow… and the camp fled" (7:22).

The Midianites escape eastwards – the only direction left "unguarded" by Gideon's men – eastwards toward the Jordan River, and beyond that to the desert wastelands that the marauders call home.[4] Gideon, however, strategically anticipating just such a development, not only rallies the people of Naphtali, Asher, and Menashe to pursue the fleeing Midianites but encourages the Ephramites (who are closest to the action) to seize the river fords, thus preventing the Midianites from crossing unmolested. Two of the enemy chieftains (Orev and Ze'ev) are captured and killed, and before the smoke of the battle has cleared, chapter 7 of the book unexpectedly ends – another glaring example of chapter and verse not only ignoring the traditional division of the text but occasionally even its natural literary structure!

---

4. The elements of Gideon's attack – 300 fighters, a surprise attack under cover of darkness, a coalition of overwhelming eastern kings pushed back to the wilderness after taking hostages – all recall Abraham's exploits, but this time without the midrashic trappings. Abraham also battled a coalition of powerful Mesopotamian kings after his nephew Lot was taken captive. He divided up his small force of 318 men and inflicted defeat under cover of darkness before turning the enemies' retreat into a rout (Gen. 14).

Judges 8:1–35

Aftermath of Strife

STRIFE WITH EPHRAIM, STRIFE WITH SUKKOT AND PENUEL

As Gideon catches up with the men of Ephraim, he is accorded a rather rude welcome:

> The men of Ephraim said to him, "What is this thing that you have done to us by failing to summon us to battle the Midianites?" And they strove with him mightily. (8:1)

At stake, of course, was not the prospect of genuine damage to Ephramite interests, but rather insult to Ephramite pride, for Gideon had failed to acknowledge the tribal hierarchy. Gideon's fighting force consisted primarily of men from his own Menashite clan of Aviezer (6:34), and it was they who had won the day by sowing panic in the Midianite camp, while the men of Ephraim were only summoned well after the enemy was already in retreat. But the Ephramites tended to regard themselves, sometimes with justification, as the linchpin of the northern tribes and as the main counterbalance to the powerful tribe of Judah to the south.

Now, however, Gideon shows his true valor in leadership, for rather than upbraiding his haughty kinsmen and thereby exacerbating the tense situation, he admirably defuses the matter by self-deprecatingly stroking their hurt egos. "Are not the gleanings of Ephraim preferable to the harvest of Aviezer?"[1] he exclaims, crediting the victory to Ephraim's pursuit of the retreating Midianites and their capture of the princes, while downplaying the pivotal role played by his own compatriots. "Did not the Lord give into your hands the Midianite princes Orev and Ze'ev? What could I have done to surpass your exploits?" Their wrath was then assuaged when he spoke those words. (8:2–3)

After crossing the Jordan River in pursuit of the remaining Midianites, his three hundred fighters are by now famished and exhausted. Gideon asks the people of the town of Sukkot for provisions, but they derisively dismiss his request: "Have you then captured Zevah and Tzalmuna [the remaining Midianite princes] that we should provide your fighters with bread?" (8:6). The people of Penuel respond as the townsmen of Sukkot, and Gideon pledges that upon his return he will exact vengeance from the leaders of both.

These brief but disturbing exchanges highlight an ongoing political problem that was the bane of all the judges who ever arose to rescue Israel from their oppressors. The feeling among certain tribes, or even towns within tribes, was that unless they benefited directly from their participation in the larger conflicts, they much preferred to leave the fighting to their compatriots who were more directly threatened. Recall how the prophetess Deborah had earlier battled the same apathy, for when she dispatched Barak son of Abinoam of Naphtali to engage Sisera in battle at the foot of Mount Tavor, the tribes of Reuben, Dan and Asher were conspicuously absent from the fray (5:16–17) while the otherwise obscure town of Meroz likewise remained aloof (5:23). The tribes still

---

1. This expression, possessing the brevity and power of an aphorism, contrasts the contribution of the tribe of Ephraim with that of Gideon's clan of Aviezer. The "gleanings" are the few undersized grapes that remain on the vine after the rest have been harvested (although the later rabbinic sources define the matter more narrowly – see Mishna Pe'ah 7:4). Gideon is saying that Ephraim's seemingly minor contribution of seizing the fords of the Jordan and capturing the Midianite chieftains, while occurring only after the main battle had been engaged by his clan of Aviezer (the "harvest"), was more consequential for securing victory over the Midianite foe. The imagery of the expression also calls to mind the cultural backdrop to the conflict with Midian and the preoccupation of the Israelite tribes with terrace agriculture, as we have seen.

had a very long way to go to forge a national identity that could transcend narrow partisan concerns in order to address the greater threats of the day. In the end, Gideon kept his cruel pledge for, upon his return from decimating the last of the fleeing Midianites that had regrouped east of the Jordan River, he struck down the seventy-seven governors of Sukkot and then destroyed the fortress of Penuel (8:16–17).

THE CAPTURED PRINCES

Finally, after the fighting had died down, the chapter records that Gideon came back from battle, with the two captured princes of Midian in his custody. What follows is an enigmatic exchange between him and the princes before they are put to death (8:18–21). Addressing Zevah and Tzalmuna, Gideon demands to know the fate of people reported killed by the Midianites at Mount Tavor. The princes respond evasively: "They were like you, the likeness of the king's children" (v. 18). Gideon then informs the princes that the murdered men were his own relatives, "my brothers, the sons of my mother," and had the Midianites spared them, Gideon would have reciprocated. Now, however, Gideon turns to his own firstborn Yeter and bids him dispatch the two, but the lad hesitates. Finally, Gideon himself slays the princes and seizes the golden moon-shaped ornaments that dangled from their camels' necks (v. 21).

Both the ancient as well as the modern commentaries offer little insight into the truncated and cryptic conversation, and what can be gleaned from the text itself is speculative. The most plausible reading is that the tense Midianite camp, stationed at the eastern reaches of the Jezreel Valley (6:33), had heard of Gideon's massive troop buildup to their south at the foot of Mount Gilboa (7:1). Besides gathering their own substantial force to counter the Israelites, they took the precaution of seizing strategic Mount Tavor to the north of the valley, perhaps taking some of Gideon's own family as hostages in order to avert or at least delay an Israelite attack. After all, the northern boundary of Gideon's tribe of Menashe extended all the way to that prominent topographical landmark, and it is plausible that some of his close kin were located there. But in the end, Gideon sent most of his fighting force home and instead struck the Midianite camp unexpectedly, as detailed above. As the Midianites retreated eastwards in hurried confusion, their princes may have decided to kill the hostages either in retaliation or else to speed their flight, since their value as bargaining chips had already been compromised by Gideon's surprise attack.

INTIMATIONS OF MONARCHY

It is clear from the text of the dialogue that critical details have been omitted. However, what is most significant about the conversation, and this is why the matter was included at all, is the Midianite princes' parenthetical remark that "they were like you, the likeness of the king's children." This passing comment, offered by the captured leaders of a vanquished enemy, is the very first intimation in the Tanakh that a leader of the Israelites had the bearing and the ability of a king!

The great question mark hanging over the book of Judges from its earliest chapters, like some dark thundercloud, concerns the matter of central and effective leadership. As the chapters of the book disappointingly unfold, we note how the tribes of Israel have slowly fallen away from their mission only to embrace Canaanite idolatry. They have jettisoned the basic unity that the early stages of the conquest of the land necessitated. In part, this was because they had not yet developed a stable political system that could impose order while ensuring continuity. Judges came and judges went, but none ever succeeded in rallying the tribes as one or in perpetuating their positive reforms for long. Furthermore, no judge ever produced a child that could rule in his or her place. Inevitably, the demise of the judge spelled the end of the all-too-brief period of peace and permanence associated with their rule, to be ominously followed by the familiar refrain: "the people of Israel did evil in God's eyes" (2:11, 3:12, 4:1, 6:1, etc.). Now, for the first time, these Midianite princes, condemned to die for their rash act of kidnapping and murder, broached the sore subject by intimating that Gideon might be a candidate for kingship.

Strikingly, the matter was immediately revisited by the Israelites themselves, for in the very next section they say to Gideon: "Rule over us – you, your son, and your grandson – for you have saved us from the clutches of Midian!" (8:22). Although the people do not use the verb form for the implementation of kingship, *limlokh*, but rather the more neutral *limshol*, meaning to exercise dominion, the thrust of their request is clear. They seek relief from the constant state of political turmoil, and from the vulnerability to foreign tyranny associated with the lack of a central authority, and recognize in Gideon's solidified rule the potential for real and substantive change. While the people seem to grasp that a desire for real kingship is premature, divided as they still are along tribal lines and still preoccupied with physically settling the land, effective regional leadership seems, for the very first time in many years, within reach.

CONFUSION OF MEANS WITH ENDS

Surprisingly, however, Gideon will have none of it. Humbly responding with noble words that recall his earlier reluctance to lead the people (6:15), Gideon says, "I will not rule over you, nor will my son rule over you. Rather, let God rule over you!" (8:23). Gideon will not don the permanent mantle of leadership as the people demand, nor will he agree to appoint his son in his stead because he feels that such innovations will have the effect of shifting communal and national focus away from serving God to concentrating instead upon man. Kingship is not a panacea, Gideon explains, as if all of the people's difficulties could be effortlessly overcome simply by appointing a monarch to rule over them. If the people of Israel are estranged from God, insensitive to His word, and loyal instead to Baal and to his vulgar cohorts, then no king will succeed in turning the tide and alleviating their plight.

This remarkable little passage, then, introduces the essence of the "king debate" and the crux of the people's awful quandary. Unwilling, on the one hand, to commit themselves wholeheartedly to the sternness and solemnity of ethical monotheism, and becoming increasingly impatient with the never-ending cycle of oppression and decline, on the other hand, the people grope for a way out. But Gideon will not accede to their request, for there can be no quick fixes for the people's sorry predicament. Recall that the major events of Gideon's career – his appointment, his marshaling of a fighting force, and his astounding victory – were all bound up with his parallel struggle against insidious Baal worship. Although the Midianites had been soundly defeated on the battlefield and beaten back to their desert redoubts, the challenge presented by Baal had hardly been engaged. Now was not the time to establish a monarchy that, if abusive, could very well entrench Baal worship to an even greater degree. Rather, Gideon's refusal suggested that the people should rather take the opportunity of the triumph over Midian, and the breathing space afforded by that triumph, to address the fundamental and underlying problems plaguing their society.

THE GOLDEN EPHOD AND THE GOLDEN CALF

The final events recorded of Gideon's career are less than flattering and bear out the hazards of kingship and the pitfalls associated with power:

> Gideon said to them, "I will make a request of you. Let each one of you surrender to me the [golden] earrings of their spoils... and they spread a garment and each one cast in his earrings of the spoils...." Gideon fashioned it into an ephod and displayed it in his town of Ofra, but all of the people of Israel strayed after it there, and it became an ensnarement for Gideon and for his household. (8:24–28)

Gideon sought to commemorate his great victory over Midian with some tangible monument. Elsewhere in Tanakh, the ephod is mentioned as one of the more ornamented outer garments of the priest that was also used in the ritual of enquiring of God and seeking His guidance.[2] Perhaps Gideon chose an ephod to recall God's guiding hand in the great victory, His willingness to bolster the warrior's spirits with signs and signals throughout the saga. But the fashioning of the image only spelled trouble, for it eventually became an object of veneration in its own right, satisfying the people's idolatrous desires. Gideon thus met the people's request for a king with a request of his own, but while he admirably deflated their misplaced aspirations, he unwittingly provided in their stead a dangerous stumbling block.

In this connection, it is intriguing to note the similarities between this account and the narrative of the golden calf, cast by Aaron the priest when Moses tarried in his descent from Mount Sinai.[3] In both cases, a

---

2. See I Samuel 23:6–12, and the proof text of Numbers 27:21.
3. See Exodus 32:1–6.

leader figure gathers golden earrings from the people, and with the best of intentions fashions them into an innocuous object that quickly becomes an idolatrous fetish. According to some commentaries on Exodus 32:4, Aaron even gathers the gold in a knotted garment (called there a *ḥeret*) just as Gideon does here, but that particular detail hinges upon an obscure word that can just as easily be read as a description of him fashioning the object with a stylus.[4] Be that as it may, the overall thrust of the narratives is the same: When precious materials are utilized to make a tangible symbol of something grand, even when the process is carried out with the purest of objectives, there will always be those who will seize the opportunity to turn the symbol into something else entirely to serve their own interests.

There is also a glaring contrast between our passage and the Golden Calf episode: There, the people demanded a god figure in Moses's stead, pressing reluctant Aaron to proceed; here it is Gideon, the leader of the people, who unleashes the tragic dynamic. Or shall we rather say that the analogue in our section to Israel's request for a molten image was none other than their desire for a king, both of them representing well-intentioned but fundamentally flawed aspirations?

REMEMBERING GIDEON

Thus Gideon's career comes to an end by ushering in the very idolatrous worship that he had so vehemently combated at the beginning of his mission. Nevertheless, posterity remembered his exploits more fondly, recalling his crushing victory over Midian as an especially impressive display of divine assistance. For the Levite poet Assaf, a contemporary of David (circa 1000 BCE) who witnessed the king's victories against powerful confederacies that sought to destroy the nascent Israelite state, Gideon's triumph provided special inspiration:

> A song for instruments by Assaf. Lord, do not remain quiet, do not be silent or still, Lord. For Your enemies roar and Your foes raise up their heads. Against Your people they plan secret schemes

---

4. Rashi mentions both possibilities in his commentary on Exodus 32:4. Rashbam and the Ḥizkuni (Ḥezekia ben Manoah) prefer to identify the *ḥeret* of Aaron with a garment, thus reinforcing the parallel with our passage.

and take counsel against Your protected ones. They say, "Let us go and cut them off from being a people, that the name of Israel be remembered no more." For they draw their hearts together and conclude pacts against you. The tents of Edom and Yishmael, Moab and those of Hagar, Geval, Ammon and Amalek, Philistia with those that dwell in Tyre. Even Assyria has joined them; they are the accomplices of the children of Lot, sela. *Act against them as you did to Midian*, like Sisera and Yavin at the stream of Kishon. *They were destroyed at Ein Dor, they were strewn like refuse upon the ground. Make their princes like Orev and Ze'ev, all of their governors like Zevah and Tzalmuna. For they have said, "We will inherit for ourselves the pleasant habitations of God."* My Lord, make them like a tumbleweed and like chaff driven before the wind, [burn them] like fire that consumes the forest and as flames that ignite the hills. So too shall You pursue them with Your whirlwind and overawe them with Your storm. (Ps. 83:1–16)

Later still, for the prophet Isaiah who lived in the eighth century BCE and witnessed the fall and exile of the northern kingdom of Israel, Gideon's triumph was the precursor to Jerusalem's own miraculous deliverance from the Assyrian monarch Sennacherib, who threatened to besiege its walls with a massive force in 701 BCE. Describing that event with prophetic foresight, seeing in his mind's eye the decimated Assyrian camp despoiled by the Israelites, he declared:

The people that walked in darkness have seen great light, and light has brightly shined upon those that dwelt in a land overshadowed with death. You [God] have made the people exalted and have increased their joy; they rejoice before You like the joy of harvest and thrill in the division of the spoils. For their burdensome yoke, the beam placed upon the shoulders, the staff that oppressed them *You have smashed like on the day of Midian*. (Is. 9:1–3)

And in another prophecy, this time pronounced as the Assyrian onslaught was underway but before they had actually reached the gates of Jerusalem, Isaiah proclaimed:

Therefore thus says God the Lord of Hosts: Do not fear Assyria, My people who dwell in Zion, for though he may strike you with the rod and raise his staff against you like the Egyptians of old, in a very short time, My anger will be spent upon their abominable words. God shall raise up a whip against them *like the striking down of Midian at the rock of Orev*, like His staff raised up against the sea, and he [Assyria] shall be carried off after the manner of Egypt! (Is. 10:24–26)

We take our leave of Gideon, inspired by his personal struggle to over-come self-doubt and by his singular victory over his people's foes, yet sadly disappointed by the events of his twilight years. The spirited Menashite, fortified by divine signs and wonders, had defeated his own fears in order to overpower the Midianites and drive them from the land. So crushing had been his triumph that his compatriots had asked him to become their appointed ruler and to perpetuate that rule through the founding of a dynasty. But humble Gideon refused, reminding the people that their true loyalties must be to God. In the end, though, Gideon's tenure was tarnished by his fashioning of the commemorative golden ephod that soon degenerated into coarse idolatry. It is therefore with a profound sense of ambivalence that his account ends.

But the saga of Gideon is not yet over. In the next section, his son Abimelech will raise the issue of kingship one last time before it is finally buried for almost two centuries, until the end of prophet Samuel's life and the ascent of Saul to the throne.

Judges 9:1–57

Abimelech the Anti-Judge

T he story of Gideon concludes with two important biographical details concerning his descendants. First, the text informs us that Gideon fathered seventy sons (!) "for he had many wives." Second, we are informed that "his concubine in Shekhem also bore him a son, and he made his name Abimelech" (8:30–31). It is this Abimelech who is the subject of our next narrative. In a stifling postscript, the chapter adds that after Gideon's death, the people of Israel once again strayed from God, this time embracing the Shekhemite fetish of Baal Brit. They forgot the God who had saved them from their enemies and, as the following events will bear out, "they did not act compassionately toward the household of Yerubaal Gideon, in accordance with all of the goodness that he had done for Israel" (v. 35).

ABIMELECH SEIZES POWER IN SHEKHEM

After his father's demise, Abimelech quickly repairs to Shekhem and enlists the help of his maternal uncles and the extended clan of his mother to convince the powerful governors of the town that the mantle of leadership ought to be passed to him. "What would you prefer," he rhetorically asks them, "that all of Yerubaal's seventy sons should rule over you, or rather that one man should rule over you? Remember also that I am your own bone and flesh" (9:2).

The important city of Shekhem, located in the hills some fifty kilometers north of Jerusalem in the tribal territory of Menashe, was not settled by Israelites only but was populated also by an indigenous Canaanite tribe that ethnically descended from the Hivites.[1] These non-Israelite inhabitants of Shekhem were not hostile to their Israelite neighbors. Throughout the lengthy account of the conquest and settlement of the land preserved in the book of Joshua, there is no mention of the city of Shekhem in any context of combat. They did not join the Canaanite confederacies of city-states that unsuccessfully battled against the Israelite armies nor is there any record in the book of an Israelite conquest of their territory. On the other hand, we do find that Joshua's inspirational and exhortative parting address to the people of Israel was delivered at Shekhem.[2] It therefore seems plausible that the Canaanite people of Shekhem, perhaps still recalling the stinging defeat inflicted upon them by the sons of Jacob centuries earlier,[3] decided that a neutral stance toward the returning Israelites would be in their best interest, and thus was born their tradition of accommodation.

For our purposes, we note that that Abimelech, the child of Gideon's concubine from Shekhem, was the offspring of a woman who was not, in all probability, Israelite in origin. Thus, he shared an ethnic affinity with the Canaanite townspeople that his other seventy half-brothers did not. This connection of blood and culture with the indigenous Shekhemites can perhaps also be inferred from the fact that when Abimelech addresses his mother's family and the governors in turn, he invariably refers to his father Gideon by his nom de guerre Yerubaal. This name, assigned to Gideon when he first threw down the idolatrous shrine in his hometown of Ofra (see 6:32), contains the root B-'A-L, *baal*, which would have been most pleasing to Canaanite sensibilities.

Abimelech's words fall on receptive ears, and after securing funds from the treasury of the local idolatrous temple of Baal Brit, he gathers a

---

1. See Genesis 34:2.
2. See Joshua 24:1.
3. See Genesis 34.

militia of vile men to do the unspeakable. Arriving unexpectedly at the home of his father's clan in Ofra, Abimelech slaughters his seventy half-brothers and then proclaims himself king over the city-state of Shekhem and over its surrounding territory. In this way, Abimelech champions his maternal connection to the Canaanites of Shekhem while displaying utter estrangement from his father's Israelite origins.

The sum of seventy pieces of silver that Abimelech receives from the shrine (9:4) corresponds exactly to the seventy brothers that he then goes on to execute. Effectively, he murders each one of his brothers in cold blood for the measly pittance of a single shekel! Abimelech's disdain for the value of human life and fraternal blood, already demonstrated at the very outset of his rule, will color the rest of his vicious career.

ALL IN A NAME

A man of resolve, ruthless Abimelech must have had his eye on the kingship from the very day that the Israelites had first broached the subject. It is reasonable to assume that at the time of Gideon's great victory over Midian, Abimelech was either not yet born or else very young, for at the killing of the Midianite princes Zevah and Tzalmuna in the aftermath of the victory, Gideon's firstborn Yeter was described as being "still a lad" (8:20). No doubt, however, the son of the concubine grew up with the stories of his father's great victory and the reports of his father's refusal to become a dynastic ruler of the people. However, Abimelech was made of more brutal stuff than his humble father was. It is more than likely that his portentous name, which means "my father is king" was not given to him by his father at all, but rather was self-assigned! A careful reading of the pertinent verse in chapter 8 implies as much, for it says, "His [Gideon's] concubine who was in Shekhem also bore him a son, *and he made his name Abimelech*" (8:31).

Generally in the Tanakh, when names are given to children by their parents, the verb *vayikra* ("he called") is used, or *vatikra* ("she called") if the mother bestows it.[4] The verb *kara* means "to call" and its usage in biblical Hebrew is quite similar to its usage in modern English – it frequently means to address another, and it can sometimes mean to

---

4. See, for example, Genesis 16:15, 19:37–38, 21:3, 29:31–30:24, et al.

assign a name. But here, the account does not say *vayikra shmo Abimelech* but *vayasem et shmo Abimlech* which translates literally as "and he made his name Abimelech." The subject of the pronoun "he" in verse 31 may not be father Gideon at all but rather Abimelech himself, and indicates that at some point the ambitious lad renounced his birth name and instead adopted a moniker that was more in keeping with his future ambitions. Instead of reading the verse as "and he [Gideon] made his name Abimelech" we may just as reliably read it as "and he [Abimelech] made his [own] name Abimelech!" Gideon refused to become ruler over his people, but Abimelech rode on his father's coattails in order to advance his own illegitimate and impious claim. "My father is king" essentially implies that "I will succeed my glorious father as king in his stead."

THE PARABLE OF YOTAM

One brother of the seventy, however, escaped Abimelech's murderous grasp. Young Yotam (whose name is a pathetic rearrangement of the letters of the word *yatom*, orphan) follows the news of Abimelech's ascent with alarm. At the time of the latter's coronation at Shekhem, Yotam climbs steep Mount Gerizim opposite and calls out to the assembly from a safe distance. Addressing himself to the governors of Shekhem who aided and abetted Abimelech's rise, Yotam pronounces what ranks as one of the most famous parables in the Hebrew Bible: the story of the trees in search of a king. The trees of the forest, he cries out, went to appoint a king. They approached the olive, the fig, and the grape, but each one refused in turn, citing their need to instead fulfill their special appointed tasks for the glory of God and for the benefit of humanity. "Shall I cease providing my sweet honey and good fruits in order to hold sway over the trees?" replied the fig (9:11). In desperation, the trees then turned to the *atad*, who ominously invited the other trees to take shelter under its shade while also warning them that should they fail to show fidelity, then "a fire shall shoot forth from the *atad* and consume even the cedars of Lebanon!" (v. 15)

While the olive, fig, and grape are well-known species, staples of the biblical diet, and mentioned in the Tanakh innumerable times, the exact identity of the *atad* is subject to disagreement. Some modern-day botanists have identified the *atad* with various species of the lycium or boxthorn.[5] These medium-height (1.5–2 meters) wild bramble bushes have a thick and stout low canopy of foliage that is full of thorns. Since the branches of the bramble often reach to the ground, the trunk is scarcely exposed and therefore the shade provided by the bush is negligible. In the summer, the bramble sheds its leaves that then dry out upon the ground and become highly inflammable. In ancient times, the bush was often planted around orchards and vineyards to discourage both human and animal trespassers.

If this is the *atad* of Yotam's parable, then his message is clear. While the other trees that were asked to become king are all productive members of the landscape, yielding delectable fruit and useful by-products, the bramble yields but thorns. It is a source of neither shade nor produce. If anything, the bramble constitutes a threat to its surroundings, for not only do its sharp thorns harm any who venture too close, but its dried leaves can spread destruction far and wide when they are ignited. So too Abimelech, explains Yotam. Though he lacks any constructive and useful qualifications to become a good king and leader, he has seized the vacant position by force. Although he promises to protect those who have been persuaded to appoint him, in the end he will destroy them and himself with his self-centered recklessness.

ABIMELECH'S DEMISE

After pronouncing his portentous parable, Yotam flees, and it is not long before Abimelech and the nobles of Shekhem have a falling out. After three years of suffering his rapacious rule (9:22), the governors fight back. By positioning their own men upon the well-traveled and well-taxed hill trails that crisscross Shekhemite territory, they are able to seize for themselves one of Abimelech's important sources of income (v. 25). Moreover, when a rabble-rouser by the name of Gaal son of Eved passes through town and openly criticizes Abimelech's rule, the governors rally around him (vv. 26–29). Zevul, who is Abimelech's local lackey, secretly

---

5. See, for example, Judah Feliks, *Nature and Man in the Bible: Chapters in Biblical Ecology* (Soncino Press, 1981), 39–42. For an alternative but no less intriguing view, see Noga HaReuveni, *Tree and Shrub in our Biblical Heritage* (Neot Kedumim Press, 1984), 58–66.

sends word to his absent boss, and when Abimelech unexpectedly arrives with his warriors shortly thereafter, a pitched battle erupts between the two sides (vv. 30–40). Gaal is easily defeated and expelled from the city, and Abimelech then prevails against it (vv. 41–45).

In the meantime, the governors flee to the town's fortress (associated with the temple of Baal Brit) and barricade themselves, but Abimelech rallies his men to quickly fell trees and gather their branches. Placing the wood at the base of the tower, he sets it alight and it topples, killing about one thousand men and women (9:46–49). The remaining opposition to Abimelech regroups and gathers at the nearby fortress of Tevetz, but the wily and ruthless ruler soon besieges it. This time, though, as Abimelech approaches its ramparts to set them alight, a woman casts down an upper millstone that finds its mark and strikes him on the head. Realizing that he has been dealt a deathblow, he beseeches his armor bearer to dispatch him, lest it be said that "a woman killed him!" (vv. 50–54). His servant complies, and thus comes to its ignominious end one of the sorriest chapters in the book. The people of Israel disperse, and the narrative concludes with the observation that the curse of Yotam was in the end fulfilled: The fire of Abimelech overtook the nobles of Shekhem as well as spelling his own doom.

AVOIDING THE PITFALLS OF MONARCHY

This first attempt in Israel to establish some sort of dynastic rule thus fails completely. The narrative is decidedly unsympathetic to any of the protagonists mentioned in the chapter, save for Yotam the surviving son of Gideon. Abimelech, of course, represents the pitfalls associated with hereditary rule, for while this system may accomplish the transition of power more smoothly than typically transpires with other forms of government, often the one who assumes that power is unfit to wield it. Abimelech had no redeeming qualities of his own and was only appointed king because of his father's merit and his own unbridled avidity. Though Abimelech may have been a gifted fighter and strategist, he used those talents only to his own advantage and not for the benefit of the people. Abimelech is the *only* judge in the book (if he may be referred to as such) who is not engaged whatsoever in the typical pursuits associated with being a biblical judge. He does not exhort and instruct like Deborah, nor does he rescue from oppression like Otniel, Ehud, or Gideon. No wonder that after his dismal end, the notion of monarchy was effectively shelved by the people of Israel for almost two centuries!

As for Gaal son of Eved, and Zevul, they too are rogues of the first order, the former an inebriated malcontent espousing no palliative reforms to counter Abimelech, and the latter an obsequious crony of the first degree. Even the oppressed governors and people of Shekhem, idol worshippers all, who were initially only too willing to support Abimelech's murderous bid for the throne, elicit no pity from the reader. It is no wonder that the main protagonists have such unflattering names, for "Gaal" means to vomit, "Eved" means a slave, and "Zevul" (at least in later rabbinic Hebrew) relates to the spreading of fertilizer!

As a whole, this chapter serves as a severe caution, providing us with a profile of the anti-ruler who must not be empowered even when the people are justifiably desperate for leadership. The anti-ruler candidate possesses a lust for power that should immediately be regarded with suspicion and alarm. He is often inspired with a healthy dose of paranoia and thinks nothing of brutally extirpating any and all who oppose him. Though he may possess cunning, charisma, and capability, he has absolutely no sense of a higher purpose and no regard for the larger good. He acts for his own advantage and views the world through the narrow prism of greed and self-gain.

In short, the chapter indicates, no judge at all is preferable to the anti-judge, for though the latter appears to alleviate social and political chaos in the short term, his narcissistic policies tend to propagate it in the long term. Without fail, the anti-judge in the end destroys himself as well as his constituents.

> God thus requited the evil of Abimelech, that which he had done to his father by slaying his seventy brothers. As for all of the evil of the people of Shekhem, God requited it upon them also, for the curse of Yotam son of Yerubaal overtook them all. (9:56–57)

Judges 10:1–18

"Renew Our Days as of Old"

T he tenth chapter of Judges, appearing about midway through the book, is transitional in character. Recall that Abimelech, the self-serving son of Gideon who seized the reins of leadership after his father's death, met his humiliating end at the hands of a woman. At the time of his demise, he much resembled the invincible general Sisera who was felled by Yael at the conclusion of Deborah and Barak's battle against the Canaanite king of Hatzor (ch. 4). In both of these situations, providence indicated that no man, no matter how powerful, can escape the consequences of his villainous deeds indefinitely. "The Omnipresent has many messengers to fulfill His decree,"[1] and therefore even valiant and ruthless warriors may unexpectedly perish in ignominy through the agency of much weaker opponents.

After the death of Abimelech, the book records that two minor judges arose to deliver the people of Israel: Tola son of Pua from the tribe of Issachar, and Ya'ir of Gilead from the branch of the tribe of Menashe east of the Jordan River. Both served for a total of 45 years but precious little is recorded of their exploits. In fact, the text does not even mention the oppressor from whom they rescued the people. As far

---

1. See Numbers Rabba 18:22.

as brevity is concerned, the account of these two is quite similar to the report about Shamgar son of Anat, who succeeded Ehud and preceded Deborah. His biography consisted of a single verse appended to chapter 3 of the book and stated only that he prevailed against the Philistines and slew six hundred of their men with an ox goad!

THE STRANGE ACCOUNT OF YA'IR OF GILEAD

The few details provided about Shamgar's success are at least appropriate for the context of the rest of the book: The verse names his foes, tallies their death toll, and describes his weapon of choice. While the text provides us with no pertinent details concerning Tola, those associated with Ya'ir are most extraneous and actually recorded in the form of a poetic couplet:

> After him arose Ya'ir of Gilead, and he judged Israel for twenty-two years. He had thirty sons who rode upon thirty donkeys (*ayarim*), and thirty towns (*ayarim*) had they. These were called Havot Ya'ir until this very day, and they are located in the land of the Gilead. Ya'ir died and was buried in Kamon. (10:3–4)

In the original Hebrew, the passage has an almost sing-song quality, for the narrator has used the same exact word to describe the donkeys and the towns, though in fact there are minor differences in pronunciation between the two. Donkeys are *ayarim*, but towns are *arim*. *Ayarot* as towns appears only in rabbinic Hebrew.[2]

The medieval commentaries offer only general insights into the passage, suggesting that the text mentions these curious details in order to indicate the importance and privileged status of this man. The comments of Radak are typical:

---

2. In the "new translation" of the Tanakh prepared by the Jewish Publication Society (1978), a valiant attempt is made to preserve the word play of the original Hebrew: "After him arose Jair the Gileadite, and he led Israel for twenty-two years. He had thirty sons who rode on thirty *burros* and owned thirty *boroughs* in the region of Gilead; these are called Havvoth-jair to this day."

This recounting is meant to inform us why he was a judge, for he was mighty and honored on account of his wealth, his offspring, and his glory. Each one of his children was a noble who rode upon a donkey…for they alone were permitted to ride in those lands. (Radak on Judges 10:4)

It is, however, odd that no other judge so far mentioned in the book was catapulted into leadership based on similar credentials. Might the text be indicating, according to Radak, that this judge came to the fore for the wrong reasons, for in the realm of judgment and leadership he possessed dubious qualifications? Might this development, according to Radak, suggest a new trend that describes a further decline in the caliber of Israel's leaders?

YA'IR JUNIOR AND YA'IR SENIOR

There is perhaps another reason for the inclusion of these details. To appreciate it one must first recognize that Ya'ir of Gilead had a mighty ancestor by the same name. Some three hundred years earlier, on the eve of Israel's entry into the land, the shepherding tribes of Reuben and Gad had decided to remain on the eastern side of the Jordan, in the fertile grazing lands that the Israelites had seized from Sihon and Og. These Amorite tyrants had refused to allow the tribes of Israel unobstructed passage through their land into Canaan (Num. 21:21–35) and met them on the battlefield only to be remarkably defeated. Eventually, some of the clans of the tribe of Menashe, led by the sons of Makhir son of Menashe, decided to join Reuben and Gad (Num. 32:39). These Menashite warriors conquered and settled the area of the Gilead, known today as the Transjordanian highlands. As related in the book of Numbers, there were other mighty men of Menashe who also settled the territory: "Ya'ir the son of Menashe captured the Amorite cities and called them Havot Ya'ir. Novah went and captured the town of Kenat and its outskirts, and he renamed it Novah after himself" (Num. 32:41–42).

Thus, the original Ya'ir was a powerful warrior who claimed extensive swaths of territory in the land of the Gilead. From the genealogical lists preserved in the book of Chronicles, we learn that this Ya'ir was not really the son of Menashe at all but rather descended from the tribe of Judah! Hetzron, the son of Judah's firstborn, Peretz, married the daughter of Makhir. Their child was Seguv, and "Seguv begat Ya'ir, who possessed twenty-three cities in the land of the Gilead" (I Chron. 2:21–22).

In other words, the original Ya'ir was a great-grandson of Makhir but in terms of tribal affiliation was actually from Judah. The fact that he was identified in the book of Numbers as a Menashite indicates that he held his grandmother's lineage (for she was the daughter of Makhir) in great esteem. And the reason for this is clear: Makhir's sons were themselves powerful warriors and the family had a well-deserved reputation among the other tribes for valor and bravery.

After all, the lands east of the Jordan River, with their lofty plateaus, verdant hills, sheep and cattle of mythical proportions,[3] and of course their colossal overlords Sihon and Og, were regarded as a frontier region that only the mighty could tame. When Makhir's sons did so, they earned their place in Israelite history. Ya'ir, who was descended from the tribe of Judah, allied himself with them and adopted their destiny as his own. The region that the book of Numbers calls Havot Ya'ir must be synonymous with the "twenty-three cities of the Gilead" mentioned in the book of Chronicles. The mention of these many towns indicates that the original Ya'ir quickly found his place in the clan of Makhir, becoming a very successful warrior, settler, and leader in his own right.

The parallel passage in the book of Deuteronomy is even more profuse in its praise of the original Ya'ir. There, Moses describes in detail the giant Og who ruled over the northern reaches of the region, called the Bashan.[4] Moses relates:

> God also gave Og the king of the Bashan and all of his people into our hands, and we struck him down leaving no remnant. We captured all of his cities at that time – there was not even one town that we did not seize from them – sixty cities that were the entire region of the Argov, the kingdom of Og in the Bashan. All of these were fortified cities with tall ramparts, double gates, and bars, besides the unwalled cities which

---

3. See, for instance, Deuteronomy 32:14; Amos 4:1; Psalms 22:13.
4. The region of the Bashan, its rugged landscape known for its fertility, is what we refer to today as the Golan Heights. It has been disputed territory for thousands of years.

were very many…. Only Og alone remained, a remnant of the Refaim, behold his bed of iron is still preserved in Rabbat Bnei Ammon, it is nine cubits long and four cubits wide, by a man's cubit…. The rest of the Gilead and the entire Bashan that was the kingdom of Og, I assigned to the half tribe of Menashe – the entire region of Argov and the entire Bashan was once known as the land of the Refa'im. *Ya'ir the son of Menashe seized the entire region of the Argov, until the border of the Geshurite and the Maakhite, and he called the cities of the Bashan by his name Havot Ya'ir until this very day!* (Deut. 3:3–14)

DREAMING OF FOREBEARS

It is now clear why our passage in the book of Judges describes our Ya'ir of Gilead in these terms. It is to draw a direct line between him and his ancestor not only in terms of a shared name and a common pedigree but also with respect to successful leadership. Just as the original Ya'ir led his men to victory over the mighty Amorites and settled the northern wild land east of the Jordan, eventually claiming twenty-three towns as his own, so did Ya'ir his descendant loyally follow in his footsteps and even surpass him. For while the original Ya'ir had only twenty-three towns to his credit, our Ya'ir had thirty, all of them called Havot Ya'ir after the name first given by his ancestor!

But now the text introduces what may be considered to be a glaring contrast between the two Ya'irs, for our Ya'ir did not manage to preserve his holdings for very long at all. After his death, we are told:

The people of Israel continued to do evil in God's eyes, worshipping the *baalim* and the *ashtarot*, the gods of Aram, the gods of Sidon, the gods of Moab, the gods of the Ammonites, and the gods of the Philistines, and they abandoned God and did not serve Him. Thus, God became angry with them and turned them over to the Philistines and to the Ammonites. They [the Ammonites] harshly oppressed the Israelites that very year, and for eighteen years thereafter, all of the Israelites that dwelt on the eastern side of the Jordan in the land of the Amorites, those that were in the Gilead. (10:6–8)

A WISTFUL MEDITATION TINGED WITH IRONY

Perhaps we should read the particulars of our Ya'ir's thirty sons, his thirty donkeys and his thirty towns as the man's wistful meditation on a bygone age remembered nostalgically, a painful reminisce of the time when the eastern tribes were ascendant and their Amorite and Ammonite enemies were overpowered and in decline. Ya'ir the younger must have tried valiantly to resurrect a past for which his oppressed people yearned, but to no lasting avail, for hostile Ammon was now more powerful than they were.

We can almost see him in our mind's eye, dressing up his sons as nobles, cloaking their donkeys in festive gear, and leading a farcical procession through the grassy highlands of the Gilead and the Bashan in an annual recreation of his ancestor Ya'ir's famous campaigns and victories. And we can almost hear the Israelite onlookers, nurtured on tales of heroism from the golden past but no strangers to the current Ammonite oppression, who immortalize the pathetic sight of proud Ya'ir and his procession with their own derisive song, a song of sons, donkeys and cities, a song of disappointment and disdain, a rhyming couplet of *ayarim*!

How much had the fortunes of the people of Israel been transformed over the intervening centuries, and all because of their poor choices! How optimistic it had all seemed when Israel first entered the land, decimating their foes and determinedly dedicating themselves to their brilliant destiny! Now, however, Israel had adopted the gods of Canaan and imbibed their twisted values, forsaking their own national mission and casting away their God.

The fact that of no other judge are such particulars mentioned, and the fact that these details are recounted immediately before the report of Israel's infidelity to God, would seem to indicate that the narrator has not only come to offer curious biographical details. Rather, he consciously employs the literary technique of irony in order to project the true feelings of the people: It would take much more than many sons, numerous donkeys, and sentimental signposts pointing to cities of the past to recreate the glorious days of Ya'ir son of Menashe. It would take, the narrator suggests, the unwavering efforts of the people to eradicate idolatry from their midst and to devote themselves sincerely to the God of Israel and to His instruction. And though Ya'ir of Gilead and his tribesmen pined for the grandeur of their illustrious forebears, they achieved none of the original Ya'ir's renown.

The glaring juxtaposition of the passages is now eminently intelligible:

After him arose Ya'ir of Gilead, and he judged Israel for twenty-two years. He had thirty sons who rode upon thirty donkeys and thirty towns had they. These were called Havot Ya'ir until this very day, and they are located in the land of the Gilead. Ya'ir died and was buried in Kamon.

The people of Israel continued to do evil in God's eyes, worshipping the *baalim* and the *ashtarot*, the gods of Aram, the gods of Sidon, the gods of Moab, the gods of the Ammonites, and the gods of the Philistines, and they abandoned God and did not serve Him. Thus, God became angry with them and turned them over to the Philistines and to the Ammonites. They [the Ammonites] harshly oppressed the Israelites that very year, and for eighteen years thereafter, all of the Israelites that dwelt on the eastern side of the Jordan in the land of the Amorites, those that were in the Gilead. The Ammonites crossed the Jordan to battle against Judah, Benjamin and the house of Ephraim, and Israel was in dire straits. The people of Israel cried out to God saying, "We have sinned against You, we have abandoned our God and instead worshipped the *baalim*!" (10:3–10)

A FAMILIAR REFRAIN

But there is more to this passage than a woeful tale of national glory departed and Israelite treachery repeated. The section continues:

God said to the people of Israel, "Did I not save you from Egypt, the Amorite, the Ammonites, Philistines, Sidonites, Amalek, and Maon who oppressed you? You cried out to Me and I saved you from their clutches! But you have abandoned Me and served other gods, therefore I will save you no more. Go and cry out to the gods whom you have chosen, let them save you in your hour of trouble!"

The people of Israel said to God, "We have sinned. Do to us what You like, but save us this day!" They removed the foreign gods from their midst and served God so that His spirit became pained by Israel's affliction. (10:11–16)

Once again, we have what appears to be a formulation that we have seen before: God reminds the people of His earlier salvation, upbraids them for their current infidelity, and seemingly abandons them to their own devices. The people in turn respond by "repenting," and then God relents, thus setting the stage for the emergence of the next judge. This convention has been employed in the book on two other occasions. It occurs at the end of chapter 2 after the demise of Joshua is reported (2:11–23), in the lengthy section that spells out for the first time the dismal cycle of the book. We see it once again in chapter 6 (vv. 7–10), after the celebrated victory of Deborah. In both of these earlier cases, and here as well, the passages of censure do not only conclude the literary section that precedes them but effectively seal the historical era as well.

As we have seen, for as long as Joshua and the elders led the people, they remained loyal to God. When he died, they began to stray. The early judges who rescued them – Otniel, Ehud, Shamgar, and Deborah – demonstrated resolve and strength of spirit and completed their careers without scandal. However, the judges that followed Deborah – Gideon, and of course ignoble Abimelech – did not achieve the same fame: Gideon was tainted by an ongoing need for divine reassurance, and he finished his term against the shameful backdrop of his ephod of gold that became an object of veneration. But he did know how to lead the people, averting internecine conflict with Ephraim and neutralizing the Midianite threat. Abimelech was, of course, no judge at all but only a poor excuse for one. It was not by his merits that during his brief tenure the foes of Israel were held at bay. Rather, it was on account of his father's lingering dread.

With the demise of the two minor judges that followed Abimelech, the book again reverts to the convention of recounting Israelite betrayal and divine displeasure, in order to indicate that we are now about to embark upon a new historical era, marked by further decline. The exploits of these final leaders who will arise after Tola son of Pua and Ya'ir of Gilead are recounted in chapters 11–16. They, in turn, will usher in the book's final dismal chapters. The last judges will neither possess the dignity nor achieve the success of even their immediate predecessors.

Judges 10:6–11:33

Yiftah Defeats
the Ammonites

After the brief mention of Ya'ir of Gilead who enjoyed a flamboyant but insubstantial career as judge, highlighted by not much other than many sons, many donkeys, and many towns, the book once again turns to ominous developments:

> The people of Israel continued to do evil in God's eyes, worshipping the *baalim* and the *ashtarot*, the gods of Aram, the gods of Sidon, the gods of Moab, the gods of the Ammonites, and the gods of the Philistines, and they abandoned God and did not serve Him. Thus, God became angry with them and turned them over to the Philistines and to the Ammonites. They [the Ammonites] harshly oppressed the Israelites that very year, and for eighteen years thereafter, all of the Israelites that dwelt on the eastern side of the Jordan in the land of the Amorites, those that were in the Gilead. The Ammonites crossed the Jordan to battle against Judah, Benjamin and the house of Ephraim, and Israel was in dire straits. The people of Israel cried out to God saying, "We have sinned against You, we have abandoned our God and instead worshipped the *baalim*!" (10:6–10)

While the people of Israel performed their perfunctory repentance in order to secure divine assistance, the Ammonites muster their forces and encamp in Gilead, preparing for a punishing assault on their grumbling vassals (10:17). The Israelites half-heartedly gather for the inevitable clash but have no leader brave enough to lead them into battle. And so it is that the governors of Gilead approach Yiftah from the district of Tov and appeal to him to be their chieftain. But this Yiftah is no blank slate:

> Yiftah of Gilead was a man of valor but he was the son of a harlot, and Gilead had begat him. Gilead's wife bore him other sons, and when the children of that woman grew up, they drove Yiftah out, saying to him, "You shall not inherit in our father's household, for you are the son of another woman!" Yiftah therefore fled from his brothers and dwelt in the district of Tov, and reckless men soon gathered about Yiftah and forayed with him. (11:1–3)

YIFTAH'S LINEAGE – TWO DIMENSIONS

Though we know nothing of Gilead the father, his name indicates that he was a respected member of the tribe of Menashe, for his tribal ancestor was none other than Gilead the son of Makhir the son of Menashe (Num. 26:29). Our Gilead's firstborn son was Yiftah, but because the latter's mother was a prostitute, he could not achieve the legitimacy that Gilead's later sons claimed for themselves. Instead, Yiftah was forcibly expelled by them, into the maw of the foreboding wilderness populated not only by nomadic shepherding tribes but also by desperate fugitives, criminals, and robbers who preyed on the more fortunate. However, Yiftah was a natural leader, and it was not long before these rootless characters gathered around him, seeking solace and support in his company. Yiftah formed them into a band of marauding men now turned against the civilization that had driven them out.

This unusual introduction to the chapter's protagonist must be read against the backdrop of two contrary frames of reference. On the one hand, Yiftah's background comes to emphasize the deterioration in the quality of Israel's leaders, a decline that directly parallels Israel's own ever-widening estrangement from God. Long gone and forgotten are the Otniels of illustrious lineage and the Deborahs of prophetic inspiration.

Now the people deserve to be guided by a man of problematic pedigree who is himself employed in the disreputable career of brigandage. Ya'ir of Gilead, Yiftah's compatriot and immediate predecessor in the narrative, could at least recall his famous forebear and point to his own successful family, substantial wealth, and deeds to numerous fertile towns east of the Jordan River, but to what accomplishments can drifting Yiftah proudly point?

On the other hand, the reports underscore a favorite biblical theme: God's salvation frequently stems from the most unlikely places, for only a person's spiritual merit determines their worth in His eyes, and their suitability, for the awesome task that He lays out before them. While most of us superficially judge others in strict accordance with meaningless externals – appearance, ancestry, and affluence – the True Judge employs other means to gauge the man. Yiftah's "promising" introduction thus recalls for us a long line of other unsung biblical heroes, people who rose from obscurity, infamy, or else the performance of questionable acts to achieve renown. Didn't Tamar the daughter-in-law of Judah rightly don the disguise of the harlot in order to secure her future that had been unjustly denied her, thus becoming the ancestress of kings?[1] Didn't Rahab the harlot and innkeeper care for the spies of Joshua and then later join the people of Israel to embrace their destiny, becoming in the process the progenitor of prophets?[2]

DAVID'S EXPULSION TO THE DESERT

It is precisely this theme that the book of Samuel will reference when it linguistically links David's ascent to the throne with our story of Yiftah. Like blameless Yiftah before him, innocent David also became an outlaw, pursued unjustly by jealous King Saul – the "legitimate" authority figure paralleling Yiftah's half-brothers – and forced to flee to the wastelands of the Judean desert in order to survive. Like Yiftah before him, providence selected David to play a pivotal role in the history of Israel, but a role seemingly incongruous with dubious desert pursuits:

---

1. See Genesis 38.
2. See Joshua 2 and Megilla 14b.

> David left from there and fled to the caves of Adulam. His broth-
> ers and all of his clan heard of it and descended there to him. *Every*
> *man who was in dire straits, every man who had creditors whom he*
> *could not pay, and every man of bitter spirit gathered to him, and he*
> *became their chief,* so that there numbered with him about four
> hundred men. (I Sam. 22:1–2)

But in glaring contrast to Yiftah's "reckless men," David's band is composed of social outcasts and men of ill-fortune – hapless debtors,[3] vaga-
bonds, and the destitute. Unlike Yiftah, David and his men do not form
a band of brigands. Instead, they eke out their subsistence from whatever
provisions they can secure in the inhospitable landscape.

In any case, the fugitive backgrounds of Yiftah and David are similar for their desperation. In general, it may be said about such men that
their humble origins and lean years of alienation and exile are divinely
orchestrated in order to offer them a unique window into the nature of
their mission. Difficult years of marginalization can imbue a Yiftah or
a David with an appreciation of the struggles that constantly face the
invisible members of society that have no champions to raise their sag-
ging spirits and no advocates to defend them from abuse. While the rich
and the powerful tend to be overrepresented among the ranks of those
that govern, it is the weak and vulnerable that are in the greatest need
of good governance. The best governor is the one who deeply understands, through the experience of his or her own life, the needs of all of
the people, especially those that are vulnerable or estranged.

YIFTAH'S FIRST MESSAGE

As the war clouds gather, the elders of Gilead approach Yiftah to lead
the people, summoning him from the otherwise-unknown "land of Tov."
This region, literally "the land of goodness," is surely more than a geographic location. It is also an ironic commentary on the curious reversal

---

3. Up until the modern era, debtors who defaulted could expect to be indentured by
   their creditors to become their slaves. See II Kings 4:1–7 for a particularly harrowing
   case. As a result, in biblical times, debtors who could find no relief for their debts
   often fled to the wilderness to evade capture.

of fortunes: Those who earlier countenanced Yiftah's unfair expulsion with studied indifference, or even active malice, now find themselves in dire straits, while the object of their scorn, whom they had forced to lead the life of an outlaw, has found a land of goodness for himself!

Yiftah secures a pledge from the elders that he will not be deposed after securing victory, thus exposing for all to see the venal and insincere nature of their well-timed request that he now return to lead the people. After all, prior to the Ammonite buildup, had any of the elders ever been troubled by Yiftah's unfair treatment at the hands of his brothers? Had any of them made even a minimal effort to restore him to his former life? But constrained by the exigencies of the hour, the elders agree to appoint him as chieftain and general, and Yiftah hurriedly attempts to avert conflict by dispatching a terse diplomatic message to the king of the Ammonites:

> What is it between me and you, that you have come to me to wage war against my land? (11:12)

The tone of the message, with its preponderance of first-person pronouns, is one of astonishment, with Yiftah clearly casting himself as the victim of unwarranted aggression. The king of the Ammonites responds in kind, accusing the Israelites of having unjustly seized his land when they came out of Egypt some three hundred years earlier! He concludes by offering an ultimatum: "Now return them [these territories] in peace!" (11:13).

SOME RELEVANT GEOGRAPHY

In order to understand the exchange, as well as Yiftah's subsequent response (10:14 –27), some geography, as well as some history, are in order. The eastern side of the Jordan River, from its headwaters north of the Sea of Galilee until the southern tip of the Dead Sea, is naturally divided up by its tributaries into a number of discrete regions. Midway along the eastern shore of the Dead Sea is an impressive narrow gorge carved by the final stretch of the Arnon. The Arnon, a perennial stream for most of its course, rises in the Syro-Arabian desert and then flows westwards some fifty kilometers while dropping some nine hundred meters in elevation, before emptying into the Dead Sea. In ancient times, the Arnon Stream formed the natural boundary between the petty kingdom of Moab to the south and the Israelite tribes of Reuben and Gad to the north.

About midway between the Sea of Galilee and the Dead Sea another tributary of the Jordan River, the Yabbok, bifurcates the landscape. The Yabbok constituted the northern border of the kingdom of Ammon in biblical times. In the fertile territories that stretched out to the north of the Yabbok, the powerful Amorites held sway. The Amorite territories were themselves divided up by the Yarmuk River (not mentioned in the Tanakh) that empties into the Jordan just south of the Sea of Galilee and forms the natural boundary between the region of the Gilead to the south and the Bashan to the north. Finally, at the southern extremity of the Dead Sea was another small stream, in Tanakh referred to as Nahal Zered, and nowadays as Wadi Hasa, which delineated the border between Moab and Edom to the south.

We may therefore speak of four main tributaries and four corresponding small kingdoms. Listed from south to north, they are the kingdoms of the Edomites, Moabites, Ammonites, and Amorites and the tributaries of Zered, Arnon, Yabbok and Yarmuk. The Edomites held sway over the regions to the south of the Dead Sea until the Gulf of Eilat. The Moabites and Ammonites ruled over the lands that stretched from the southern extremity of the Dead Sea past the Arnon and northwards to the Yabbok, while the Amorites controlled the mountainous plateau that rose beyond the Yabbok and continued past the Yarmuk until the lofty mountain range of the Hermon in the north.

Moab and Ammon were neighboring peoples that shared hegemony over the Transjordanian highlands from the Arnon until the Yabbok. Moab and Ammon were not only adjoining realms, they were also related by ties of kinship. Recall that Lot, Abraham's nephew, had long ago (perhaps some seven hundred years before Yiftah) dwelt in the fertile region of Sodom, the area of the "plain of the Jordan."[4] In the aftermath of Sodom's overthrow, he and his two surviving daughters fearfully retired to a cave and there he concluded his life in infamy by

---

4. See Genesis 13:10–12.

fathering through them two grandchildren: Moab and Ammon.[5] Moab and Ammon the descendants of Lot, bound by blood, common history and shared culture (i.e., the same gods), soon raised clans of their own and settled down along the length of the Jordan plain. By the time the Israelites left Egypt, they were already established kingdoms.

In addition, the nations of Moab and Ammon were connected by the international trade route that traversed their lands: The great south-north highway that began at Eilat and continued all the way to Damascus, crisscrossed here and there by secondary caravan routes leading westwards through the arid Sinai Peninsula to Egypt, and eastwards through the barren Arabian peninsula to Mesopotamia. The Moabite capital of Kir, as well as the Ammonite capital of Rabbat Bnei Ammon, were both located along this road, referred to in the Tanakh as "the king's highway" (Num. 20:17), or simply "the paved way" (Num. 20:19). Incidentally, the memory of the ancient Ammonites lives on in the name Amman, the capital of present-day Jordan that is situated on the ruins of ancient Rabbat Bnei Ammon but shares nothing with the Ammonites historically, ethnically, culturally, or linguistically.

SOME RELEVANT HISTORY

Based on the above, the king of Ammon seemed justified in decrying the Israelite possession of territories east of the Jordan that had been considered his patrimony. But there was one significant historical detail that the Ammonite king neglected to mention, and it was this point that Yiftah singled out with special emphasis. Sometime before the Israelites began their march to Canaan, the kingdoms of Ammon and Moab had been attacked and overrun by the mighty Amorite king, Sihon, who hailed from the north. The two petty kingdoms were easily defeated and Sihon seized some of their territory: The Ammonites were pushed back from the banks of the Jordan and confined to a narrow strip of land around their capital of Rabbat Bnei Ammon (located some thirty kilometers east of the Jordan), while the Moabites lost all of their holdings north of the Arnon.

---

5. See Genesis 19:30–38.

Sihon soon cemented his hold on his newly won territory by establishing his capital at refurbished Heshbon, located on the international highway about midway between the Arnon and the Yabbok. Sihon's crushing victory, which introduced Amorite hegemony to the southern region east of the Jordan River, was regarded by the surrounding peoples with awe and dread. A fragment of an ancient ballad, preserved by the Torah in the book of Numbers, describes the triumph:

> For a fire has gone forth from Heshbon, a flame from the city of Sihon, it has consumed the city of Ar, Moab, and the chieftains of Arnon's high places. Woe to you, Moab, you have been destroyed, oh people of the god Kemosh, for he has made his sons into refugees and his daughters into captives to the king of the Amorite, Sihon. (Num. 21:27–29)

The historical facts, then, are these: when Israel neared Canaan, they requested passage through Edomite and Moabite territory, but they were rebuffed by both.[6] Circling around to the east of Edom and Moab, a maneuver that lengthened their journey considerably, Israel then requested of the Amorite king to traverse just north of the Arnon, through the newly won territory of Sihon. The ogre not only refused, but came out to engage them in battle; miraculously, Israel prevailed. Therefore, argued Yiftah, the Israelites did not seize Ammonite territory at all, but rather *Amorite* territory, for Sihon had already conquered the land from the Ammonites before Israel won it in turn! As Yiftah explained:

> The people of Israel sent messengers to Sihon king of the Amorites and king of Heshbon, and they said to him, "Let us pass through your land until we reach our place." But Sihon did not allow Israel to pass through his borders. Sihon gathered all of his people, encamped at Yahatz, and fought against Israel. God the Lord of Israel gave Sihon and all of his people into the hands of Israel and they struck them down, and Israel possessed all of the lands of the Amorites that dwelt in that region. They possessed

---

6. See Numbers 20:14–21 and especially Deuteronomy 2:2–37

the entire Amorite territory, from the Arnon until the Yabbok and from the desert until the Jordan. Now that God Lord of Israel has driven out the Amorites from before His people Israel, will you now possess it? .... While Israel dwelt for three hundred years[7] in Heshbon and its villages, in Aror and its villages, and in all of the towns that are next to the Arnon, why did you not rescue [your territory] during that time? (Judges 11:19–26)

As the talmudic sages would later put it: "These territories of Ammon and Moab were purified (that is, made permissible to the Israelites) by Sihon."[8] In effect, the counter-claim of Yiftah invoked a principle of international law that is considered to be relevant even today: Territory that is won from an aggressor in the course of a defensive war need not be surrendered and especially not to a hostile entity that did not exercise jurisdiction over the territory at the time of the conflict.

After his reasonable entreaties to the Ammonite king were rebuffed, Yiftah leads the tribes into battle. Miraculously, his force of irregulars handily defeats the Ammonite hordes on the battlefield and goes on to destroy twenty of their towns, and thus it is that Yiftah returns Israelite hegemony to the disputed lands.

---

7. Yiftah's offhand remark about "three hundred years" is arguably the most important chronological marker of the book. It indicates that from the time that the people of Israel crossed the Jordan and entered the land until this moment three hundred years had elapsed. This allows us to insert the judges mentioned thus far – the years of enemy oppression and the years of stability that the judges bestow – into a larger frame, along with the events of the book of Joshua.

Commentaries ancient and modern have valiantly attempted to do just that but it is difficult to get exact results. What does seem clear for the medieval commentaries is that we must not count the years of oppression separately but rather *include* that number as part of the years of stability. See Rashi and Radak on 11:26 and Ralbag (Gersonides) on 11:40. The modern commentaries, on the other hand, argue that Yiftah's number is close to a century too short – unless we assume, as I argued in the introduction, that not all of the judges are sequential and that sometimes their stories overlap. In any case, it is clear from Yiftah's remark that the book of Judges as a whole covers a much longer time span than the book of Joshua.

8. Gittin 38a; Ḥullin 60b.

Judges 11:29-40

Yiftah's Vow

The tribes of Israel, having strayed once again from God, were subjected to eighteen years of harsh oppression, this time at the hands of the Ammonites. These Ammonites, centered around their capital of Rabbat Bnei Ammon, had not only terrorized the Israelite tribes east of the Jordan River but had also crossed the river and subjugated Judah, Benjamin, and Ephraim.

Providence selected an unlikely hero to rescue a chastened Israel: Yiftah of Gilead, a well-liked local brigand, the son of a prostitute, who had earlier been expelled by his legitimate half-brothers from the family homestead.

A TIME FOR VOWING

On the eve of his departure to battle, Yiftah made a vow with the intent of securing divine favor, namely that he would offer a sacrifice to God upon his triumphant return. Such conduct is itself unremarkable and should not be misconstrued as a mercenary attempt to "bribe" the deity. In fact, there are a number of other biblical episodes that employ the vow motif in a similar fashion. For instance, after Jacob our forefather had fled from home and hearth into the uncertainty of exile because of the murderous wrath of his brother

Esau, he eventually came to a place which he would later call Beit El. Resting his weary head within a protective cordon of stones, Jacob was soon awakened from his fitful sleep by a heavenly vision of divine concern and care. On the morrow, Jacob took one of the larger stones and poured oil upon it in order to set it up as a marker of the place where he had encountered God. Then, he pronounced a vow to be fulfilled if God would only preserve him on his journey, sustain him, and return him one day in peace to the land of Canaan: "This very stone that I have set up as a marker shall be a place of worshipping God, and from all that You shall give me I will offer a tithe to You" (Gen. 28:10–22).

Much later, in a similar situation to our context, the people of Israel undertook a vow on the eve of their battle with the Canaanite king of Arad who attacked them as they neared the promised land at the conclusion of the wilderness wanderings:

> The Canaanite king of Arad who dwelt in the Negev heard that Israel had traversed by the way of the Atarim. He made war with Israel and captured captives from them. Israel undertook a vow to God and said: 'If You will allow me to wholly prevail against this people, then I shall utterly dedicate their cities [and the victory to You, by not taking from the spoils].' God listened to the voice of Israel and gave over the Canaanites to them so that Israel utterly destroyed them and their cities. They therefore called that place Horma. (Num. 21:1–3)

In both of these situations, one taken from the world of worship and the other from the world of warfare, the vow is utilized as an incentive, spurring on the supplicant to undertake a superhuman effort in a hostile situation. Through exercising the vow, one's trust in God becomes the means by which resolve is maintained in the face of difficult odds and devastating despair. The vow becomes an expression of steadfast faith that God will not disappoint, even when the situation may seem dire. We may go so far as to argue that a vow undertaken in such circumstances demonstrates humility, as if the one who takes the vow recognizes that he does not possess sufficient merit to deserve divine favor, if not for the power of the pledge to "secure a loan."[1]

A QUESTION OF CONTENT

What is remarkable concerning Yiftah's vow, however, relates to its content, for while the warrior indicates that he will sacrifice to God upon his triumphant return from battle, he is vague concerning *the object* to be sacrificed:

> Yiftah declared a vow to God, and he said: "If You completely surrender the Ammonites into my hands, then that which shall go forth from the portals of my house to greet me when I return in peace from Bnei Ammon will be for God, and I shall offer it as a burnt offering!" (11:29–31)

The ancient rabbis, in commenting upon this episode, declared:

> Said R. Shemuel bar Naḥmani in the name of R. Yoḥanan: Four biblical figures initiated vows. Three of them asked inappropriately but God nevertheless responded appropriately, while the fourth asked inappropriately and God responded in kind. The first was Eliezer the servant of Abraham for he stated, "The maiden to whom I shall say, 'Please tilt your pitcher so that I might drink,' and she shall respond, 'Drink! And I will also water your camels,' it is she whom You have proven to be the one for Isaac" (Gen. 24:14). And what if she had been a Canaanite maidservant or a prostitute? Nevertheless, God brought about that it was Rebecca.
>
> The second was Caleb, for he stated, "I shall give my daughter Akhsa in marriage to the one who shall capture Kiryat Sefer" (Josh. 15:16). And what if he had been a Canaanite or else a slave? Nevertheless, God brought about that it was Otniel.

---

1. Other notable vows in the Tanakh include barren Hannah's heartfelt pledge that if God would only remember her and grant her a child then she would dedicate that very child to God's service at the Tabernacle of Shilo forever (I Sam. 1:11).

The third was King Saul for he stated, "The one who strikes him [Goliath] down shall be given great wealth by the king, and he [the king] shall also give him his daughter" (I Sam. 17:25). And what if he had been an Ammonite, a Canaanite or a *mamzer* (the offspring of an adulterous or incestuous relationship)? Nevertheless, God brought about that it was David.

The fourth was Yiftah, for he stated, "That which shall go forth from the portals of my house to greet me when I return in peace from Bnei Ammon will be for God, and I shall offer it as a burnt offering." And what if it had been a camel, a donkey, or a dog? Would he still have offered it? This time, however, God responded by bringing about that it was his own daughter![2]

EXERCISING CARE WITH ONE'S WORDS

In three of the examples quoted above, the protagonists in question made ambiguous commitments that related to marriage and that concerned the identity of potential spouses for their children. Eliezer, the loyal steward of Abraham, should have been more specific about the qualities of the woman that he was seeking as a match for Isaac, Abraham's son. Caleb should have been more careful to indicate what other traits ought to characterize a potential suitor for his daughter, over and above valor and courage. Saul, in attempting to encourage someone to step forward to battle the Philistine giant Goliath, should have stated his challenge to the people of Israel with greater detail, clarifying that mighty but otherwise unsuitable individuals need not apply. Nevertheless, in all of these situations, divine providence smiled upon these leaders, and their rash words did not come back to haunt them. But Yiftah, alone among them all in dedicating his vow exclusively to God's glory – "that which shall go forth from the portals of my house…will be for God, and I shall offer it as a burnt offering" – lived to regret his impulsive offer, for it was his own daughter that came out to greet him!

The rabbis, truth be told, could not imagine that Yiftah intended anything other than to offer an animal as a sacrifice to God. When they

---

2. This rabbinic source, widely quoted by the medieval commentaries, is found with variations in Taanit 4a, Leviticus Rabba 37:4, and *Yalkut Shimoni* II:25.

wished to emphasize the impetuousness of his vow, they stated simply that Yiftah should have exercised more caution, for instead of a permitted species fit for sacrifice such as a sheep, goat, or cow, he could have also been greeted by "a camel, a donkey, or a dog." However, it is less clear why this lack of specificity should have aroused so much divine displeasure. After all, didn't Yiftah undertake the vow in the best tradition of meeting adversity with a call to piety, and with God's glory alone in mind?

CONSIDERING THE *AKEDA*

The answer is to be found in a striking series of parallels between this episode, which culminates in the sacrifice of Yiftah's daughter, and its most natural analogue in Tanakh – the *Akeda*, the episode of the binding of Isaac, recounted in Genesis, chapter 22. While it is beyond the scope of our analysis to analyze the *Akeda* in depth, we may nevertheless note the following similarities as well as some of the glaring differences. In both situations, it is the relationship with God that is highlighted – Abraham is called upon to demonstrate his absolute loyalty while Yiftah seeks to show his dedication and gratitude. In both episodes, the one singled out by God for immolation is an only child described in the original text as *yahid* (Gen. 22:2) or *yehida* (Judges 11:34). In both passages, there is a period of dreadful anticipation between the pronouncement of the plan and its fulfillment – three days journey separate God's command to Abraham from his building of the altar upon Mount Moriah, while two months pass between Yiftah's return from battle and the sacrifice of his daughter. In both situations, it is the parent-child bond that is sorely tried, with the parent showing superhuman readiness to carry out the terrible deed, and the child demonstrating herculean resignation, staggering acceptance and extraordinary trust. At the same time, as the awful moment draws closer, there are words of affection that pass between the parent and the child, with the child invariably addressing the parent as *avi* or "my father," while the father, in turn, refers to "my son" or "my daughter" (Gen. 22:7; Judges 11:35-36).

There are, as well, a number of stark contrasts. At the *Akeda* it is God who demands the unthinkable of Abraham as a trial of faith, while in our chapter it is Yiftah who initiates the challenge in order to secure victory upon the battlefield. At the *Akeda*, God specifically selects Isaac as the intended sacrifice, while it seems to be happenstance that singles out Yiftah's daughter. At the *Akeda*, Isaac's words are not recorded (could his response have been anything other than awesome silence?), while in our passage Yiftah's daughter not only fails to discourage her father from carrying out the act but actually *encourages* him to do so saying, "Father, you have made a vow to God, therefore do to me what you did declare since God has performed great vengeance upon your enemies, the Ammonites!" (11:36). And, most tragically, at the *Akeda*, God in the guise of an angelic voice from heaven stays Abraham's hand at the last moment, while here there is no divine intervention to save Yiftah's daughter from her father's fulfillment of his reckless vow.

AN INESCAPABLE CONCLUSION

The startling conclusion to be drawn and the shocking explanation for the *Akeda* parallels is therefore the following: Yiftah *did not* intend at all to offer an animal as a sacrifice to God upon his return, but rather a *human being!* When he stated "then that which shall go forth from the portals of my house to greet me when I return in peace from Bnei Ammon will be for God, and I shall offer it as a burnt offering," he was not referring to an animal, but rather to a living person. "The first person," said Yiftah, "that shall come forth from my home, passing the threshold of the doorway, shall be dedicated to God as a burnt offering!" It is critical to note that in Hebrew there are no gender-neutral pronouns and therefore the original Hebrew verse, phrased in the masculine, can be convincingly rendered as:

> If You completely surrender the Ammonites into my hands, then *he* that shall go forth from the portals of my house to greet me when I return in peace from Bnei Ammon will be for God, and I shall offer *him* as a burnt offering!

Other evidence for Yiftah's true intent includes the fact that there is no reference in this passage to gates or to barns, to fields or to sheepfolds, but only to "the portals of my house." And though in ancient times, animals lived in close quarters with their human masters, they nevertheless did not share with them the actual living space implied by "house." The expression "the portals of my house" is therefore a poetic way of saying "the first member of my household whom I encounter." That person whom providence would fatefully select could be a servant or slave, a cousin or clan member, a loyal supporter or else a casual visitor, but Yiftah surely did not expect it to be "his only child!" His stunning surprise at her sudden appearance was not due to the fact that a person came forth to greet him (for that was his hope all along) but rather that it was, tragically, his own beloved daughter.

LEXICOGRAPHICAL EVIDENCE

The idiom used, both in Yiftah's vow as well as in its aftermath, to describe the act of going forth to greet – *latzet likrat* (11:31, 34) – occurs almost forty times in the Tanakh. Sometimes it is used to describe a hostile encounter such as going forth to meet the enemy on the battlefield,[3] often it is used in the more neutral sense of rendezvousing, or else the friendly sense of greeting,[4] but it is *never* used to describe anything other than an encounter between two or more human beings. In fact, the term *likrat* by itself, though it occurs well over a hundred times, only once refers to a human meeting a non-human.[5]

We must therefore amend our understanding of the episode: Yiftah's vow was no innocent show of devotion but rather a repugnant and twisted act of misplaced piety. The vow was met blow for blow by God's own ironic and thundering response of disapproval: It was none other than Yiftah's only daughter who went forth to meet him "with drums and with dances" (11:34). It is for this reason that Yiftah did not merit a divinely orchestrated turn of events for the good, as did the other three who impulsively took vows, for though God may be forgiving concerning imprecise language, He will not forego the monstrous crime of murder in His name. There must be consequences for such villainy, and let them fall upon the head of the perpetrator in the most unexpected but forceful fashion! In the larger context, this episode confirms that which we sorrowfully suspected: Israel and its leaders, in this horrific culmination of an insidious process underway since the book began, have become indistinguishable from the Canaanite idolaters.

---

3. See, for example, Numbers 20:18, 20; Judges 20:31; II Chronicles 2:35:20.
4. See, for example, Exodus 18:7; Judges 4:18; Isaiah 7:5.
5. See Judges 14:5, concerning Samson's unexpected encounter with a young lion.

RECALLING THE INFAMY OF THE CANAANITES

The Canaanites were technologically more advanced, politically more astute, and culturally more aware than their Israelite neighbors, but none of that "enlightenment" was translated into a heightened moral sensitivity (is it ever?). Over and over again, the Torah wages a war of words against the Canaanite infatuation with idolatry, sexual immorality, magic, and cruelty, but the most serious indictment against their societies is stated in the following passage, and it concerns, of all things, the act of worship:

> When God your Lord cuts off the nations [from the land] that you are going to inherit, and you drive them out and inhabit their land, then be careful lest you become ensnared by them after they have been destroyed from before you, and lest you enquire after their gods saying, "How did these nations serve their gods? I will do so as well." Do not do so to God your Lord, for all the abominations that God hates they perform for their gods; *they even burn their sons and daughters in the fire to their gods!* [Rather] you shall observe all of the things that I command you; do not add to it nor subtract from it. (Deut. 12:29–13:1)

The above text from the book of Deuteronomy clearly links devotion to the gods with human or child sacrifice, while making it abundantly clear that the God of Israel abhors both. The *Akeda*/Yiftah matrix is thus reinforced: To Abraham, God forcefully demonstrates that while He truly desires utter devotion and trust, He *will not* countenance the sacrifice of Isaac. The drama is only an exploration of the makings of profound faith, never intended to be carried out. It is simultaneously a harsh polemic against prevailing Canaanite practice. As Abraham raises his hand to murder his child in His name, God stays his hand and proclaims: "What I truly desire is your sincerity and devotion to My commands, nothing more. Isaac is your and Sarah's future and the fulfillment of My promise. Could I have demanded from you to immolate him in My name?!" Yiftah, though he is a leader in Israel and a seeming servant of all that is just and holy, demonstrates by his vow that he is also a product of caustic Canaanite culture that will guarantee victory upon the battlefield by vowing to sacrifice an innocent human being! Did he never study the story of the *Akeda*?

ANOTHER EXAMPLE

Lest the reader object to the fundamental premise that Canaanites were capable of such things, consider the following episode from the second book of Kings, chapter 3. The context concerns a battle that takes place between a confederacy composed of the king of Judah, the king of Israel, and the king of Edom on the one hand, and the king of Moab on the other. The Moabites desperately attempt to defend their borders, but they are routed and overrun. This prompts their king to do a desperate but not unthinkable act:

> He took his firstborn son, who would have ruled after him, and he offered him as a burnt offering upon the ramparts so that there might be great fury upon Israel. (II Kings 3:27)

There is more than a passing similarity here to our own passage, for in both situations it is defeat on the battlefield that must be averted. Could it be that Yiftah, who preceded this king of Moab by some three centuries, also thought that God desires desperate acts of devotion in order to secure His favorable response in desperate situations? Could it be that Yiftah believed that he would secure divine sympathy by offering that which is most precious and dear to the deity, namely inviolable human life? Could it be that his vow to God must be read as literally as the original Hebrew suggests? Does it not state explicitly that no sacrificial animal is intended at all, but rather a person?

> Yiftah declared a vow to God, and he said: "If You completely surrender the Ammonites into my hands, then *he* that shall go forth from the portals of my house to greet me when I return in peace from Bnei Ammon will be for God, and I shall offer *him* as a burnt offering!" (11:9–31)

THE RESPONSE OF YIFTAH'S DAUGHTER

The most telling indication that our interpretation is correct is provided by Yiftah's own daughter, for her response to the turn of events is nothing short of startling. Should she not have cried out against her father's monstrous vow? Should she not have engaged God Himself in heated and desperate debate? Her explicit approval of her father's pledge and her utter willingness to become his sacrifice (11:36) can only mean one thing: She herself regarded his vow of killing another human being for the sake of God as a pious pronouncement even as it found her as the unintended target. Like her own father and the morally corrupt Israelite society around her, she had imbibed cherished Canaanite beliefs. Initially, Israelites adopted human sacrifice as part of their worship of Canaanite gods. Later, those twisted devotions were employed for their worship of God Himself!

What else could one of the later prophets have meant when he solemnly declared:

> With what shall I approach God and show deference to the Lord of heaven? Shall I approach Him with burnt offerings or with one-year-old calves? Shall God desire thousands of rams or tens of thousands of rivers of oil? *Shall I offer my firstborn for my transgression, the fruit of my womb to atone for the sin of my soul?* Man may have declared to you what he thinks is good, but what does God require of you? Only to perform justice, to love compassion and to walk humbly with your Lord! (Mic. 6:6–8)

Micah, who lived in the eighth century BCE and railed against injustice, social inequality, and insincere worship, here presents us with an ascending list of things that, intuitively, we might expect God to desire: a standard burnt offering, an especially choice one-year-old calf, thousands of expensive rams, and tens of thousands of rivers of precious oil. Surely, the God of Israel, like the others gods of Canaan, Egypt, Moab, Ammon, Edom, and all of the other innumerable tribes and peoples of the region, would be impressed with such gifts! As the crescendo to this catalog of pleasing sacrifices, Micah suggests that perhaps God desires the ultimate: "My firstborn for my transgression, the fruit of my womb to atone for the sin of my soul"! Man has declared what he thinks is good and if that man is a polytheistic idol worshipper then, indeed, his gods could ask for nothing more precious than a human sacrifice, a child sacrifice! But for Micah this is all a rhetorical question, for what God of goodness and morality would ask His practitioners to murder a human being for His service? No, says Micah in his thundering rejection of what many men call holy; what God truly desires – and all that He desires – is for us "to perform justice, to love compassion and to walk humbly with your Lord!" The *Akeda* therefore brackets Yiftah on one side of the timeline while Micah's condemnation brackets it on the other, unequivocally denouncing his vile vow as an outrage fit for the gods, but not for the God of Israel.

REVISING OUR (MIS)CONCEPTIONS

We must accordingly revise our mental image of the episode. Now we see in our mind's eye brave Yiftah preparing to go out to battle, anxious and uncertain but brimming with a confidence inspired by his vindication at the hands of the elders of Gilead who have appointed him as their leader. As he prepares to take his leave of the assembly of the people who had apprehensively witnessed his investiture at Mitzpah, Yiftah casts one last long look toward the verdant hills that stretch out in the direction of his own home. His mind races with a thousand desperate thoughts and plans, his heart pounds with the enormity of the task that lies before him. But Yiftah, after all, though a brigand by trade, is a servant of God in spirit. How will he appease this stern deity and cause His blessings to shower him with victory?

Taking a cue from his cultural surroundings, and still possessed by the thought of the home and family that he fears he may never see again, Yiftah pronounces his fateful vow: "Oh mighty God, if You but grant me triumph, then I will present You with the most valuable offering of all: A member of my own household, perhaps a relative or a dear friend! The sacrificial victim will understand our desperate situation, he will not protest this act of extreme devotion perpetrated upon his being, for such has been the hallowed practice among the peoples of this land from time immemorial!"

Remarkably, God grants Yiftah his astonishing victory and he returns home flushed with excitement. The accolades of the people are still ringing in his ears as he expectantly retraces his path toward his beloved homestead. In the distance he can hear the rhythmic beating of the drum and the sound of song, and he absentmindedly wonders who might it be that has come forth to greet him. "God was pleased with my vow," he remarks, as he draws closer, "and now I must repay Him with joy!" But soon the figure is recognizable, her sweet voice suddenly familiar, and Yiftah falls to the ground, doubled over in grief. How unexpected was the victory against the Ammonites, and how unexpectedly has merriment turned to tragic and indescribable mourning! His only daughter (how innocent her smile was but a moment ago) attempts to raise him up, his other family members rush to his side, but no one can make out the incoherent words that issue forth, punctuated by heartbreaking sobs.

Slowly, he regains his composure. Picking himself up from the ground, he inaudibly pronounces the ineffable words through his clenched lips: The vow to God (cursed be the day that it was ever pronounced! Cursed be the people who could countenance such things!) must be fulfilled. Silence falls upon the family now, joined by all the concerned onlookers who have hurriedly come in response to the commotion. All eyes are upon Yiftah's daughter, his only child and truly that which is most beloved to him in the entire world. Her drum still lies in the dust where it fell when she ran to greet her father as he collapsed, and her young and shapely shoulders, still draped in the brightly colored robe that she had specially donned for her father's return, are now stooped and broken. Though her eyes brim with tears, her voice is soft and comforting: "Father, you have made a vow to God, therefore do to me what you declared since God has performed great vengeance upon your enemies, Bnei Ammon!"

GOD'S RESPONSE

All are struck by her earnestness and by Yiftah's steely resolve, the people nod approvingly if hesitantly, and even the blue skies above seem pleased by the outcome. But there is much consternation in heaven as God disappointingly looks on, not at all indifferent to what has transpired but determined to let human beings exercise their dismal choices. Later, His thoughts will be articulated by Jeremiah, the First Temple prophet who lived to see Yiftah's evil decision played out a thousand times around the outskirts of Jerusalem and in the verdant valley of Ben Hinnom just to the west of the city wall:

Thus says God of hosts the Lord of Israel, behold I will bring evil upon this place so that all that hear of it – their ears shall ring. This is because they have abandoned Me and have made this place unrecognizable. They have offered incense there to other gods that neither they, nor the kings of Judah, nor their ancestors knew, and they have filled this place with the blood of the innocent. They have built high places to Baal upon which to burn their children by fire as sacrifices to Baal. These are things that I did not command, nor did I say, nor did I ever contemplate! (Jer. 19:3–5)

Our conception of the episode must therefore be recast. Far from being an innocent victim of divine capriciousness and cruelty, a casualty of Kafkaesque circumstances that have conspired to destroy him, Yiftah himself has chosen the course that has brought him to this terrible moment. It was not an innocent or ill-considered slip of the tongue that condemned him to the loss of his own beloved daughter, but rather a conscious and deliberate pronouncement of iniquitous malevolence. And rather than an innocent and pure victim of her only sin of loving her father too much, Yiftah's daughter ought to be regarded as an accomplice to his act of infamy.

As for all of Israel that stood by in the aftermath of that terrible moment, we need only compare their acquiescence to another instance of a rash vow pronounced in battle, this time by King Saul who battled the Philistines about a century after Yiftah.[6] King Saul forbade his army, on pain of death, to partake of any food or drink until the discomfited Philistines had been completely routed. Saul's own son Jonathan, however, had not been present when the vow was uttered, and he tasted from the wild honey that he found during the course of pursuing the enemy. Though Saul felt compelled to stand by his vow and to put his own son to death, "the people redeemed Jonathan so that he did not die." But in our passage, Israel did nothing to avert the decree, thus indicting themselves of having succumbed to the very Canaanite evil that God had repeatedly called upon them to extirpate from their midst so that they might avoid being consumed by it in turn.

6. See I Samuel 14:20–45.

As we have seen, the ancient rabbis refused to entertain the notion that Yiftah could have contemplated the outrageous act of human sacrifice. In their noble capacity for exoneration of the culpable, they therefore transformed his indiscretion from an appalling moral failure into a foolish ritual infraction: rashly pronouncing an impulsive and imprecise vow. In similar fashion, so evil was the deed of immolating his own daughter in the final fulfillment of the vow that some of the medieval commentaries were unable to countenance such an abomination in ancient Israel. They preferred to interpret the actual "offering" to God to mean her dedication to a monastic life, so that she led a life of hermitage and isolation, barred from marriage and separated from society.[7] In support of their view, the biblical text itself was adduced, for it states that "he did to her in accordance with the vow that he had made" (11:39) and makes no explicit mention of sacrifice.

There are therefore four possible readings of the story, ranked according to increasing severity: (1) Yiftah's vow was to offer a pure animal but he was imprecise. His daughter fatefully appeared instead, and he fulfilled his vow by dedicating her to a reclusive life. (2) Yiftah intended a human sacrifice. His daughter fatefully appeared instead, and he fulfilled his vow by dedicating her to a reclusive life. (3) Yiftah's vow was to offer a pure animal but he was imprecise. His daughter fatefully appeared instead, and he sacrificed her to God. (4) Yiftah intended a human sacrifice. His daughter fatefully appeared, and he sacrificed her to God. The ancient rabbis preferred the third reading, the medieval commentaries the first, and our analysis the fourth! By choosing the fourth possibility, we must assume that Yiftah's initial intentions were morally malevolent, as the straightforward reading of the relevant verses indicates. Therefore, Yiftah's intention in pronouncing his vow was to carry out an act of human sacrifice upon an altar, and this he did in due course to his own daughter. As for the ambiguous biblical language concerning the fulfillment of the vow, we may say (in contrast to the medieval commentaries) that the Tanakh

---

7. See Radak on 11:31; Ralbag on 11:34–40. See also Ibn Ezra's commentary on Genesis 22:1 where he entertains a similar possibility regarding the *Akeda,* but then rejects it.

chose to describe the terrible deed with delicate but unmistakable circumlocution.

Whatever interpretation of the episode is ultimately adopted, it is clear that the ancient rabbis, and the medieval commentaries after them, certainly had little positive to say concerning Yiftah, and he is not remembered in our tradition as a role model in any sense of the term. Quite the contrary. When they wanted to teach us that every generation suffers the leaders that it deserves, they rabbis said: "Yiftah in his generation is like Samuel in his generation... even a man who is the least of men but has been appointed as an overseer of the community, must be accorded due respect."[8] The former became a paradigm for poor leadership while the life and career of the latter constituted an ideal.

And what of God in all of this? What was His role? As is most often the case, God remained silent, allowing people to make their evil choices and to live or die by the consequences. It is a basic premise of biblical theology that human beings are free to make decisions of destiny. Though we recoil from human acts of violence and cruelty, we simultaneously champion our freedom to choose. The latter is truly only possible if we are willing to accept the possibility of the former. But God's silence in the arena of human history should not be misconstrued as absence or approval. Patiently, He waits, hoping that we will choose the good. And relentlessly, through the Tanakh and the teachings that constitute His message to Israel and to mankind, He makes His expectations of us clear. God is therefore never silent, for His words continue to reverberate across the cosmos and down through the generations until the end of time.

As we leave this chilling episode behind, we recognize once again the basic progress of the book: With each passing generation, with each unfolding era of oppression, with each new leader that arises to save them, the tribes of Israel slip farther and farther away from their destiny and from the lofty challenge of ethical monotheism that God has set before them. How well placed indeed are the rites of mourning yearly practiced by the daughters of Israel in commemoration of the young girl's demise

---

8. See Rosh HaShana 25a–b.

(11:40), for truly there is much to mourn as this sorry tale concludes. As for us, a nagging question resurfaces with greater urgency: How will the tribes of Israel ever succeed in changing the course?

Judges 12:1–15

The Legacy of Yiftah

Chapter 12 of the book of Judges describes the aftermath of Yiftah's victory over the Ammonites. Recall that the kingdom of Ammon, centered on an upper tributary of the Yabbok Stream at the city of Rabbat, about forty kilometers east of the Jordan River, had harshly oppressed the Israelite tribes of Reuben, Gad, and Menashe that lived in the highlands of Gilead. Eager to reverse three hundred years of history, Ammon denied any Israelite claim to the fertile lands that had first been settled by those tribes after the trouncing of Sihon and Og, the mighty Amorite kings, by Moses and the Israelites (see Num. 21:21–35, 32:1–42). The expansionist Ammonites also pressed westwards, subjugating the tribes of Ephraim, Benjamin, and Judah that all dwelt on the opposite side of the Jordan River. Yiftah, brigand and outlaw, had been hastily summoned by the elders of Gilead to counter the Ammonite menace. After his peace overtures were rebuffed, he confidently led a force of Israelite irregulars drawn from all of the tribes east of the Jordan River (but especially Menashe) into battle. Unexpectedly, Yiftah inflicted a crushing defeat, and the Ammonites were pushed back all the way to the edge of the desert, while Israelite hegemony was reestablished over the disputed lands.

The national triumph, however, was marred by Yiftah's personal tragedy, for he had uttered a vow on the eve of his entry into the battle.

Upon his triumphant return, his only daughter came forth with timbrels to joyously welcome him, and Yiftah doubled over in grief. In the end, after she had mournfully wandered for two months accompanied by her maidens, lamenting her fate among the verdant hills of Gilead, her father fulfilled his distorted pledge of devotion and immolated her in the name of God.

THE EPHRAMITES' CLAMOR

While the demise of Yiftah's daughter is recorded at the end of chapter 11, this is for the sake of literary considerations. Appending her sacrifice to the victory over Ammon emphasizes the tragic quality of the events while neatly completing the account of the shocking episode in its entirety before moving on to speak of other matters. In reality, though, the events of chapter 12 happened *before* the daughter of Yiftah met her final fate, for the tribe of Ephraim actually clamor against Yiftah as soon as the smoke of battle has cleared:

> The people of Ephraim were mustered and passed over [the Jordan] toward the north, and they said to Yiftah: "Why did you traverse [the river] in order to battle the people of Ammon while neglecting to summon us to accompany you? We will burn down your house upon you with fire!" (12:1)

Yiftah's reaction to the Ephraimite provocation is swift and harsh. Rebuking them for their initial failure to join him in battle against the Ammonites, Yiftah wastes no time in gathering his compatriots, the people of Gilead who dwell east of the Jordan, and engaging the Ephraimites in hostilities. Overwhelmed, the Ephraimites attempt to flee but to no avail. Quickly, Yiftah seizes the fords of the Jordan in order to prevent the Ephraimites from escaping back over the river and then proceeds to slaughter them to a man:

> The Gileadites secured the fords of the Jordan of Ephraim, so that if a fugitive from Ephraim would say, "Let me traverse," the people of Gilead would say to him, "Are you then an Ephramite?" If he would respond "No," then they would say to him, "Say now *shibbolet*." If

he answered "*sibbolet*," for [Ephramites were] unable to pronounce the word,[1] then they would seize him and slaughter him at the fords of the Jordan. At that time, 42,000 Ephramites perished. (12:5–6)

THE PRECEDENT OF GIDEON

Exploiting the inability of the Ephramites to pronounce the sibilants properly, Yiftah's men are easily able to ferret them out and kill them. The Ephramite losses are, of course, staggering, exceeding any other Israelite casualty number recorded in the book! Considering the matter from the point of view of leadership, we may say that Yiftah fails here miserably. This is not the first example of wounded Ephramite pride recorded in the book of Judges, nor is it the first time that a judge has been placed in such trying circumstances. We must compare Yiftah's conduct to that of his predecessor Gideon, who earlier overcame a different oppressor from across the Jordan that had penetrated into the heartland of the Israelite settlement to the west. In the heated aftermath of warfare, Gideon also faced an Ephramite challenge to his rule, but he met it in a radically different and infinitely more constructive way.

Under circumstances not unlike those faced by Yiftah, similarly confronted by a large and well-armed enemy force, Gideon assembled a coalition of tribes to engage the Midianites but conspicuously omitted summoning the Ephramites who were beyond the geographic range of the oppressor. It was not until the rout of the fleeing foe that Gideon called upon the Ephramites to secure the western fords of the Jordan, in order to prevent the nomadic Midianites from escaping across the river eastwards toward the desert. This the tribe duly did, but then they strove with Gideon "mightily:"

> The men of Ephraim said to him, "What is this thing that you have done to us by not summoning us when you went to fight the Midianites?"… But he responded: "Have I done anything as

---

1. Parenthetically, this encounter highlights the fact that the Israelite tribes employed slightly different dialects from each other that betrayed their origins. Clans are naturally more loyal to their own members, where membership is formed through a complex mix of common culture, history, language and dialect.

valiant as you have done now? Are not the gleanings of Ephraim preferable to the harvest of Aviezer? Did not the Lord give into your hands the Midianite princes Orev and Ze'ev? What could I have done to surpass your exploits?" Their wrath was then assuaged when he spoke those words. (8:8:1–3)

Here, Gideon was confronted by an Ephramite provocation born out of the proud tribe's frustration with being excluded, but, unlike Yiftah, he defused the situation with soothing words. By employing a strategic mix of self-deprecation and glowing praise of his interlocutors, he was able to overcome the Ephramite hurt and to win them over to his side. Rather than exacerbating the existing tribal rivalries, always a source of great grief in the book, Gideon attempted to heal the natural rifts and to foster unity. Because of his willingness to exercise humility, he was successful.

THE CONTRAST WITH YIFTAH

However, Yiftah was cut from different cloth. A brigand at heart, the charismatic outlaw had been called from the desolate highlands to do battle with the Ammonites, and with his fighting spirit he prevailed. Faced, however, with a quarrel among his own splintered polity, he could not and would not bring the tribes together. By championing his own compatriots and their decisive role in the victory and by denigrating the Ephramites that were angered by their exclusion from the rout, he stoked the coals of strife, and tens of thousands perished by his word!

In fairness, Yiftah claims in his rebuttal to Ephraim that the tribe had remained deaf to his entreaties to assist in the battle, at least until the Ammonites were already put to flight. A paraphrase of 12:2–3 might read as follows: "As long as the threat of the Ammonites was still upon you, you would not dare to join us despite my urgent appeals," said Yiftah, "but now that I have scattered them so that they are in withdrawal from your territory, you complain about your exclusion from the fray!" In this aspect, his situation differed markedly from that of Gideon who had never called upon the Ephramites to join the battle, since Menashe and the more northern tribes were the ones to endure the worst of the nomads' devastating invasion (see 6:33–35). It was only when the Midianites began their retreat toward the southeast that Gideon sent his messengers to the Ephramites and requested them to seize the river fords, ahead of the fleeing Midianite hordes. Yiftah's indignation at the Ephramites, therefore, was certainly valid. An urgent appeal unanswered is a more serious offense than an initiative not taken. Nevertheless, with the enemy vanquished and the unity of the tribes now put to the test, Yiftah should have responded with greater magnanimity.

It is with this infamy that Yiftah's term concludes, for nothing else is recorded of his short six-year rule (12:7). And while it may be said that in beating back the Ammonites, Yiftah admirably fulfilled his mandate as judge, posterity remembers him more for his fits of excess. His rash and reckless words were his undoing, condemning both his kinsmen to the slaughter as well as his own daughter to the flames. No wonder that when the ancient rabbis pondered the curious epitaph that records his burial "in the cities of Gilead" (v. 7) they darkly concluded that he must have suffered from a debilitating illness that caused his limbs to wither away and drop off one at a time, so that each one was buried in a different town of his realm.[2] Thus, the Scriptures could literally claim that he was, in fact, buried "in the *cities* of Gilead"! But with the disturbing imagery of limbs severed and strewn, were the rabbis perhaps more soberly alluding to Yiftah's legacy, to his sowing of divisiveness and discord, to his penchant for breeding schism among the tribes – the body of Israel, as it were – over which he exercised his rule? Were the rabbis perchance referring to the striking down and sacrificial dismemberment of his own daughter, his own flesh and blood and a metaphorical limb of his body, in a twisted and perverse act of devotion to God? For the rabbis, who often couched profound interpretation in fanciful language, Yiftah's ultimate fate was a perfect reflection of his most grievous failures as a leader of the people and as a man of God.

THE CONCLUDING PASSAGE

The account concludes with the mention of three minor and obscure judges, each one receiving only two or three verses of text. Of Ibzan from Beit Lehem it is said only that he judged for seven years and had many sons and daughters; of Elon from Zebulun it is recorded only that

---

2. See Genesis Rabba 60:3.

he judged for ten years; and of Abdon son of Hillel from Piraton it is stated only that he ruled for eight years and had many sons and grandsons. Thus it is that the long narrative of Yiftah ends with a concise list of little-known personalities, much as the Gideon saga similarly concluded with the mention of two minor judges named Tola and Ya'ir (10:1–5). The arc of inexorable decline that is the book's abiding feature is in no way relieved by the mention of these obscure judges, and their terse biographies serve as a fitting introduction to the book's final cycle of failure that will be ushered in by its last judge: Samson of Dan.

The geography of Elon and Abdon indicates a more northern locus for their exploits, as the tribe of Zebulun settled west of the Sea of Galilee while Piraton is found in the hill country of Ephraim. Based on this scant information alone, we might have concluded that Ibzan of Beit Lehem similarly hailed from the region, for in the territory of Zebulun there is a town by the name of Beit Lehem (Josh. 19:15).

The more famous Beit Lehem, however, at least insofar as the biblical narratives are concerned, is Beit Lehem (Bethlehem) of Judah, located just south of Jerusalem. If Ibzan came from Beit Lehem of Judah, then he is the second judge from that tribe recorded in the book. The first was Otniel son of Kenaz whose exploits in capturing Kiryat Sefer won him glory as well as the hand of hoary Caleb's daughter in marriage (1:8–15). Later, Otniel defeated the tyrant Kushan, thus earning his place as the first of the judges (3:7–11). Ibzan, coming at the *end* of the book from Otniel's tribe, serves as the closing bracket to Otniel's promising beginning. His mention extends to us an invitation to ponder further the steep curve of deterioration traced by the lives and times of the judges.

For some of the rabbis, however, the mention of Ibzan provided a ray of hope. In Bava Batra 91a, Rabba bar Rav Huna remarks in the name of Rav that "Ibzan is Boaz," and this identification is widely quoted by the classical commentaries.[3] Boaz of Beit Lehem Judah is one of the heroes of *Megillat Ruth*, a compassionate man who cares for Naomi, the indigent widow of his deceased relative Elimelech, as well as for Ruth her Moabite daughter-in-law. The Megilla, whose events take place "during the time of the judges" (Ruth 1:1) is a poignant tale of loss, loyalty,

---

3. See Rashi's commentary on Judges 12:8 et al.

and love, and furnishes us a telling glimpse into the lives of ordinary rural Israelites who lived in the hill country of Judea in the town of Beit Lehem. Theirs was a tight and supportive community that provided assistance to those in need as well as comfort to those that were in pain. There are, in fact, few books in the Tanakh that can compare to *Megillat Ruth* for sheer empathic power. And while our analysis of the book of Judges has painted that age as being dark, chaotic and nasty, Ibzan of Beit Lehem reminds us that nestled among the rocky hills were plenty of upright Israelites who honorably eked out their subsistence, cared for the less fortunate in their midst, and died unremarkably. While theirs is not the account of the book of Judges, the Tanakh nevertheless preserves their story in *Megillat Ruth* to serve as a counterbalance to our unremittingly bleak tale.[4]

---

4. An intertextual approach to the study of Tanakh assumes that biblical stories – though they may be separated by centuries of time and much intervening textual material – are intrinsically connected. Sometimes this connection is linguistic or thematic, sometimes it is historical or chronological and sometimes it is literary or stylistic. Sometimes the linkage is about comparing and often it is about contrasting. Effectively, an intertextual approach asserts that the earliest interpretation of the Tanakh is the Tanakh interpreting itself, by suggesting a linkage between texts so that they can shed light on each other and yield new insights about each one in turn.

Judges 13:1–25

The Birth of Samson the Nazirite

The people of Israel continued to do evil in God's eyes, and God delivered them into the hands of the Philistines for a period of forty years. (13:1)

Once again, in the book's final gasp, the sorry cycle of Israelite treachery followed by divine wrath is repeated, but this time the oppressors have a new identity. Gone are the Canaanites, Moabites, Midianites, and Ammonites of earlier cycles. They are now replaced by a foe far more menacing and fierce: the Philistines.

The Philistines, whose ascendancy began toward the end of the period of the judges and continued until David vanquished them about one hundred and fifty years later, were a militaristic, technologically advanced people that dwelt in the coastal plain of Israel. Scholarship, basing itself upon the biblical text,[1] archaeological evidence, and extra-biblical records, places their origins in the area of the Aegean Sea, among the Greek islands such as Crete that gave birth to the civilization of Minoa. Sometime during the thirteenth century BCE, waves of these

---

1. See, for instance, Genesis 10:14; Deuteronomy 2:23; and especially Amos 9:7.

maritime peoples, some of whom boarded ships and traveled eastwards with the winds while others journeyed overland along the coast of Asia Minor, began to settle upon the shores of the eastern Mediterranean from Lebanon in the north down to Egypt in the south. Pharaoh Rameses III, who ruled over the "Two Lands" toward the end of the twelfth century BCE, commemorated his victory over a large invading force of these so-called Sea Peoples with a series of monumental stone reliefs for his mortuary temple at Medinet Habu. In the foreground of these reliefs, the tall raiders are depicted with plume-crested helmets, braided hair, long swords, and armor upon their upper bodies, while in the background can be seen the carts and wagons that convey their women and children. These were the families that accompanied the warriors on their expeditions for the Sea Peoples arrived not only as conquerors but as colonizers as well. Appropriately enough, modern Hebraists derived a new term from the word "Philistine," divesting it of ethnic designation or a description of geographic origins. They used it more generically to mean simply "invader."[2]

THE PHILISTINES' RISE TO POWER

But while the wily Rameses III employed a brilliant strategy combining sea and land maneuvers to defeat the invaders, and succeeded in beating back their onslaught from the borders of the Egyptian delta, the Philistines were able to easily establish themselves along the Canaanite coast to the north. Eventually, they formed themselves into a powerful pentapolis, a confederacy of five towns each of which was ruled by an independent governor.[3] In hindsight, the Egyptians welcomed the development; after coming to terms with the newcomers, they made use of the Philistines' mercenary tendencies to continue their rule over the land of Canaan, but this time by proxy.

The Philistines, settled in the coastal cities of Gaza, Ashkelon, and Ashdod, as well as in the cities of the plain, Gat and Ekron, quickly adopted the local Canaanite culture and pantheon, but, nevertheless,

---

2. Hence the modern Hebrew usage of the root P-L-SH.

3. In biblical Hebrew these governors are known as *seranim*, which some scholars associate with the "tyrants" of the archaic and classical Greek periods.

maintained some peculiar traits that betrayed their non-Canaanite origins. Thus, their painted bichrome pottery was quite similar to Mycenaean ceramics of the same period, while their burial practices were analogous to those of other Aegean cultures.[4]

It was, however, their advanced knowledge of metallurgy and of the process by which iron is extracted from its ore that proved most decisive for the region. In all probability, this science, and the potential for improved weapons that it introduced, was acquired by the Philistines from their sustained maritime connections with the Anatolian coast. The potent combination of militarism, metallurgy, and mercantile interests that characterized Philistine society from its inception proved to be fateful for those tribes of Israel that were settled in close proximity to their burgeoning coastal cities. By the end of the period of the judges, the Philistines had become a force to be reckoned with, for their expansionist aspirations soon turned toward the interior of the country of Canaan and to the lucrative trade routes that crisscrossed its hills. Pressing inland and armed with fearsome chariots of iron, they easily extended their oppressive hegemony over the hapless southern and central Israelite tribes in their way, most of whom were primitive agrarian homesteaders with inferior bronze implements and no martial tradition of which to speak. The Israelites were subjected to taxation and the hated corvée, while their large towns were kept in check by garrisons manned by professional Philistine soldiers.[5]

---

4. Keeping their likely Greek origins in mind, is it any wonder that the account of Samson their nemesis has all of the trappings of a Greek myth?

5. Parenthetically, it should be emphasized that the name "Palestine" was imposed on the province of Judea by the Roman emperor Hadrian after he had cruelly suppressed the Bar Kochba revolt in the second century CE, more than a thousand years after the events of our book. Hadrian's renaming was a conscious evocation of the ancient animosities, although by that time, the Philistines had long ceased to exist. The Romans, fed up with Jewish resistance and ongoing opposition to their harsh and rapacious rule, decided to commemorate their bloody victory over the Jews by derisively renaming these lands Syria Palaestina, so that Israel's ancient connection to the place might be expunged from memory in favor of their implacable foe who had harshly oppressed them some thirteen centuries earlier! Therefore, it is one of history's greatest ironies that the present-day conflict between Israel and its mortal enemies, who dwell in Gaza and call themselves Palestinians, echoes, at least in name, this early and decisive clash.

THE OPENING OF OUR CHAPTER

It is against this backdrop that the events of Judges chapter 13 must be appreciated, for the birth of the judge heralded in the narrative, Samson of Dan, occurred at a time when Israelite fortunes were at a low point. The narrative of the book of Judges is far less interested in the historical data presented above, and much more interested in the strange circumstances that surrounded the birth of Samson:

> There was a man from Zora from the clan of the Danites whose name was Manoah, and his wife was barren and had not borne children. An angel of God appeared to the woman and said to her, "Behold, though you are barren and have not borne children, you shall nevertheless conceive and give birth to a son. Now, therefore, be careful not to drink wine or intoxicating drink and do not eat anything that defiles. This is because you shall become pregnant and bear a son, and no razor shall touch his head, for the child will be a *nazir* of the Lord from the womb, and he will begin to save Israel from the clutches of the Philistines!" (13:2–5)

The "barren woman" motif that introduces our tale recalls the stories of Sarah (Gen. 21:1–3), Rebecca (25:19–21), Rachel (29:31), Hannah (I Sam. 1:2), the Shunamite woman (II Kings 4:8–17), and even the ruined city of Zion, who expectantly waits, like a childless woman, for the return and restoration of her exiles (Is. 54:1–8). In all of these cases, it is nothing less than divine intervention that changes the dismal fortunes of the barren woman, and this intervention, in the form of unexpected pregnancy and birth, is foretold ahead of time.[6] The birth of a child under such circumstances is a portentous event, and

---

6. These pregnancies and births never negate the laws of nature. Each one of the barren women in the Tanakh is married to a man and the child conceived is the product of their union. The "immaculate conception" and "virgin birth" of early Christian tradition, familiar tropes in ancient (especially Greco-Roman) mythologies, are nowhere to be found in the biblical motif of the "barren woman" and were anchored in a deliberate mistranslation of Is. 7:14. The "annunciation" of the Gospels, on the other hand, was certainly inspired by the visitation of angelic messengers to Sarah and to the wife of Manoah.

the offspring so brought into the world is destined for a special mission in life. In this respect, the account of Samson's birth does not divert substantially from the pattern.

However, something is eminently lacking from our account that is a centerpiece of the other contexts: a record of the future mother's heartfelt prayers for offspring. Sarah, Rebecca, Rachel, and Hannah all expressed terrible longing for a child and engaged in intense conversations with their husbands and/or devotions to God in order to secure one. Zion sat bereft and forlorn, mourning her exiled children and praying for their redemption. However, the "wife of Manoah" as she is known, nowhere asks for her husband's support or for God's attention to her plight. There are no tearful supplications or profound entreaties. Furthermore, unlike the others, who all are named explicitly, the wife of Manoah will remain strangely anonymous throughout the account. What is her name and where is her prayer?

THE UNIQUE CIRCUMSTANCES OF SAMSON'S BIRTH

While the birth of Samson the "savior" figure is announced, like the others, from the outset, this announcement comes with a unique set of conditions. They are placed upon the mother even prior to the moment of conception, and upon the child from the moment of his birth. The wife of Manoah is to abstain from "drinking wine or intoxicating drink and eating anything that defiles," while the child is to be subject to the strictures of naziriteship from birth. Nowhere else in the book of Judges, whose pages are filled with the celebrated exploits of leaders who arose in Israel to save their people from oppression, do we have anything that remotely resembles our account in this matter. Nowhere else in the entire Tanakh is any man or woman set aside by God from birth for the onerous nazirite vows!

The closest parallel is in the story of Samuel, in which barren Hannah vows to dedicate her offspring – if God will but answer her prayers – to a life of service at the Tabernacle at Shilo, even imposing upon him certain constraints that are naziritic in origin: "No razor shall touch his head" (I Sam. 1:11). But while the ancient rabbis debated whether, in fact, Samuel was a nazirite in the full sense of the term,[7] no one could deny the

---

7. See Nazir 66a with the Mishna.

fundamental difference between the two circumstances. Hannah accepted the nazirite vows for her child as her free and autonomous choice, as an act of dedication and devotion to God who alone could fulfill her prayers. But in our account, the state of naziriteship is divinely imposed, with no introduction or warning, upon a nameless woman and her unborn child who nowhere expressed an interest in such a challenge!

Perhaps an analogue to our story is to be found elsewhere, in the account of Jeremiah the prophet whose reluctance and fear were forcefully overcome by God's proclamation of an imposed calling:

> The word of God came to me, saying, "Before I fashioned you in the belly I knew you, and before you went forth from the womb I sanctified you; for a prophet unto the peoples I have designated you." But I said, "Woe is me, almighty God, behold I know not how to speak, for I am but a lad!" But God said to me, "Do not say 'I am but a lad', for concerning all that I shall send you, you shall go, and all that I command you, you shall speak. Do not fear them, for I am with you to save you," says God. (Jer. 1:4–8)

In a similar vein, one could argue that imposing the nazirite vows upon the unborn child of our passage is an emphatic statement of his future mission, a mission that is from the outset enforced and compulsory, binding and non-negotiable until the bitter end. While this may be the case, imposing the strictures of naziriteship from before birth seems peculiar and exaggerated, for we may have expected God to have sufficed with an adamant declaration of His intended role for the offspring. Alternatively, could Samson not have been selected for his mission at some later point, designated as a savior figure once he reached adulthood and maturity, just like Jeremiah?

THE PASSAGE OF THE NAZIR

In order to gain a broader perspective on these matters, we must consider the subject of the *nazir* in its original context. The provisions of this unusual practice are spelled out at length in Numbers 6:1–21 and we will suffice with a brief overview. The *nazir* is a man or woman who freely chooses to observe a period of abstention from certain behaviors that are otherwise permitted. The commitment is formalized by pronouncing a vow of naziriteship in which the devotee declares himself a *nazir* for a set duration of at least one month.[8] The abstentions, effectively prohibitions, are limited to three main categories: consuming all grape products, cutting any hair, and having any contact with a human corpse. While the Torah neither spells out the significance of the vow nor the meaning of the proscriptions, it does unequivocally link the matter of the *nazir* to the realm of holiness and sanctity: "All the days of his naziriteship, he shall be sanctified to God" (Num. 6:8).

The ancient rabbis disagreed over the desirability of becoming a *nazir*, with some of them decrying the autonomous imposition of additional prohibitions over those already mandated by the Torah for the average person, while others saw in the onerous rites a legitimate aspiration for the more spiritually inclined.[9] While the early rabbis may have expressed ambivalence about embracing naziriteship, the medieval commentators were almost unanimous in their enthusiastic endorsement of the matter.[10] The sentiments of Rabbi Abraham Ibn Ezra are typical of this approach:

> There are those who explain that the word *nazir* is related to *nezer* or crown, as the verse states that "the *nezer* of his Lord is upon his head" (Num. 6:7). This interpretation is not unlikely. Understand that all people are enslaved to the desires of this world; the true king who wears upon his head the crown of dominion is the one who has achieved freedom from desires. (Ibn Ezra on Num. 6:7)

For Ibn Ezra, the *nazir* is a type of monarch, for he too exercises dominion. But unlike the temporal king whose rule extends over earthly realms and whose power is measured by his wealth and armies, the *nazir* is instead king over his inner drives, over the terrestrial desires that hold

---

8. This minimum duration is not stated in the text of the Torah explicitly and was derived by the ancient rabbis through interpretation. See Mishna Nazir 1:3.

9. See Taanit 11a.

10. Maimonides, however, adopted the more critical interpretation. See *Mishneh Torah, Laws of Opinions* 3:1.

most of us in their sway. Therefore, the *nazir* abstains from wine that clouds judgment, numbs the senses, and is often, when consumed to excess, merely a hollow escape from more pressing challenges and concerns.[11] He does not cut or tend to his hair, a rejection of the prevailing infatuation with appearance and fashion that consumes so much of our energy and resources. He avoids contact with any corpse defilement because his life is dedicated to eternal life, to the service of God whose essence is timeless and immutable existence. The *nazir* wears a "crown," his long and unshorn locks attesting to monarchy of another more exalted sort: mastery of the self. No wonder that the rites of the *nazir* are quite similar to those pertaining to the high priest, and that the latter is also described as being crowned by the *nezer*:

> The priest who is more exalted than his brethren, the one who has had the anointing oil poured upon his head and has been designated to wear the [special] garments, shall neither cause his hair to grow long nor rend his clothing [as signs of mourning]. He shall not come into contact with any dead bodies, not even to defile himself for his mother or his father. He shall not leave the precincts of the Temple and thus desecrate the Temple of his Lord, for the crown (*nezer*) of the anointing oil of his Lord is upon him, I am God. (Lev. 21:10–12)

THE SELF-CONTRADICTION OF IMPOSED NAZIRITESHIP

In essence, then, the *nazir* is also a type of high priest. But unlike the high priest, whose suitability for office is a direct function of noble lineage and who does not choose but is rather chosen, the rites of the *nazir* may be freely adopted by anyone. Any man or woman, whether of humble origins or exalted birth, may aspire to the sanctification of the *nazir* as a matter of free will. The *nazir* represents the possibility

---

11. The Tanakh provides us with a number of cautionary tales concerning wine and intoxication: the pathetic account of Noah's drunkenness in Genesis 9:18–29, the infamous story of Lot and his daughters in Genesis 19:30–38, and possibly the tragic demise of Aaron's sons in Leviticus 10:1–11. These are reinforced by the praise heaped upon the clan of the Rechabites in Jeremiah 35 for heeding the injunctions of their ancestor Yonadav, which included abstaining from wine.

afforded to any Israelite to experience the overarching presence of God. We mistakenly believe this encounter to be the exclusive preserve of the high priest who alone may enter the holiest precincts of the Temple, but actually the rites of the *nazir* indicate that all who seek Him in sincerity can experience His presence!

If our analysis is correct that the *nazir* is a positive role model for sanctified living precisely because of the autonomy involved in the acceptance of the rites, then our introduction to Samson is all the more puzzling. Why would God impose naziriteship upon the unborn child and upon his mother, when imposition is antithetical to the sincere striving for holiness that is the hallmark of the sensitive and God-searching soul? While we may have found in Jeremiah an analogue for sanctification from birth for a particular task or mission, there is no precedent for the imposed naziriteship that serves as the critical introduction to Samson's birth.

These, then, are the salient facts of the story: Samson's barren and anonymous mother, introduced abruptly without any further elaboration, is unexpectedly visited by a messenger of God, who announces that she will imminently give birth. Most remarkably, the messenger also indicates that she is to desist from wine and other intoxicants derived from grapes, that she is to avoid anything defiling, and that she is to take care never to cut the hair of her new son, for the child will be a nazirite from his birth until the day of his death, and "he will begin to save Israel from the clutches of the Philistines" (13:5).

THE FORTITUDE OF THE NAZIR

The dearth of a parallel to our account is for a simple reason: To be a *nazir* is to freely and independently choose to constrain oneself from a limited number of otherwise permitted things, in order to nurture one's spiritual awareness through the exercise of precious self-mastery. How can such serious and transformative vows be imposed from above while bereft of conscious choice from below? How can such a lofty mission be coerced from without if its very touchstone is sincere submission from within? Even the naziriteship of the prophet Samuel that we considered earlier, declared before conception by his righteous mother Hannah, was not the product of coercive divine decree but rather the natural consequence of her own mindful and deliberate will:

She uttered a vow and said: "Oh God of hosts, if You shall surely be cognizant of your maidservant's plight, and shall remember me and not forget Your maidservant so that You grant your maidservant offspring of men, than I shall set him aside for God's service for his entire life, and no razor shall touch his head!" (I Sam. 1:11)

Samson's naziriteship is therefore a unique and peculiar phenomenon. How are we to understand it, and what might be its meaning in the larger context of the book of Judges? Why does the book conclude the story of the judges with the account of a man whose most unusual qualities were forced upon him by God Himself?[12]

The medieval commentaries, too, were puzzled by the imposed nazaritehood of Samson, and they offered several possibilities. According to one school of thought, the strictures placed upon Samson were intended by God as a kind of prophylactic, a divinely administered inoculation, as it were, against the allure of Philistine women and their wiles. Knowing that Samson's challenge would involve an exaggerated libido, God sought to create a framework of restraint so that Samson might have a fighting chance to overcome his desires. Abstention from wine, from haircutting and from contact with death and defilement offered Samson exercises in self-discipline and pointers toward spiritual sensitivity. In this formulation, the imposition of naziriteship was aimed at providing Samson with the tools that could help him succeed in his mission.[13]

Another school of thought maintains that the naziriteship of Samson was intended as some sort of "power booster" so that he might successfully fight the Philistines. Samson's physical strength depended upon his hair remaining long and intact. As soon as it was shorn, he was reduced to normal abilities (16:19–20). When it began to regrow, his

---

12. In Mishna Nazir 4:6 the possibility is raised of a naziriteship that is pronounced upon a child by his father. Such a vow can only have standing if the child, his mother, or other family members do not object. Although there is an element of coercion in the father's initial pronouncement of the vow, in the end there must be free acceptance by the child and others in order for it to stand. There is therefore no halakhic precedent for a vow of prenatal naziriteship such as that of Samson.

13. See Ralbag, 13:1–5.

strength was restored (16:22–30). According to this view, being a *nazir* from birth was no burden at all. It was actually a divine gift – a miraculous bestowal of superhuman strength that no other *nazir* was granted.[14]

AN UNUSUAL JUXTAPOSITION

These early commentaries, while offering plausible interpretations, do not succeed in dispelling our questions entirely. If Samson was made a *nazir* from the womb so that he might rein in his overactive id, the safeguard seems to have failed miserably. Samson never succeeded in overcoming his desire for Philistine women, and all of his dangerous adventures were triggered by unwholesome trysts with them. On the other hand, while naziriteship does seem to confer superhuman strength upon him, it remains unclear why this should be the case. There are other nazirites mentioned in the Tanakh and none of them share Samson's prowess.[15] If God had been determined to bless Samson with unusual might, it could have been accomplished through any number of means. David the warrior king, for instance, early on defeated the Philistine giant Goliath and later was responsible for finally vanquishing Goliath's people entirely, all of it accomplished without recourse to anything resembling naziritehood. Why should Samson have been any different?

To begin to frame an answer, we turn to the insightful interpretation of the ancient rabbis, who were struck by the Torah's unusual juxtaposition of the nazirite laws with the account of the *sota* or wayward woman, in the book of Numbers, chapters 5 and 6. There, the Torah describes the trial by ordeal of the woman suspected by her husband of disloyalty and treachery, of having embraced a paramour even while her husband has unequivocally warned her not to do so. With witnesses to any explicit wrongdoing lacking, even while serious suspicions of impropriety exist, the woman is taken to the precincts of the Tabernacle and into the custody of the officiating priests. There, if she continues to

---

14. See Rabbi Yosef Karo, 13:4–5.
15. In Lamentations 4:7–8, the nazirites of Jerusalem are remembered for their fine appearance – "whiter than snow, redder than rubies, sculpted as sapphires" – and not their physical strength. In fact, they waste away and perish just like everyone else from the famine gripping the besieged city.

protest her innocence, she is ceremoniously made to drink bitter waters, into which the inked words of a scroll containing divine curses have been dissolved. Should she be guiltless, her husband's accusations being without foundation, then the cursed liquid has no effect. But should she be guilty of surreptitious and serious wrongdoing, then "her belly shall swell and her thigh shall fall away so that the woman shall be a source of scorn among her people!" (Num. 5:27).

Immediately following this account of the *sota* are the provisions of the *nazir* who, as we have seen, chooses to temporarily adopt three specific strictures that proclaim what Ibn Ezra understood to be the truest kingship. As he commented, "All people are enslaved to the desires of this world; the true king who wears upon his head the crown of dominion is the one who has achieved freedom from desires." Commenting upon the juxtaposition of the passages, R. Judah remarked:

> Why was the section of the *nazir* placed adjacent to that of the *sota*? It is to indicate that whosoever sees the *sota* in her disgrace shall constrain himself from wine! (Sota 2a)

It is beyond the scope of the present study to investigate the matter of the *sota* in greater detail. We must leave the specifics of those unusual laws for our studies of the book of Numbers. But this much is obvious: At its core, the matter of the *sota* is a commentary upon the dissolution of society's most basic foundations, namely the reciprocal trust that informs the relationship of husband and wife. Whatever else may be said about the subject, the husband's jealous accusations are hurled against the backdrop of a relationship that has failed because mutual respect, reliance, and conviction have withered and died. Truly, when we read the painful account, we do not know who is to blame: Has the husband lasciviously sought companionship elsewhere so that his wife has succumbed in turn to the seductions of a secret lover? Has the wife broken the sacred vows of marriage and thrown her loyalties to the wind, so that her husband is now driven into a jealous rage? Or are perhaps both to blame for having neglected their relationship for too long, even while finding excitement and interest in the company of others? This much is certain: The marriage, human society's most sacrosanct commitment, has foundered because both partners have ceased to believe in the uniquely human capacity to maintain and to foster trust. And the implications of that failure are profound: What society can continue to meaningfully function when the nuclear relationships that are its very glue have become undone?

A VOW OF REACTION

This, then, was the meaning of R. Judah's trenchant remarks. Confronted with social dissolution and moral decay, breach of sacred trusts and treachery, the concerned and thoughtful person can do only one thing: Recoil in disgust and retreat. For R. Judah, the vows of the *nazir* are therefore primarily a *reaction*, a response to society's breakdown and collapse. The *nazir* who has "witnessed the degradation of the *sota*" abstains from wine and the cutting of the hair, thereby withdrawing from the world of people and their shallow fascinations. He will not come into contact with a corpse, with a symbol of the moral death that surrounds him on all sides, because his life is lived in protest of their villainy. Instead, he will draw back into the world of the spirit, finding his solace in absolute God and in His presence, until such a time as he has gathered the necessary spiritual strength to return to that society so that he might confront its failings and then enthusiastically begin the process of its restoration. It is as if R. Judah argues that any meaningful repair of the frayed fabric of the world must be preceded by an honest assessment of its faults, a profound recognition of its imperfections and by an impassioned protest against its failures. A *nazir* cannot be a passive figure, one who accepts offensiveness with a shrug of the shoulders and then goes on with his day. A *nazir* reacts mightily, and in that reaction the long and arduous process of transformation tentatively commences.

Returning to our context, we may now consider it from this remarkable perspective. As we have seen, the book of Judges describes the story of the steady and incremental decline of the people of Israel. With the initial ardor of the settlement long ago dissipated, even while most of the Canaanite population remained entrenched, Israel struck down their roots in the new land. But slowly (or was it swiftly?) the people of Israel succumbed to Canaanite culture and to its insidious features, and they strayed from God; and with each successive cycle of woe, the slope of their decline increased. Each new judge was but a reflection of his or her era, and so over the course of the book, the caliber of each correspondingly deteriorated. Enter the final cycle in the book, as the people of Israel chafe under the yoke of the ascendant Philistines. In all of the earlier stories of extended oppression they pathetically cried out to God for relief (2:1, 3:9, 3:15, 4:3, 6:6, 10:10, 15), but here Israel's entreaties are glaringly absent, as if they too have become numbed and desensitized to the sorrow of their plight.

Suddenly, a woman is introduced, anonymous and obscure, a vehicle for God's final attempt to change the trajectory of Israel's self-destruction. Like the wayward *sota*, Israel has strayed and without a correction, all is lost. It is precisely in order to highlight God's intervention into the story that the barren woman, the wife of Manoah, must remain unknown and silent. She has no name or background, and she has no prayer, in spite of her barrenness, because the birth of the child will not be the product of her initiative.

Unexpectedly, a mysterious messenger appears to her, indicating that she will soon conceive and give birth to a figure that will initiate the arduous process of Israel's rescue from the Philistine tyranny. But how strange is the messenger's news, for she must abstain from wine and strong drink and must not cut the new child's hair, for "a *nazir* of the Lord shall the child be from the womb." This divine imposition of unusual force, this burden borne until the "day of his death," is a clarion call to the people of Israel whom Samson will rescue that now is the decisive moment of choice. The people of Israel must decide – embrace the pagan culture of the Canaanites and Philistines, serve their gods, immerse in their way of life, abandon God and perish, or else react against the scourge of intermarriage and the amorality of idolatry, arrest the decline and live!

SAMSON'S CHARGE TO THE PEOPLE

Samson, therefore, like all of the judges who came before him, is an embodiment of the challenges of his own age, a reflection of his people's failures, a likeness of their ignominy, and also an expression of their hopes for deliverance. The strictures of the *nazir* inexplicably placed upon him by divine fiat are an emphatic declaration that for Israel to survive as a nation in Canaan, for Israel to succeed at preserving its unique patrimony in a world inimical to their mission, for Israel to arrest their precipitous decline and to break the cycle of their betrayal and treachery, they must react! And that reaction, like that of the sensitive soul struck dumb by the degradation of the *sota* and by the implied collapse of all of the sacred trusts invested in the bond of marriage, must initially be one of abrupt and unequivocal withdrawal and alienation from the pervasive culture that seductively and destructively beckons them from all around. Samson, in the symbolism of his unusual way of life, is therefore to proclaim to his people the only possibility for their restoration that remains: "Overcome apathy and spiritual torpor, protest against immorality and idolatry! Break ranks with corrosive Canaanite beliefs and practices that have brought us to the brink of self-destruction, even as the seditious satyrs continue to enthrall!"

Perhaps this is the meaning of the curious arrival on the scene of the woman's husband Manoah, who otherwise contributes little to the advancement of the story. After the messenger has appeared to her and transmitted God's communication, she shares the news with her incredulous husband who then requests of God that the messenger return (13:2–8). Return he does, communicating nothing substantially new, except this: "All that I said to the woman you shall observe… all that I commanded her you shall do!" (13:13–14). Though Manoah attempts to show deference to the visitor, his entreaties are curtly rebuffed, and when the caller betrays his angelic origins by ascending heavenwards in the flames of the makeshift altar, Manoah fears death. Again, his wife reassures him and proves herself to be, undoubtedly, the more sensible and discerning of the two.

Manoah, then, whose name means "rest, cessation, and complacency," represents that part of the people's psyche that prefers inertia over the challenge of growth, Canaanite comforts over Israelite mission, reluctance to culturally disengage in contrast to his wife's enthusiastic embrace of the visitor's startling words. The angel's barb is therefore well-placed indeed: "All that I said to the woman you shall observe… all that I commanded her you shall do!" While the anonymous woman is slated to soon become the instrument of God's salvation, her husband Manoah will quickly fade back into the murkiness that is his wish, for though he remains part of the account throughout chapter 14, he is never mentioned by name again.[16]

It is not, of course, that Israel are to suddenly adopt the nazirite lifestyle of Samson en masse in some sort of superficial and absurd literalism, but rather that they are to begin to internalize the uniqueness of their rescuer's calling, recognizing that their own response to their dire situation cannot be one of "business as usual." Rather, they must cry out, not against the political oppression that weighs so heavily upon them, but rather against the social injustice and the communal hurt, the moral devastation and religious ruin, the denial of meaning and higher purpose, and the headlong embrace of spiritual shallowness that all go hand in hand with enthusiastic worship of the Canaanite pantheon, the bankrupt gods that champion ritual over content and empty incantation over that which is noble and pure.

From Samson's perspective, however, he is placed in the most difficult situation of having to adhere to an upright way of life that is not of his own choosing but rather has been thrust upon him from even before his birth! As we shall see, this unusual arrangement will introduce no small amount of complications, as Samson enters the fray and begins to engage the mission that he cannot avoid.

---

16. In this connection, we might wonder about Samson's name as well. It derives from *shemesh* and the suffix (*on*) may signify a diminutive: "little sun." In the epic of Gilgamesh, Shamash the sun god assists Gilgamesh in his epic adventure to secure cedars from the slopes guarded by the ogre Humbaba. In ancient Egypt, the sun was worshipped as a god during all periods. Known as Ra, he was represented as a falcon (Horus) or as a sun disc (Aten). Therefore, the name Samson recalled, of all things, the pagan sun god that was so enthusiastically worshipped – in one form or another – by all ancient peoples of the Fertile Crescent!

Isaac was so named because of the joy that he brought to the world (Gen. 17:15–17), Jacob because he grasped his twin brother's heel (Gen. 25:26), Joseph for his mother's hopes that she would have another child (Gen. 30:22–24), and Samuel because he was "requested of God" (I Sam. 1:20). But what might the name Samson have signified to his parents? It is a name that incorporates nothing of the mission or majesty of their child's birth! If ever there was a child that demanded an auspicious name it was surely the offspring of Manoah's wife, the simple woman whose very diet was dictated in deference to the one who "will begin to save the Israelites from the clutches of the Philistines" (Judges 13:5)!

Judges 14:1–16:31

The Tragedy of Samson

SAMSON AND THE TIMNITE WOMAN

Samson's exploits, extending over the course of three chapters in the book of Judges (14–16), can be divided into two main parts that are separated by a brief interlude. In the first part, soon after he is moved by the spirit of God "at Machane Dan, between Zora and Eshtaol," Samson sees and is attracted to a Timnite woman. He goes with his reluctant parents to meet her, kills an attacking lion at the vineyards of Timna (whose carcass is later occupied by a swarm of bees), and becomes engaged to her. When he returns to marry her sometime later, he discovers honey in the carcass, eats it barehanded and shares it with his parents.

During the marriage celebration, Samson pronounces an impossible riddle to his thirty Philistine friends, inspired by the honey in the carcass of the lion: "Out of the eater came something to eat, and out of the stalwart came something sweet" (14:14). Samson challenges them to solve the puzzle by identifying the subject within the seven-day period of the marriage feast or else to forfeit to him thirty outfits of clothing. If they should succeed in solving the riddle, he commits to providing them with thirty suits of clothing in turn. The Philistines agree and when faced with failure, they force his Timnite wife under fear of death to extract the answer from him, thus triumphing just before sundown of the seventh day. Samson slays thirty men in Ashkelon, seizes their clothing to meet his debt, and abandons his new wife in a rage. Concluding the lethal affair, the father of the Timnite bride marries her to one of Samson's friends instead.

Sometime later, during the season of the wheat harvest, Samson attempts to reclaim his Timnite wife but is denied by her father, who now offers him her younger sister. Enraged, Samson captures three hundred foxes, ties torches to their tales, and burns the Philistine fields in revenge. The Philistines retaliate by burning the Timnite and her father alive, and Samson slaughters them in turn. He then retreats to the cleft cliffs of Eitam in the wilderness of Judah.

The Philistine forces now mass at Lehi, demanding Samson's extradition. Three thousand men from the tribe of Judah, fearful of Philistine retaliation, turn over Samson whom they have bound using two new ropes. As he approaches the jeering Philistines, Samson breaks the bonds and slays one thousand Philistines with a jawbone of an ass. Faint after his smashing triumph, he cries out in thirst to God who answers with a miraculous fountain that issues from the rock.[1]

The second half of Samson's story comes after a brief pause at the beginning of chapter 16, in which Samson dallies with a prostitute in Gaza while the Philistines lie in wait. In the middle of the night, Samson uproots the ponderous gates of the walled city and carries them off to the outskirts of Hebron, some sixty kilometers to the east of Gaza and some one thousand meters higher in elevation!

SAMSON AND DELILA

In the second part of Samson's story, Samson falls in love with a Philistine woman of Nahal Sorek, known as Delila. The Philistines bribe her to discover the source of his superhuman strength. She makes four

---

1. The curious Hebrew phrase *hamakhtesh asher baleḥi* in 15:19 might mean that the fountain emerged from the depression in the rock at Lehi (the site of the battle) or, more creatively, from the "socket of the jawbone" of the ass. According to this second possibility, Lehi (literally: "cheek bone") is so called because of the victory that Samson secured there with the jawbone of the ass. The image of the saving waters issuing forth from the jawbone of the ass is a literary parallel to the honey that Samson earlier extracted from the carcass of the lion. In both situations, life-giving sustenance emerges out of something dead, decaying and defiled.

attempts to extract the secret, each time harassing him with claims of feeling unloved. Samson deceptively responds that he can be defeated if:

1. He is bound with seven moist cords [of gut] that have not been dried.
2. He is bound with new ropes that have never been used.
3. His seven locks are woven into the warp of the loom.

After each revelation in turn, Delila subdues Samson as he indicates, with the summoned Philistines lying in wait and ready to attack. But each time, Samson breaks the bonds, fights off his attackers and exposes the ruse.

Finally, after much cajoling, Samson reveals the truth of his power to Delila – if his locks of hair are shorn, he will be bereft of his strength. After he finally reveals his secret, Delila lovingly lulls the hero to sleep and then dispassionately cuts his hair as the Philistines look on. Samson is then captured, blinded, brought to Gaza as a prisoner, and set to labor turning the grindstone. Soon thereafter, the Philistines gather in the temple of their deity Dagon to celebrate their victory, singing songs of triumph and making sport of Samson. The humiliated Israelite, pathetically propped up between the pillars that support the temple, grasps them forcefully, fervently prays for divine assistance, and brings down the entire edifice, killing himself along with three thousand Philistines. Samson's story ends with his brothers and kin retrieving his body and burying him "between Zora and Eshtaol" at his father Manoah's sepulcher; "and he judged Israel for twenty years" (16:31).

Armed with a good grasp of the basic storyline, let us proceed to consider the protagonist more closely. We begin by noting that Samson's entire career as judge is informed by his failed relationships with Philistine women. Invariably, he is attracted to them, initiates some sort of liaison with them, and then discovers that they are not trustworthy or faithful. The progression is pronounced: A young Timnite bride fearfully betrays his riddle, a prostitute in Gaza callously ensnares him, and Delila of Nahal Sorek treacherously divests him of his strength – as he sleeps in her lap – for the promise of monetary gain. Samson's entire behavior in this regard stands in glaring opposition to the shrill alarm consistently sounded in the book of Judges, to avoid intermarriage with the idolaters at all costs: "The people of Israel dwelt in the midst of the Canaanites.... They took their daughters for wives and gave their own daughters to their sons, and they served their gods" (3:5–6). To intermarry with the Canaanites means to ultimately adopt their gods, a dynamic that invariably leads to moral ruin. How much more so for a judge in Israel, who was to serve as an example to his people, and especially a nazirite judge charged with living a life of restraint and self-control!

UNDERSTANDING SAMSON

Radak was rightfully perplexed by Samson's astonishing behavior and offered the following trenchant remarks:

> We must wonder how the one commanded by God to be sanctified from the womb could have defiled himself with the daughters of the uncircumcised! It appears that the women whom Samson took at Timna, Gaza, and Nahal Sorek were converted by him and turned by him to the Israelite religion. God forbid that the judge of Israel and their savior should marry Philistine women and abrogate the biblical command of "you shall not intermarry with them" (Deut. 7:3), a grave infraction that brings a man to denial of the Creator blessed be He, as the Torah says, "For he will turn your son away from Me" (Deut. 7:4). We nowhere find in the text that he was punished for this behavior or that he "did evil in God's eyes." On the contrary, God granted him success in everything that he did.
>
> The text says that "it was from God," meaning that his taking of Philistine wives was inspired by God and His will was thus accomplished, for surely he converted them and turned them to the religion of Israel. In spite of this, it was a pretext from God that he should take Philistine women in order to execute vengeance upon them.... So too the swarm of bees in the carcass of the lion or Samson's wife who was given to his fellow; all of these were causes for Samson to execute vengeance upon the Philistines. Blessed be God who alone reckons events and causes, and everything is from Him. (Radak on Judges 13:4)

Radak suggests that Samson did not marry idolatrous Philistine women at all but rather fresh converts to the faith of Israel![2] While this interpretation succeeds in addressing the technical, halakhic aspects of the matter, it falls short of providing us with a compelling reading. There is nothing at all in the text to suggest that the Timnite or Delila joined their destiny to Samson or to his people, and for Radak to include the Gazan prostitute in this grand journey of spiritual transformation borders on the farcical!

At the same time, Radak's comment that all of Samson's actions in this regard were a pretext for executing vengeance upon the Philistines is a brilliant attempt to solve the problem that may absolve us of the need for the "conversion" argument at all. Essentially, Radak argues that Samson's intentions[3] all along were to antagonize the Philistine overlords

---

2. Maimonides makes a similar argument in his *Mishneh Torah, Book of Holiness, Laws of Forbidden Relations* 13:14–16, but his reading is much more circumspect: "Solomon converted women and married them and Samson also converted them to marry. But it is well-known that these women only converted for the matter [of marriage] and therefore the *beit din* did not approve. The text also regarded them as gentiles who maintained their forbidden status. Moreover, it is clear from the end of the story that their original intentions were insincere, for they continued to serve their idols and also built high places to serve them. The text holds Solomon responsible, for it states that 'Solomon then built a high place for Kemosh the abomination of Moab.' (I Kings 11:7)." For Maimonides, our tale provides us with much food for thought as far as insincere conversions are concerned. Samson may have fulfilled his "halakhic obligation" in keeping with the letter of the law, but for Maimonides his choice of mates was ultimately ruinous.

3. The text is ambiguous concerning Samson's intentionality in the matter. The critical phrase explaining his irrational desire for the Timnite woman states that it was "from God, for he sought a *pretext* to engage the Philistines and at that time the Philistines ruled over Israel" (14:4). The unusual Hebrew word *to'ana* and its root A-N-H indicate an unexpected confluence of events, often with a threatening undertone (see Ex. 21:13; II Kings 5:7; Ps. 91:10; Prov. 12:21). The phrase may therefore imply less about conscious decision-making on Samson's part and more about his reckless desire. But that impulsive desire was in accordance with God's overarching plan for Samson to engage the Philistines in battle. We can heighten that divine role by reading the phrase this way: "It was from God, for *He* sought a pretext to engage the Philistines and at that time the Philistines ruled over Israel." Radak, however, understands that it was Samson who made the choice: "His original intention was positive – to seek a pretext to engage the Philistines. But then desire overtook him when he saw her, for she was fair in his eyes. He then forfeited his godly intention for a bestial one.

so that he could coax them into battle and defeat them, thus freeing his people Israel from their clutches. What better way to foment friction than the time-honored trigger of ethnic strife known as intermarriage! Ironically, Radak's interpretation on this point could be reinforced were we to assume that the Philistine women in question were *not* converted to the faith, thus creating a cultural mismatch likely to generate even more hostility as far as tribal loyalties are concerned. If that was Samson's intention, then we must submit that he succeeded admirably but at a terrible personal cost.

UNDERSTANDING SAMSON'S PREDICAMENT

Let us attempt to unravel the enigma of Samson by considering the matter from a different angle than that proffered by Radak. From a literary perspective, it is obvious that we are intended to read the story of Samson as an integrated whole. This is suggested by the refrain that provides the geographic backdrop to Samson's exploits: "between Zora and Eshtaol." This phrase first introduces us to the budding hero who is moved by the spirit of God "at Machane Dan, between Zora and Eshtaol" (13:25). It is repeated once more at the very end, after Samson's untimely death when his body is retrieved from the ruins of the temple of Dagon by his brothers and kinsmen who bear his remains to the family sepulcher "between Zora and Eshtaol" (16:31).

Furthermore, the numbers associated with Samson's exploits indicate a defined literary unit that slowly but surely proceeds to a climactic conclusion. His first encounter with the Philistines involves thirty male wedding guests and then thirty male victims in Ashkelon (14:11, 19). In his next attack, after his attempts to reclaim his Timnite bride fail, he makes use of three hundred foxes and eventually claims one thousand Philistine casualties (15:15). The unnerved men of Judah, who fear a Philistine reprisal and are determined to betray Samson, number three thousand (15:11). This number is duplicated when the temple of Dagon comes crashing down, and about three thousand Philistines, "men and

---

Therefore, he was punished and the Philistines gouged out his eyes, measure for measure." This latter statement, holding Samson liable even as he fulfilled God's will, echoes an early rabbinic reading in Sota 9b–10a.

women who had come to see Samson's disgrace," perish in the ruins (16:27). Clearly, these numbers are intertwined, increasing in a linear fashion, typically by multiples of ten.

Finally, the literary unity is emphasized by the triad of Philistine women that propel the plot forward from its innocuous beginnings to its dramatic end, a story that is told in two parts as outlined above, with a brief interlude consisting of Samson's dalliance with the Gazan prostitute. The parallels between the two halves of the story are pronounced: Both begin with a Philistine female in whom Samson takes an unhealthy romantic interest; both pivot on some kind of mystery regarding Samson and his strength that must be unraveled by his nemeses; and both conclude with a lethal confrontation that leads to Philistine casualties. The interlude in Gaza incorporates this *femme fatale* theme while simultaneously highlighting the Philistine astonishment at a man who could uproot the bolted city gates and bear them on his shoulders while ascending to the hills of Hebron!

Most intriguingly, there is an element of constraint, of Samson repeatedly being bound, that informs both halves as well as the interlude. It is this feature that holds the key to understanding the essence of the story. After Samson binds the foxes and lets them loose with torches to burn the Philistine fields, the enemy masses for attack and the men of Judah, hoping to avert a Philistine onslaught, arrest their errant judge in order to turn him in. Samson makes no attempt to resist and only extracts a pledge that the men of Judah will not kill him – incidentally highlighting his utter refusal to fight his own kinsmen. The men of Judah agree and bind him with "two new ropes" (15:13), presumably because these are more sturdy than ropes that have already been worn down through use. As Samson approaches the cheering Philistines who eagerly anticipate his capture, "the spirit of God came upon him and the ropes that were on his arms were like flax burnt by fire; his ties melted off of his arms!" (15:14).

In the interlude, there is no explicit binding of the hero but there is an implicit one, for the city of Gaza is surrounded by stout walls and the gates of the city are bolted with heavy beams. Samson is effectively held captive in Gaza as the Philistines bide their time, confident that he will not escape their grasp. But at midnight, the hero arises to surprise them and "breaks his bonds" by lifting the locked gates off of their foundations and marching away into the night.

As for the second half of the story involving Delila, it emphasizes this theme of constraint to the extreme. Four times, she asks the hero the secret of his strength "and how you may be bound in order to subdue you!" (16:6, 10, 13, 15). Each time Samson offers her an answer, and she immediately implements it with no attempt to conceal her vicious intentions. Every one of Samson's successive responses intensifies the means of binding: For the first attempt, he must be bound with seven new, moist cords (of sinew or plant fibers) that have not been dried; in the second, with new ropes that have never been used; and in the third, his seven locks must be woven into the warp of the loom, thus holding his head (and, by extension, his body) firmly in place. Each time, Samson reacts to Delila's whoop of "the Philistines are upon you, Samson!" by severing the bonds, breaking loose and attacking the enemy.

PAYING CLOSER ATTENTION TO THE DETAILS

At first glance, this extended frolic between Delila and Samson seems droll if not somewhat depraved. A "love affair" indeed, in which the woman makes it abundantly clear on multiple occasions that her intentions are malicious and the man continues to comply, fully aware that the story will end with his downfall by her hands! As mentioned, each one of Delila's requests for the answer to the secret of Samson's strength pivots around an attempt to subdue him, which he gladly entertains. However, there are two small details which merit closer attention. First of all, we notice that as Delila's appeals progress, Samson comes closer and closer to revealing the truth. His first response is non-committal and simply suggests that new and moist cords are needed. Moist gut or plant fiber is of course very flexible but possesses much less tensile strength than material which has been dried and then spun to form cords. To use moist gut or plant fiber to bind someone is not the most dependable method, and perhaps Samson is preying on Delila's pagan superstitions by suggesting a magical quality to the act. In any case, in his first "admission," Samson draws no attention to the fact that his long mane of hair is the true source of his strength.

The theme of binding is now repeated in his second response: new ropes. While reminding us of Samson's binding by the men of Judah earlier (15:13), it does not suggest much else to Delila other than the possibility of Samson's capture. The third response, "if you will weave the seven locks of my hair into the web" (16:13), is more intriguing and indicates for the first time that somehow, Samson's strength is connected to his hair. But, of course, in spite of Delila's faithful attention to his instructions, Samson is unsubdued, even as she goes one step beyond the weaving and securely holds down his locks with the peg.

Parenthetically, it should be noted that here our narrative forcefully parts ways with the "Hollywood" portrayals. The Philistines are consistently astonished by Samson's strength and go to great lengths to ascertain its source. This is a sure indication that Samson's physique was nothing other than completely unremarkable. If Samson had possessed the muscular build of a titan, there would have been little mystery about the source of his superhuman strength. But because his physique was like that of an ordinary man, Delila and the Philistines could not figure out Samson's mysterious might.

THE SECRET OF THE HAIR

The progression therefore is as follows: Samson feeds Delila with answers that he knows to be incorrect but with each successive reply he draws closer and closer to revealing the truth of the matter. Finally, he comes clean with his fourth response[4] "after she had nagged him and coerced him with her entreaties constantly, so that he was weary to death" (16:16):

> He told her everything that was in his heart and said to her, "A razor has never touched my head, for I am a nazirite of God from my mother's womb. If I am shorn then I shall be bereft of my power; I will weaken and become like any other man!" (16:17)

---

4. In the Tanakh, a series of three things followed by a final fourth often indicates a climactic end: "Thus says God: for three transgressions of Judah and for four I will not relent" (Amos 2:4, et al.). Bilaam's donkey was struck three times and then opened its mouth to rebuke him (Num. 22:21–30); Bilaam himself utters three prophecies at Balak's behest before offering the fourth climactic vision unsolicited.

A final tantalizing detail may help us assemble the pieces into a coherent reading. While Samson's first replies to Delila appear to offer dead-end clues to the source of his strength, we noted that the third response is more revealing, while the forth divulges the secret. Examining the responses more closely, however, highlights a common literary thread. While the first three responses revolve around constraints that are then broken, they all generate similar imagery. Cords, ropes and an incomplete web on the loom all have filament-like features that form both the main part of the item as well as its extension. A length of biblical rope, for instance, is made of date palm fibers that are tightly twisted together to form a coil; at its ends, the rope unravels to become loose threads. Long, supple cords of animal sinews or plant fibers are composed of individual strands that are spun together, but at the extremities they begin to untangle. The web of the loom is where the threads of the warp are painstakingly inserted into the woof in order to form the textile. But at the ends, there is no weave but only unconnected vertical or horizontal threads.

In short, all the items under consideration have a certain *hair-like appearance*, and each time this "hair" is first held in check and then let loose! The three items in question, therefore, are not simply about constraint, but they are all reminiscent of hair that is bound and then let loose. Samson alludes to all of this in his penultimate revelation to the treacherous Philistine: "If you will weave the seven locks of my hair into the web…" The nazirite's hair did not grow loose but was gathered into seven discrete locks, now fraying at the ends, which actually resembled the cords and the ropes all along!

A DELIBERATE REVELATION

We are now in a position to understand the true nature of Samson's replies: Samson intended to reveal his secret to Delila all along, hoping that his hints would be enough for her to guess the correct answer on her own. "The answer, Delila, has to do with cords and ropes, with warps and woofs and locks of hair!" It is as if Samson longed for Delila to solve his terrible secret so that she might finally cut his locks and rid him of his nazirite freight forever. The tragedy of Samson is the tragedy of a man who was burdened with an identity that he did not choose, with a mission for which he did not ask, and with a destiny that he could not avoid: "For the child will be a nazirite from his birth until the day of his death, and he will begin to save Israel from the clutches of the Philistines" (13:5).

This then is the hero's predicament – the source of his strength is the nazaritehood that offers restraint and self-control, precious values in short supply even as the Israelites slide deeper and deeper into the morass of Canaanite idolatry and relativism. But that very strength is itself a terrible existential weight, for it was placed upon Samson before his birth to become his self-fulfilling prophecy. In this light, the otherwise bizarre features of Samson's narrative can now be illuminated. Samson, chosen by God to rescue his people, burdened with a message of austerity and self-discipline, devotion to God and a higher calling, chafes against his election, for what man can embrace a mission imposed with rigor? Thus, he seeks out those who represent the antithesis of his calling, the Philistine sirens who promise him succor in the form of mindless living, descent into decadence and self-gratification, and worship of the pagan gods of wine and song who ask nothing of their adherents except that they surrender their souls!

Viewed this way, Samson's behavior is anything but impulsive or irresponsible. It is the conscious (or perhaps subliminal) choice of a man who will not submit to God's uninvited meddling. The Timnite, the Gazan harlot, and Delila are all cut from the same Philistine cloth that Samson longs to hold and feel: A warm and safe cover under which a man may sleep and briefly forget his troubles. "Cut my hair!" he cryptically cries out to Delila each time, "divest me of my calling and let me find rest!" But like every man who knows that revealing his overwhelming secret will spell his self-destruction, that removing the terrible weight of his calling will lighten the burden but simultaneously rob him of his deepest identity, Samson can only come to that moment incrementally. It will take four discrete and deliberate steps, but with each self-taunting revelation to Delila he makes it more and more clear to himself that there can be no turning back.

At the beginning of his mutiny, Samson tied the foxtails together and then set them alight. The frightened creatures ran helter-skelter among the Philistine fields of grain as they tried desperately to free themselves of the bonds, but to no avail. Sowing destruction in their wake, the animals quickly succumbed to the flames and expired in a flash of heat and light. Could Samson have possibly realized that the exhilarating moment was, in fact, a premonition and that their fate was to be his? Seeking to be unloosed from the constraints of his calling, Samson replayed the scene: the broken bonds, the desperate attempt to flee, the uncontrollable destruction, and the self-immolation.

But there can be no rest for those chosen by God, no place in which to hide from the fateful calling that God imposes. *As Samson himself realizes.* Even as he willingly surrendered his magical locks of hair to the Philistine siren and her razor, he could not surrender his identity or his mission. Even as he languished in a Gazan prison, shorn of his locks and forlorn, shackled in bronze fetters like a lowly slave to turn the grindstone, and at long last summoned as a derision to be scorned, "his hair, which had been cut, began to grow back" (16:22). In the end, Samson embraced his calling as he uttered a profound prayer to the unfathomable deity that selected him from before birth to save Israel from their oppressors:

> Samson called out to God and said, "Almighty God, please remember me and please strengthen me just this once, Lord, so that I might avenge even one of my two eyes from the Philistines!" (16:28)[5]

With that, Samson fully embraces his mission, bringing the temple of Dagon crashing down and dispatching the arrogant Philistine tyrants. Thus, as the blind judge who only now sees the meaning of it all, Samson meets his tragic end. Of all the judges, Samson is most heartbreaking;

---

5. Viewed as a literary character, Samson is often accused of arrested development, of showing little or no progress during the course of his story. But even a cursory comparison of Samson's prayer at this final moment with his earlier utterance at Lehi (15:18) clearly indicates otherwise. At Lehi, Samson indignantly demanded, here he sincerely implores. At Lehi, Samson never referred to God by name; here he does so three times. Samson's challenge, then, is to move from denying his mission to accepting it. In the woeful ending, he will even hold it dear, as he brings the temple of Dagon crashing down upon himself.

of all the leaders, the most terribly alone. No other judge in the book labors in such isolation, with none of his own people at his side to face down the enemy. Essentially, Samson's life is a splendid study in alienation, a profound glimpse into the process that unfolds when a man withdraws from his community, people, and himself. Bereft of tribal ties, estranged from parents and family, Samson is alone. Only in the final scene, after he has perished in the process of reclaiming his mission, is he reunited with his people and the father and mother whose sage advice he had earlier spurned: "His brothers and father's clan came down and carried up his body. They ascended and buried him between Zora and Eshtaol, *in the sepulcher of his father Manoah*, and he judged Israel for twenty years" (v. 31).

With this dénouement, the last of the judges leaves the scene, his greatest exploit an exercise in self-destruction. At a moment such as this, we are left to pensively ponder one distressing and melancholy question: What might have been? If only Samson had accepted his calling, if only his nazariteship had been broadcast to Israel as the precious gift that it was, what might have been?

Before we move on, we dare not ignore the larger question that Samson's calamity glaringly raises, even as the story of the judges now comes to its sorry end: Is it possible that Samson's personal challenge is merely a reflection of the larger national tragedy that has unfolded in the book? For like the judge who was chosen against his will, so too were the people of Israel chosen. Like the judge burdened with a precious gift that demanded self-mastery as the prerequisite for success, so too did the people of Israel feel burdened. Like the nazaritehood foisted upon the unborn child while he yet dreamily drifted in his mother's womb, so were the people of Israel given their holy charge unsolicited. And like the judge who sought unrequited love among the Philistines who could never understand, so too did Israel expend their best energies in an attempt to intermingle with the Canaanites, pagans incapable of fathoming the meaning or mission of the chosen people.

Micah's Idol

T he last chapters of the book of Judges are unremittingly bleak. Gone are any judges to lead the people of Israel, gone are any short-lived moments of stability or success, and gone are any pretenses of a happy ending. Instead, the final lengthy narratives of two discrete yet intertwined stories, confirm our worst fears: Canaanite idolatry, with its heavy emphasis on violence and bloodshed, has not been rejected by the tribes of Israel – it has been embraced!

The first of these accounts, chapters 17–18 of the book, is referred to in early rabbinic literature as *pesel Mikha*, the "idol of Micah." The second, chapters 19–21, is called *pilegesh beGiva*, the "concubine at Giva." One might succinctly summarize the matter by saying that the "idol of Micah" is about the tribe of Dan's embrace of idolatry, while the "concubine at Giva" is about the tribe of Benjamin's endorsement of rape and homicide. Put differently, the final stories of the book of Judges, while offering the usual fare of tribalism and emphasizing its deleterious effects, also comprise an unholy trinity of evil acts that halakha would later codify as cardinal crimes that must not be committed even on pain of death.[1] A pathetic refrain is repeated (with slight variations) no less than four times in these final chapters: "In those days there was no king in Israel; every man did what was fit in his own eyes" (17:6, 18:1, 19:1, 21:25).

CHRONOLOGICAL CONSIDERATIONS

Before considering the chapters in depth, a preliminary question must be asked. Given that the first sixteen chapters of the book, containing the accounts of twelve judges (and one anti-judge – Abimelech), are presented in sequential order, can we assume that the final chapters are also in chronological order? Or might the absence of any explicit judge figure in these stories intimate that their placement at the end of the book of Judges was a literary choice rather than a chronological necessity? In other words, did the story of Micah's idol or that of the concubine at Giva happen after the demise of Samson or at some earlier time during the period of the judges? And if earlier, how much earlier?

There is no consensus among the early commentaries on this critical point. Rashi, who mirrors early rabbinic opinions, states in his commentary on 17:1 that these final chapters do not follow the order of the rest of the contents of the book:

> Even though these two sections were recorded at the end of the book…they took place at the beginning of the period of the judges, during the days of Otniel son of Kenaz. This is indicated by the fact that the tribe of Dan "set up for themselves the idol of Micah that he had made, for all of the days that the House of God was at Shilo" (18:31). From this we understand that Micah's idol existed during the entire period that the Tabernacle stood at Shilo. As for the concubine at Giva, it states concerning Yevus – which is Jerusalem – that "we will not turn aside to go to a heathen city," thus indicating that Jerusalem had not yet been conquered

---

1. The Talmud's formulation, in Sanhedrin 74a, is to the point: R. Yoḥanan said in the name of R. Shimon son of Yehotzadak, "In the upper chamber of the house of Nitze at Lod, the rabbis voted and then ruled that concerning all of the transgressions of the Torah, if they (the idolaters) say to a person 'transgress or die!' he should transgress, with the exception of idolatry, sexual immorality and murder."

[by the Israelite tribes]. But it was conquered immediately after Joshua's demise as related at the beginning of our book (1:8).

Rashi's conclusion is therefore categorical: the final events reported in the book actually transpired much earlier, at the very beginning of the period of the judges, for Otniel was the first recorded savior in the story (3:9) as well as the son-in-law of Caleb son of Yefuneh, Joshua's contemporary (1:12–13). It should be noted that Rashi's view is based upon the *Seder Olam Rabba* (ch. 12), a classic rabbinic chronology composed in the second century CE.

In contrast to Rashi, and after a thorough review of his evidence, Radak asserts that the final events of the book occurred exactly where they are placed in the text – after the death of Samson and before the ascent of Eli the priest at the beginning of the book of Samuel:

> These matters transpired between Samson and Eli who was a judge for Israel. During this interregnum, there was no judge for Israel, and each person did what was fit in his own eyes…. Micah made his idol and the tribe of Dan set it up, while the tribe of Benjamin committed the evil deed concerning the concubine at Giva. (Radak on Judges 18:1)

For Radak, there is no need to rearrange the final narratives of the book; they occurred exactly at the moment that they appear in the story. Everything is recorded sequentially and one chapter follows the next without interruption. To assume that the book as a whole follows the same ordering principle from beginning to end implies consistency and textual integrity. However, it should be noted that besides the evidence adduced by Rashi, there are a number of additional time markers in these final chapters that make Radak's assertion difficult. First of all, the book reports that at the time of Micah, the tribe of Dan had not secured their tribal territory (18:1), a situation that best fits a much earlier epoch when the tribes of Israel were still fully engaged in that pursuit. Secondly, when the identity of the priest appointed by Micah is finally revealed (18:30), he appears to have been active just a couple of generations after Moses, placing the events shortly after Joshua. Finally, when the people of Israel prepare to battle Benjamin for a second time and make enquiry of God, the book reports that Pinhas, son of Elazar, son of Aaron the priest was officiating (20:28). Since this very Pinhas is explicitly named toward the end of Moses's life (Num. 25:1–15) and is prominently mentioned at the conclusion of the book of Joshua (ch. 22), it stands to reason that the episode of the concubine at Giva occurred shortly after Joshua's death when the first judges were leading the people.[2]

If we adopt Rashi's view that the final narratives are not presented as the chronological conclusion to the book, their placement at the end of the book cannot be arbitrary or capricious. The question must be asked: Why would the author have suddenly decided to adopt a different strategy in recording the last chapters of the book so completely out of order relative to when they occurred? What possible advantage would such a literary decision offer?

According to Rashi, there must be a deliberate *thematic* motive for the non-chronological placement of these chapters.[3] Recall that the book presents us with a series of judges that inspire less and less as the chapters unfold. Otniel, Ehud, and Deborah all led the people with nobility and grace, but Gideon lacked faith and, in the end, unwittingly built an idol of gold instead of a monument to victory. Yiftah immolated his own innocent daughter, while Samson, the final judge, pursued Philistine women to self-destruction. The overall trajectory of the book of Judges

---

2. Ralbag (Gersonides) also adopts the view that the final events occurred "in the early days, when there was no judge, during a period of oppression. Perhaps it was before the days of Otniel son of Kenaz, perhaps before Ehud, or perhaps before one of the judges that followed them" (Ralbag, 17:1). But while Rashi dogmatically assigns the stories to the days of Otniel, as indicated in the *Seder Olam Rabba*, Ralbag is more flexible. Of course, for Radak to maintain a chronological reading, Pinhas would have to be approximately four centuries old at this point, making his reading unreasonable!

3. In a more midrashic vein, some commentaries draw a link between the story of Samson and the idol of Micah based upon the 1100 silver pieces that appear in both. The Philistines offer multiples of this amount to Delila to ascertain the source of Samson's strength (16:5), and Micah reports this to his mother as the stolen sum (17:2). Continuing the idea, Ralbag remarks that both stories concern the downfall of the tribe of Dan because of ill-gotten gains – Samson is a Danite, and the idol that they erect becomes Dan's tribal deity (Ralbag, 17:1).

is unmistakably downward and the message is crystal-clear: The people of Israel, in aping the beliefs, values, and practices of their Canaanite neighbors have entirely lost their way! How better to emphasize the utter depravity of the situation than by locating the stories of Micah's idol and the concubine at Giva at the end *as if* these stories naturally follow what precedes and thus seamlessly complete the account of infamy.

In other words, had the two episodes been presented to the reader during the opening chapters of the book when they actually occurred chronologically, we would have remained incredulous and unconvinced: Could these events really have happened so soon after Joshua's inspired leadership came to its glorious end? However, at the end of the book, the idol of Micah and the concubine at Giva make *perfect* sense: We cannot imagine a more fitting conclusion to the sordid and miserable deterioration narrated in our book! Thus it is that strict chronology must be sacrificed now, not for dramatic effect (though there is drama in the telling) but for the sake of something more important: the cautionary message for us.[4] When societies forfeit their ideals, the downward spiral often ends with a devastating moral collapse.

THE CASTING OF THE IDOL

The story of Micah's idol can be divided into three discrete scenes that unexpectedly converge only later. In the first scene (17:1–6), the protagonist Micah is introduced as hailing from Mount Ephraim. Suddenly, he confesses to his mother that it was he who stole her eleven hundred pieces of silver. Though she had pronounced a curse on the thief, she now blesses her son in the name of God. After he restores the funds to her, she dedicates them to the making of a sculpted idol and molten

---

4. The book of Samuel also ends with a number of sections (all of them in chapters 21–24 of II Samuel) that appear to be chronologically out of order with the rest of the story. Just as here, the commentaries wrestle with the possibilities and fail to achieve a consensus. As here, a sequential conclusion is contradicted by various details that are provided, and the concluding chapters are best understood as the *thematic* end to the story of David's reign, offering the reader a profound summary of his character and accomplishments in place of a strict chronological rendering of the events. Intriguingly, the ancient rabbis ascribed both Judges as well as Samuel to the same author: Samuel the prophet (see Bava Batra 14b).

image[5] as an expression of gratitude. She gives two hundred pieces to a metalworker who prepares a sculpted idol and a molten image that are placed in Micah's house. Micah now builds a shrine or "house of God" that includes an ephod and *terafim* (household gods) and appoints one of his sons to serve as priest. The section concludes with the remark that "in those days, there was no king in Israel; every man did what was fit in his own eyes."

With this deplorable introduction, our story begins. We note that the idol of Micah is a bastard-child born out of grievous theft and woefully misguided piety. Micah had stolen money from his own mother, she had harshly cursed the unknown thief, and with his sudden admission of guilt, the adverse dynamic was transformed by her blessing. But instead of generating a positive dénouement of repair and restoration, her blessing in God's name now triggers a dedicatory act of paganism. It is the first time in the Hebrew Bible (at least since the episode of the Golden Calf in Ex. 32) that we meet an Israelite who overtly prepares an idol for worship.[6] The mother's invocation of God's name even as she offers up the silver for the fashioning of the idol highlights the syncretism that has plagued the people of Israel throughout the book. Micah's mother blesses, Micah acquiesces, the metalworker happily obliges, and the idol is prepared and set up. The irony is in the word pair of *pesel umasekha* – the sculpted/molten image that echoes one of Deuteronomy's many harsh admonitions on the matter: "Cursed be the man who will fashion *pesel umasekha* that is an abomination to God, the work of a craftsman to be set up in secret! All of the people shall respond: 'Amen!'" (Deut. 27:15).

---

5. In the Hebrew, these are referred to as *pesel umasekha*. The first word implies something sculpted, probably from wood or stone. The second term indicates something made of molten metal, here the silver funds. It is not clear if, or how, the two elements are combined to form one idol.

6. Obviously, the Tanakh has reported many generic instances of the people of Israel worshipping idols up to this point. See, for instance, Joshua 24:23; Judges 2:1–13, 3:7, 6:25–32, 8:27, 33, 10:6. However, this is the first time that the Tanakh describes how a particular Israelite actually *commissions/fashions* an idol and *sets it up* for worship. This is the first time that such an act is not explicitly or implicitly censured by the text. The distinction may seem trivial on a practical level but it indicates a profound ideological shift in ancient Israel: Idol worship is no longer a stigma.

But here, there is no secrecy, no embarrassment, and no shame. What an Israelite of an earlier generation would have done only under cover of darkness in the private confines of his own home, fearful of exposure and its harsh consequences, has now become a public act of piety, as Micah's house is quickly transformed into a "house of God."[7]

A WANDERING LEVITE

The second part of the story (17:7–13) introduces a wandering Levite lad who leaves his home in Beit Lehem (Bethlehem) of Judah to seek his fortune and arrives at Micah's house in the hills of Ephraim. With excited promises of room, board, and a clothing allowance, Micah tries to convince him to remain and to become the priest of his shrine. The Levite obliges and becomes like "one of his own sons" (17:11). Micah is pleased with the turn of events, and understands it as a good portent: "Now I know that God will bestow goodness on me because the Levite has become my priest" (17:13).

Levites had no tribal territory of their own in ancient Israel and lived in cities that were scattered among the other tribes (see Num. 18:20, 35:1–8). As a result, it was not unusual for them to lead a vagabond life. For this reason, the Torah often groups the Levite with the convert, orphan, and widow – vulnerable members of society requiring special support. Our Levite therefore relocates from Beit Lehem in the south to Mount Ephraim in the north, and when Micah makes him an offer, he cannot refuse. We should take note of the fact, however, that the reason for Levite powerlessness was precisely so that the tribe would remain true to their calling: To instruct the people of Israel in the ways of God. After all, had they not proven themselves deserving at the episode of the Golden Calf, so many centuries before, when they rallied to Moses's side

---

7. It should be noted that while the text keeps referring to Micah's *beit elohim* or house of God, the early rabbis were loath to translate the term as referring to God. The Aramaic translation consistently renders it as *beit ta'uta* or house of error, no doubt taking the plural form of this name of God to mean "the gods." Micah, then, never succeeds in setting up a true House of God – that would be an absurdity given the facts of the story. At the same time, however, we should bear in mind that the text is reporting what Micah and the Israelites *think* of the matter; for them, pathetically, it is a house of God.

to slay the idol worshippers (see Ex. 32:25–29)? As Moses so memorably declared on the eve of his death when he blessed the Levites for their single-minded devotion:

> He said of his father and mother, "I see them not;" he did not favor his brothers, and his own children he did not know, for they kept Your charge and guarded Your covenant. They will teach Your laws to Jacob and Your statutes to Israel; they will offer incense before You and sacrifices upon Your altar. (Deut. 33:9–10)

The earlier irony of Micah's mother dedicating her recovered lucre to God by commissioning an idol is here magnified tenfold by the Levite, erstwhile servant of God, who, for a modest fee, readily agrees to staff the pagan shrine and function as its priest, in direct contravention of his tribal history and calling! All of this is extremely gratifying to Micah himself, a self-styled devotee of God, who has now succeeded in securing an authentic Levite for his shrine, in place of his own son. The priesthood in ancient Israel (like all tribal identities) was hereditary, handed down from father to son throughout the generations. Micah knew that his own son could at most masquerade as a bona fide priest, even as he went about his ceremonial duties in the family shrine with relish. Having finally secured a real priest[8] to minister to the gods, Micah is now certain that God's beneficence will be bestowed.

THE DANITES RELOCATE

The third and lengthiest part of the story now takes a detour with the entry of the tribe of Dan. The Danites are introduced as the tribe that did not succeed in securing their territory, as indicated at the very beginning of the book (1:34) and intimated even earlier in the book of Joshua (19:47). They were originally allotted land on the coastal plain, extending from Jaffa eastwards to the lowlands near Beit Shemesh. This land was bordered to the

---

8. Actually, only the direct descendants of Aaron the priest could offer sacrifices to God. The Levites who were their kin played a supporting role in the service in the Tabernacle or Temple but did not approach the altar. But for Micah, such distinctions were evidently picayune.

south by the tribe of Judah, to the east by Benjamin and Ephraim, and to the north by Menashe. But the Canaanite inhabitants were too strong for them, and the tribe of Dan managed to settle only a small part of the allotment.

The tribe therefore sent a surveying party of five men to scout out other possible sites to settle, and this party makes its way from Zora and Eshtaol in the southern lowlands to Mount Ephraim in the northern hill country. In a serendipitous turn of events, they lodge at the house of Micah (who presumably runs an inn as part of his shrine business) and "recognize the Levite's voice" (Judges 18:3). We are not informed how the Danites know the Levite. Perhaps he had made their acquaintance during other unreported travels near Beit Lehem. Alternatively, the text may mean that they noticed that the Levite had a different accent than the other Ephramites and they, also being strangers, struck up a conversation. It is this convergence between the Danites and the Levite that will be crucial for what follows.

After the polite introductions are completed, the Danites beseech the Levite to enquire of God concerning the success of their mission. This he does and the divine response that he extends is singularly encouraging: "Go in peace. The way that you will travel upon is guided by God" (18:6). It should be noted that, invariably, when supplicants beseech a false priest or false prophet for His blessing, the response is positive and upbeat. The reason for this is obvious – no one wants to pay good money for a negative or pessimistic answer! If Micah's priest fails to please, then he will quickly be out of business.[9]

The Danites now make their way northwards, scouting as they go, and eventually come to the town of Layish, located far away at the headwaters of the Jordan River. Inhabiting the town and the surrounding fertile area are peaceful people who are Sidonites in origin but have no treaties with surrounding tribes. The Danites quickly return to their compatriots and advise: "Arise and let us attack them, for the land that we saw is very good!" (18:9). Six hundred armed Danite warriors and their families, a significant part of the tribe, now begin the trek northwards, first pausing at Kiryat Ye'arim and then continuing through the hill country of Ephraim.

---

9. See I Kings 22 and Jeremiah 28 for two blatant examples. In Temple times, false prophets and priests were often part of the king's court and received a stipend for their efforts.

When they arrive at the house of Micah, the scouts attempt to seize the idolatrous images and the other equipment of the shrine. When the Levite priest protests, they make him another offer that he cannot refuse:

> Be silent! Put your hand upon your mouth! Go with us and be our patron and priest. What is better for you, to be a priest in one man's house or to become a priest for a tribe and clan in Israel? (18:19)

The Levite readily agrees and accompanies them as they make their escape. But now the alarm is sounded by Micah's neighbors and he quickly pursues them. When he catches up with them, however, they threaten him with violence; realizing that he is outnumbered, Micah relents.

The Danites continue their northward trek. Arriving at Layish, they massacre the inhabitants and burn the town to the ground, "and there was none to save them" (18:28). They rename the town "Dan" after their eponymous ancestor and set up the idol of Micah as their deity. Finally, at the end of the story, the identity of the pivotal Levite priest is revealed:

> Yehonatan, son of Gershom, son of Menashe, and his children served as priests for the tribe of Dan until the land was exiled. The idol of Micah served as their god as long as the House of God stood at Shilo. (18:30–31)

THEFT AND VIOLENCE

One might say that this third and last part of the story unfolds unexpectedly insofar as plot is concerned, but completely predictably insofar as theme is concerned. That is to say that the shrine that is eventually set up in the tribe's new northern territory is entirely due to the fortuitous meeting that took place earlier between the Danite survey party and the Levite who served as priest at the house of Micah. Presumably, it could have turned out differently had the acquaintance not been made. But with respect to the thematic trajectory of the first and second parts of the story, what happens in this third part is utterly unsurprising. If Micah stole from his mother, and out of that theft an idol was born, so why shouldn't the Danites steal that very idol from him in order to make it into a bigger god? If our itinerant Levite was ready to betray his mission in order to serve as a two-bit priest in the house of Micah, then why should we be surprised when he betrays his master as well as his calling a second time when a larger offer presents itself?

These two intertwined vices of theft and betrayal that color the first two parts of the story are now underscored by a third more ominous one in this final section: violence. The threat of violence is everywhere: The Danites who steal the idol and its appurtenances convince the protesting Levite that he has a brighter future with them, but the advice to "Be silent! Put your hand upon your mouth!" (18:19) is a veiled threat as well. This violence becomes more explicit when Micah protests. The Danites caution him: "Do not raise your voice at us, lest bitter men among us kill you and your household!" (18:25).

The most grievous expression of this might-makes-right mentality is the extirpation of the peaceful Sidonites who dwell at Layish. The Danites quickly identify the possibilities – "they dwell securely...quiet and safe...there are no threats...they dwell far away from the Sidonites and have no dealings with other men" (18:7). Having identified the dwellers of Layish to be easy targets with none to come to their aid, the Danites act with impunity: "They came upon Layish, upon a people who were quiet and safe, and they struck them down by the sword and burnt the town to the ground" (18:27).

THE IDENTITY OF MICAH'S LEVITE

There is one final indignity, which lands like a hammer blow on the unsuspecting reader. As pointed out above, it is only at the very end that we learn the identity of the Levite. This contrasts with Micah who is named at the outset and is never referred to as "an Ephramite." While the dramatic effect is clearly enhanced by withholding the crucial information until the end, there might also be another agenda at play. The Levite, of course, has a name that we will eventually learn, but for the entire story he is simply "a Levite," a representative of a once-proud tribe. His personal identity is bound up with his tribal identity in a way that is not the case for

Micah. The reason is, as we pointed out above, that the tribe of Levi has a special mission that sets them apart from the other tribes. This Levite, then, betrays not only his own personal integrity in ministering to false gods but the integrity of his tribe and its mission. However, there is more.

> The tribe of Dan erected the idol and Yehonatan, son of Gershom, son of Menashe, and his children served as priests for the tribe of Dan until the land was exiled. The idol of Micah served as their god as long as the House of God stood at Shilo. (18:30–31)

Who exactly is Yehonatan, son of Gershom, son of Menashe? Why is his grandfather's name also provided when the usual biblical convention is to suffice with mention of one's father's name? The ancient rabbis preserve a shocking tradition that the original name of this Levite was slightly different. This tradition is based upon the fact that the name Menashe is written in a highly unusual fashion, with the Hebrew letter *nun* slightly suspended above the others:

יהונתן בן גרשם בן מ‎נ‎שה

There are, according to the Masoretic tradition, only three other letters in the entire Hebrew Bible that are written this way.[10] Rashi quotes the rabbinic tradition:

> For the sake of Moses's honor, a *nun* was added in order to change the name. But the added letter was written suspended, in order to indicate that the real name is not Menashe but rather Moses! (Rashi on Judges 18:30)

In other words, the Levite of our story was named Yehonatan, a beautiful if innocuous name. His father was Gershom, also not a remarkable name in its own right. But Gershom's father was not some otherwise unknown Menashe but rather illustrious Moses, the celebrated lawgiver himself! It thus emerges that it was Moses's own grandson who ministered at the idolatrous shrine at Dan, and after him, his children, and

---

10. The other three are found in Psalms 80:14 and Job 38:13, 15.

his children's children, "until the land was exiled!" While this tradition would certainly place the episode early in the book of Judges, as Rashi explained above, that is the least of its significance. Much more importantly, it suggests that the people of Israel, or at the very least some very prominent members of the people, did not take long at all to embrace idolatry and to surrender their precious patrimony in the process.

Great men, and even the greatest of men, come and go. Their children and their grandchildren will remain behind to make their own moral and religious choices, in spite of the best values and education that a parent can inculcate and bestow. While parental involvement, guidance, and expectations go a long way toward ensuring the successful transmission of an ethic for living, it cannot be the entire story. While the environment that we craft for raising our children is critical for their development, it is not necessarily the only determining factor. In the end, each person must choose for himself how he will live his life and what moral and religious choices he will make. How painful and disappointing it can be when a child chooses a different path, especially when the parent understands that path to be ruinous. But such is the lot of men. The precious gift of free will, a human being's most essential expression of what casts us "in God's image," is for each person to actualize as they see fit. The Torah can hold us accountable for our actions only if we truly have the ability to choose; the ability to freely choose without coercion must also include the ability to choose poorly.

A DEARTH OF HEROES

There are no heroes in our story. Micah is a charlatan, and the Levite a desperate fraud. Micah's mother is a naïve and misguided soul. The Danites are highhanded thieves and merciless killers. The only characters to receive any sympathetic treatment in the story whatsoever are the non-Israelite inhabitants of Layish! What a harsh indictment of the people of Israel at this sorry juncture in biblical history.

As far as our narrator is concerned, the debacle is primarily due to a lack of strong government that could hold individuals accountable. Recall that our story twice invokes a refrain in quick succession: "In those days, there was no king in Israel" (17:6, 18:1). The first time, the phrase elaborates: "Every man did what was fit in his own eyes." In other words, in the absence of strong leadership, anarchy reigns. Like many other nations in the region, ancient Israel was arranged into a loose tribal confederacy that was ruled by patrician tribal elders. That meant that government tended to be local, at most regional, and necessarily quite weak. When an enemy oppressor appeared, these tribal leaders were typically too feeble to defend their territory and an inspired "judge" arose to win the day by rallying the people and raising a militia. But no judge in our book created a standing army, a complex government or a tax regime to finance projects for the general welfare of the citizens. None managed to unify the tribes of Israel into a single bloc or to conclude useful treaties with surrounding peoples. And when the judge passed, the people again were effectively leaderless.

Under such conditions, the individuals decide how they will behave and survival of the fittest is the order of the day. Moral calculations become secondary for most. Thus, Micah fashions his local fetish, the Danites steal it and adopt it as their god and no one protests. For the biblical narrator, the correction must take a form appropriate to the time and place: monarchy.[11] While the monarchical form of government in ancient Israel comes with its own acute challenges, this much is clear: A king sets policy for his kingdom with a power that no judge or tribal elder can ever muster. Ideally, the king's good governance can transform society while holding the nefarious at bay.

The book therefore enters the final stretch by offering the following parting reflection on the era: Judges can be charismatic leaders, fierce warriors and even sources of spiritual inspiration. But as a form of government, rule by judges is necessarily limited. Their careers are short, there is no mechanism for succession and their reforms cannot be sustained. They emerge from a tribal culture and are subject to its limits. Forging a national identity is no job for a judge; fostering a national mission is simply beyond a judge's capabilities. While rule by a judge is better than no rule at all, as the idol of Micah episode makes clear, the tribes of Israel will need to develop a different mode of government if they are to successfully embrace their task in the world.

---

11. Obviously, biblical Israel was not a republic or a parliamentary democracy in which the people choose their representatives and there is a clear division of powers – these forms of government being relatively recent developments.

The Concubine at Giva

The last narrative of our book is unparalleled in the Tanakh for its viciousness. It is a harrowing account of violent rape, cruel homicide, and brutal, internecine warfare. It begins as a personal tragedy but quickly becomes a national catastrophe. It is the ultimate nightmare of those who subscribe to ethical monotheism as their system of values.

A LEVITE AND HIS CONCUBINE

The story begins with a Levite from Mount Ephraim who takes a concubine[1] from Beit Lehem in Judah. She strays[2] from him and returns to her father's house, remaining there for a period of sixteen months. Her Levite husband finally follows in order to bring her back and, when he arrives, his father-in-law is happy to see him. The Levite and his

---

1. It is beyond the scope of this study to analyze the halakhic and historical aspects of concubinage. Briefly, while there is a lively debate about the acceptable parameters of the practice, there is agreement that the status of a woman who is a concubine is, except in the case of divorce or widowhood, comparable to that of a wife.
2. The critical phrase in verse 2 is *vatizne alav*. This term typically indicates faithlessness and betrayal but here may simply mean that she abandoned him. See Rashi and *Targum Yonatan*. A brief talmudic discussion can be found in Gittin 6b and Tosafot on *zevuv matza la*.

concubine remain with the father-in-law for three days, eating, drinking, and lodging there. On the fourth day, they arise early to return to Mount Ephraim, their servant lad and donkeys in tow, but the father-in-law prevails upon them to remain longer. On the fifth day they arise early again; once more the father-in-law fetes them so that they do not begin their journey until the afternoon. As they make their way northwards from Beit Lehem along the ridge of the hill country, the sun begins its descent. It is already setting when they reach the non-Israelite town of Yevus (Jebus), later called Jerusalem. While the servant boy of the Levite advises that they lodge in Yevus, the Levite will have none of it: "We will not turn off to a heathen town that is non-Israelite. Let us rather continue to Giva … of the tribe of Benjamin" (19:12).

We begin by noting that, like our account of Micah's idol, a Levite is once again central to the story. The locations of Beit Lehem and Mount Ephraim also featured earlier, except that Micah's Levite traveled from Beit Lehem to take up residence in Mount Ephraim while here the Levite hails from Mount Ephraim and makes his way to Beit Lehem to reclaim his concubine. The point of the reportage is to alert the reader to the interconnections between the two events and to suggest that both represent moral and spiritual failures of the highest order.

The father-in-law of the concubine is a very hospitable man. Perhaps he is meant to serve as a foil for the hostile people of Giva whom we shall meet shortly or for the inhabitants of Yevus whose lodgings must be avoided. Yevus is the formidable Canaanite town that resisted Israelite conquest until the time of David (Judges 1:21; II Sam. 5:6–10). The Levite's refusal to lodge there, even as the sun is setting and traveling the trails after dark can be dangerous, highlights his conviction that idolaters cannot be depended upon either for hospitality or for moral behavior. This quickly turns out to be an ironic assumption.

INTIMATIONS OF SODOM

At Giva, the forlorn travelers make their way to the town square but no one offers them hospitality. This is despite the fact that they have their own provisions and require only lodging, and despite their destination being "the House of God" (19:18–19) and they are therefore pilgrims. Only an old man who lives in Giva but hails from Mount Ephraim takes an interest in their plight. His generous invitation to them concludes portentously: "But do not sleep in the square" (v. 20). Bringing them home, he offers provender for the donkeys, water to wash their feet, and food and drink. No doubt relieved, they feast with him and are enjoying themselves when a group of hooligans gathers around the house and a threatening knock is heard at the door. Their vile demand now follows: "Bring out the man who has come into your house so that we may rape him!" (v. 22).

The old man goes out to face the mob and attempts to dissuade them by appealing to the ancient law of hospitality. When this fails to convince them, he offers them his own virgin daughter and the Levite's concubine. In the end, the Levite seizes his concubine and hands her over to them. She is abused by them all night long.

The critical elements of our dismal tale are familiar to us from the similar story in Genesis: Lot's hospitality to the wayfarers in Sodom (Gen. 19). There, as here, vulnerable visitors arrive late in the day, and no local townspeople offer them hospitality. A passerby who is himself a foreigner takes them in and prepares a festive meal for his guests. In Sodom, as in Giva, the house is surrounded and the calm is suddenly interrupted by threatening knocks that are followed by an outrageous demand to commit sexual abuse. In both episodes, a desperate attempt to assuage the mob with noble appeals to conscience fails, and then a misguided and horrific offer is made to surrender innocent victims.

The connection between the episodes is reinforced by the deliberate use of similar language. In both accounts, the evildoers "surround the house" (Judges 19:22; Gen. 19:4), they demand to "bring him out so that we may rape him" (Judges 19:22; Gen. 19:5), and the host goes out to mollify the crowd by saying, "My brethren, do not do evil" (Judges 19:23; Gen. 19:7). He then offers his own virgin daughter(s) to them: "I will bring them out to you and you may do to them what is fit in your eyes, only do not harm the man" (Judges 19:24; Gen. 19:8).

Clearly, the intent of all of this is to draw a cohesive parallel between the behavior of the Sodomites, who represent the epitome of evil, and the people of Benjamin who viciously attack the visitors in their midst. This parallel also extends to the respective hosts, the old Ephramite and Lot, who are prepared to do the most loathsome of deeds in order to preserve their guests. While the desire to save their visitors is laudable, to sacrifice innocent victims in their stead is reprehensible. Ultimately, of course, it is not the host but the Levite himself who surrenders his concubine!

In fairness, there are important differences between the two accounts as well. The most significant of these is indicated by Nahmanides, in his lengthy comments to Genesis 19:

> Know and understand that the matter of the concubine at Giva, even though it resembles the episode at Sodom, is not nearly as vile. Those wicked Benjamites had no intention of deterring visitors from their midst.[3] Instead, they were lascivious and wanted to rape the male traveler.... Also, not all of the Benjamites took part as was the case in Sodom where the text reports that "the people of the city, the people of Sodom surrounded the house, young and old, every single one of them" (Gen. 19:4). But here, it was "people of Giva, the scoundrels" (19:22). This refers to the powerful nobles...this is why the other townspeople did not protest. (Nahmanides on Gen. 19:8)

As Nahmanides points out, the criminals at Giva were a small but powerful group; the crime of the townspeople was their failure to intervene. But even as we take note of the critical distinctions, it is clear that the overall thrust of our author is to create an equivalence with the Sodomite episode. In so doing, the basic thesis of these final chapters is reinforced: The people of Israel were chosen by God to break with idolatry and its corrosive values and to instead create a different paradigm predicated upon ethics, morality, and accountability. It now emerges that they have not at all succeeded.

---

3. The people of Sodom attack with the goal of deterring any visitors to their town, as implied by Ezekiel 16:49: "Behold this was the sin of Sodom...pride of plenty, peace and tranquility were enjoyed by her and her surrounding villages, yet they refused to support the poor and downtrodden." In rabbinic literature, the inhospitality of the Sodomites takes on epic proportions. The point of Nahmanides is to highlight that the scoundrels of Benjamin had no such intentions – instead, they were motivated by lust.

DEATH AND DISMEMBERMENT

What follows next in the narrative is most disturbing and is best presented by the verses themselves. With the break of dawn, the concubine is released by her tormentors. Somehow, she manages to return to the house, falling down at the locked and bolted door until sunrise. Her master the Levite now arises and opens the door to resume his journey:

> Behold, the woman, his concubine, was fallen down at the entrance to the house, with her hands on the threshold. "Arise and let us be on our way," he said to her, but there was no response. He put her on the donkey, arose and went to his home. He came to his house, took the carving knife, grasped his concubine and cut her into pieces, limb by limb, into twelve pieces, and he sent them throughout all of the borders of Israel. Whosoever saw it said, "Nothing like this has ever happened; nothing like this has ever been seen from the time that the people left the land of Egypt until this very day! Consider it carefully, take counsel and discuss it!" (19:27–30).

The abject helplessness of the concubine is contrasted sharply with the acts of the Levite. She has fallen at the threshold while he arises. She is placed on the donkey while he leads the way home. She lies still while he fetches the knife. But his enthusiasm now only raises more disturbing questions: Did he sleep soundly as his concubine was being raped throughout the night? Did he not worry about her fate such that he might have discovered her earlier lying at the threshold from dawn until daybreak, even as he kept the door firmly closed? Having discovered her now, has he no words of sympathy or alarm? Does he expect his curt summons – "Arise and let us be on our way" – to be promptly obeyed as if nothing has happened during the intervening night of terror?

Most disturbing of all is what is not stated but only haltingly intimated. Many commentaries reasonably assume that by daybreak, the concubine was dead. They argue that when there was no response to the Levite's summons, it indicates that she was no longer alive. But the text nowhere actually states that she was dead. It is not impossible to imagine that he places her on the donkey and takes her home while she is moribund. Arriving home, he now dismembers her; but is she *dead*? The mind shudders to think of the possibilities that are now reinforced by one more parallel: The Levite uses a large knife to do the deed. In the Hebrew, this instrument is referred to as a *maakhelet*, and comes from a root that means "to consume." It is a knife that is reserved for dismembering animals. In the book of Proverbs, it is compared to a sword: "A generation whose teeth are like swords and whose incisors are knives (*maakhalot*), to consume the poor of the land and the needy from among men" (Prov. 30:14). There is only one other use of the term in the Tanakh and that is from the *Akeda*! In Genesis 22:10, Abraham stretches forth his hand and "takes the *maakhelet*" to slaughter his son, before an angel of God stays his hand. Effectively, our story is implying that the concubine too has been sacrificed, but our Levite is no Abraham. In the *Akeda*, Abraham's love for his son Isaac is incontestable, his fear of God unsurpassed. For the Levite, his concubine is an object, his God an afterthought. While granting that the surrender of his concubine to the mob was a desperate and dire response to a life-threatening moment, his conduct toward her after the outrage is itself outrageous.[4]

THE ISRAELITE REACTION

The reaction of the people of Israel to the gruesome sight is immediate. Four hundred thousand armed men gather "as one, from Dan to Be'er Sheva and the land of the Gilead" (20:1) at Mitzpa. There, the Levite recounts the events (neglecting to take any responsibility for his own behavior!), and the congregation decides to attack Giva. All the men of Israel gather to the town "united as one man" (v. 11). Nobly, before beginning hostilities, the tribes of Israel send a delegation to the Benjamites, demanding the extradition of the perpetrators, but they are rebuffed. Instead, the Benjamites gather twenty-six thousand fighters of their own. The tribes of Israel enquire of God and then attack but

---

4. As *Midrash Tanḥuma, Vayera* 15 explains, quoted by Nahmanides in his earlier comments: "The nature of the world is that a man will surrender his life to save his daughters or his wife; he will kill or be killed. But this one (Lot) turned over his daughters to be abused!" We might add that "this one" – the Levite – turned over his concubine to be raped and then he dismembered her body!

they are defeated, losing twenty-two thousand fighters. After the battle is lost, they cry out to God and enquire whether they should persist on the morrow. The divine response is unequivocal: "attack them" (v. 23), but the next day, the Israelites are defeated again, this time suffering eighteen thousand casualties.

The people cry before God again, fast, and offer sacrifices. Now, God's response is categorical: "Attack them, for tomorrow I will give them into your hands!" (20:28). This time, the tribes station an ambush force of ten thousand men next to Giva. In the meantime, the main Israelite force attacks but quickly feigns retreat, drawing the Benjamites out of Giva as they anticipate another rout. The ambush force now attacks Giva unopposed, kills all of the inhabitants and lights the town on fire. When the pursuing Benjamites look back and see the pall of smoke, they realize the ruse, but it is too late. The ambush force pursues them, the retreating Israelites counterattack and the Benjamites are caught in between and almost totally annihilated – twenty-five thousand are killed and only six hundred manage to escape to Sela Harimon. All of the Benjamite towns are struck down and burnt. With this, the battles end.

UNITED TO DESTROY

Israel's desire to uproot evil and to punish the perpetrators and those that harbor them indicates that there is yet hope for justice. Not every vestige of ethics has been lost. Moreover, it is the first time in the book of Judges that we see the tribes of Israel come together, including those east of the Jordan River who elsewhere tended to be apathetic to the fate of their comrades (see 5:15–17, 8:4–9). At long last, Israel arises to do what is right and pure, free from the terrible scourge of tribalism that plagued and hampered the mission of every single judge in the book. Without doubt, both of these developments are encouraging. Paradoxically, however, all of this positive momentum is for the sake of extirpating another tribe in Israel. Finally charged with a moral vision and unified "as one," the people of Israel utilize their newfound concord to destroy Benjamin!

The irony is amplified by the careful language that the text employs. When they prepare for the first battle and enquire of God, "Who from among us shall go up first to battle Benjamin?" God responds,

"Judah shall be first" (20:18). This verse, coming near the end of the book, is a mirror image of its beginning. Recall the first verse of the book:

> It came to pass after the death of Joshua, that the people of Israel enquired of God saying, "Who shall go up for us first to do battle against the Canaanites?" God said, "Judah shall go up, for behold I have given the land into his hands." (Judges 1:1)

The terrible difference is that at the book's opening, the tribes united to do battle with the common enemy: the Canaanites. Here, the tribes of Israel once again come together to destroy the common enemy, but it is not the Canaanites against whom they are fighting but rather their own compatriots!

The memory of better days, when the tribes shared a destiny that knit them together as one, is also highlighted in the final battle. The exact dynamic of this battle as described above occurs in only one other place in the Tanakh, and that is at the battle of Ai in the book of Joshua. In chapter 7 of that book, the tribes of Israel under Joshua's leadership are handily defeated by the Canaanites of Ai. The people are distressed by the loss and Joshua enquires of God. When the Israelite forces regroup (in Josh. 8), they place an ambush of hidden fighters to the west of the town. Joshua and his men fall back in retreat, the defenders of the Ai pursue them and leave the town wide-open, and the ambush enters and burns it down. As the smoke billows heavenwards, the men of Ai realize that they have been duped, but it is too late. They are completely wiped out by the Israelite force.

Our text, therefore, while purporting to tell us the story of the battle against the Benjamites, is also consciously reminding us of an earlier battle against the Canaanites. However, whereas in the days of Joshua, the tribes of Israel came together to fight their shared foe the Canaanites, here the foe is one of their own. Formulating the matter slightly differently, we might reduce it to the following analogues: The Benjamites of Giva, whose terrible orgy of violence precipitates the crisis, parallel the Canaanites of the Ai. More specifically, we might say that the Benjamites resemble the Sodomites, who championed a particularly noxious strain of Canaanite immorality. The tribes of

Israel who unite to do battle against Giva remind us of Joshua's spirited men who waged war against the Ai. Although they were defeated the first time, they put their trust in God and then, by employing an ambuscade, prevailed.

Noting this intertextuality may help us resolve a difficult exegetical issue. If it is the case that the tribes of Israel gathered together to do what is right and to uproot evil from their midst, if their entreaties to Benjamin to turn over the criminals went unheeded and they were forced to attack their brethren, why do they suffer defeat in the first two attempts? If they enquired of God before battle and were given divine assurances, why do the Benjamites succeed in routing them twice and in killing forty thousand Israelites? While historians may admit to the unpredictable role of fortune in occasionally determining the outcome of warfare, the Hebrew Bible allows for no such possibility. In the Tanakh, triumph or defeat on the battlefield is the exclusive purview of God and is a direct function of human merit or culpability. In other words, when Israel sins, they are defeated; if they are worthy, they prevail. Why then are they defeated twice by the Benjamites, who are clearly the culpable party in the conflict?

EXPLAINING ISRAEL'S DEFEATS

Commentaries ancient and modern have attempted to answer this question with only partial success. Radak, echoing Rashi and drawing on an ancient tradition from the Talmud, offers the following formulation:

> The rabbis explained that this punishment [of defeat] befell Israel because of the transgression of Micah's idol that happened at that time.... Behold, Israel was zealous for the matter of the concubine at Giva, but they were not zealous to extirpate the idol of Micah. They should have been zealous and attacked [the tribe of Dan] in order to destroy that shrine from Israel just as they destroyed this evil. Therefore, they were punished in this conflict. The Holy One blessed be He said to them: "You did not protest when it came to My honor. When it comes to the honor of flesh and blood you now protest?!" (Radak on Judges 20:21, based on Sanhedrin 103b)

In this interpretation, the defeat of the tribes of Israel in the first two battles against Benjamin is not due to any failure on their part insofar as the immediate context is concerned. The tribes of Israel are liable due to another, unrelated indiscretion – their tolerance for the idolatrous shrine of Micah that continued to function "for as long as the House of God was at Shilo" (18:31).

This explanation has the advantage of strengthening the linkage that we noted earlier. The idol of Micah and the concubine at Giva are not simply two terrible episodes narrated at the conclusion of the book that together highlight the risks of weak government and the downward moral spiral of the people of Israel. According to this reading, there is an intrinsic link between the episodes – the first constitutes an affront against God, the second an affront against man. How can the people of Israel completely ignore one while acting fervently for the other? Is not the moral mission of Israel founded upon the bedrock of their acknowledgment of God's sovereignty? Can idolatry be tolerated even as immorality is not?

At the same time, the text nowhere actually draws a connection between Israel's defeats at Giva and their tolerance for the idol of Micah. This is especially troubling given the fact that Israel enquires of God on the eve of both battles against Benjamin and even while God responds, He nowhere shares His displeasure about the idol of Micah. In contrast, when Israel was defeated at Ai and Joshua enquired of God, He was forthcoming with a litany of indiscretions to explain the setback, leaving no room for doubt:

> The people of Israel have sinned and have also abrogated My covenant that I commanded them, and have also taken from the consecrated property, and have also stolen, and have also denied and have also placed [it] in their vessels. The people of Israel will not be able to stand before their foes, for they will flee from before them, for they have become banned. I will no longer be with you if you do not destroy the banned matter from your midst! (Josh. 7:11–12)

A different answer is offered by Ralbag (Gersonides), who pays careful attention to the language employed when Israel enquired of God:

> The people of Israel said: "Who from among us shall go up first to battle Benjamin?" and God responded, "Judah shall be first"

(20:18). But they did not finish the enquiry for *they should have asked whether they would win or be defeated*. If God had told them that they would be defeated, they would not have engaged in battle. This is why setback befell them: Because they did not enquire properly the first time or the second. However, the third time they did enquire properly: "Shall I continue to go out to battle against my brother Benjamin or shall I desist?" (20:28)…This time, the response was complete, and God said, "Go up, for tomorrow I shall give them into your hands." (Ralbag on Judges 20:18)[5]

For Ralbag, there is a proper way to enquire of God, in which the questioner leaves nothing open ended and no room for doubt. The error of the people is therefore not an axiological lapse but rather a technical fault. In not phrasing their enquiry with watertight precision, the tribes of Israel left themselves open to misinterpretation of the divine response, with all its tragic consequences. While this interpretation limits the scope to our immediate context and does not depend – like Radak – on extraneous and perhaps tenuous linkages, it also is prepared to forfeit forty thousand lives for imprecise words.

Among the medievals who relate to this point, Rabbi Yosef Kara is the most resourceful. Combining the features of Radak's reading with Ralbag's thesis, Kara adds one crucial factor to the mix:

They enquired of God utilizing the *urim* and *tumim*,[6] But they did not test their question carefully by enquiring if they would win or lose. Rather they said: "Who from among us shall go up first to battle Benjamin?" (20:18), *thinking that they would triumph*. Therefore, they did not enquire if they should attack Benjamin or desist. That which they asked was answered. Their defeat was because of

---

5. A fuller version of Ralbag's remarks can be found at the end of his commentary on chapter 21 of the book of Judges, where he provides his readers with a lengthy list of key conclusions from the story; see no. 16 on his list.

6. The *urim* and *tumim* are understood to be mysterious names of God enclosed within the folds of the breastplate of the high priest (see Ex. 28:30). According to Numbers 27:21, the *urim* and *tumim* are essential for the protocol of enquiring of God. See above, chapter "Israel's Tragic Lethargy (1:1–36)."

the iniquity of the idol of Micah that they did not protest, while concerning the concubine at Giva they did protest. (Rabbi Yosef Kara on Judges 20:18)

In this formulation, Rabbi Kara deftly combines the earlier elements – a procedural error in not enquiring carefully as well as a more profound misstep in neglecting to address idolatry. But, he suggests, the reason why the tribes neglected to enquire more fully was that they were convinced that they would triumph. Considering the numerical superiority of their fighting force (400,000 versus 26,000), there was no need to entertain the possibility of defeat and therefore their enquiry was only about who should lead the battle against Benjamin and not whether the battle should be fought at all. In other words, the tribes of Israel were guilty of the classic human foible of hubris. While the ultimate cause for their defeat was their indulgence for the idol of Micah, the direct cause was their pride in their own power.

A DIFFERENT EXPLANATION

Applying a literary approach to the problem yields a different solution, soundly based upon our earlier analysis that linked the battles against Giva to the defeat of Ai in the book of Joshua. Recall that our text drew a parallel between Canaanite Ai and Israelite Giva on the one hand, and between Joshua's army and the tribes of Israel on the other. In this analogy, the criminals from Benjamin are recast as Canaanites because of their diabolical behavior, whereas the united tribes of Israel, noble and just, are like the fabled army of Joshua. But Joshua's army, in spite of its virtue, was defeated in their first skirmish with the defenders of the Ai and only prevailed the second time. The reason for their initial rout was because in their midst was an offender by the name of Achan who had taken from the spoils of Jericho in spite of Joshua's explicit ban. It was only after Achan was extirpated that Joshua was victorious.

The critical lesson from that story, as developed at length in our commentary on the book of Joshua,[7] was that all of the people of Israel are responsible for each other, and all the more so are the soldiers of

---

7. See Hattin, *Joshua: The Challenge of the Promised Land,* 124–127.

Israel who fight shoulder to shoulder. Only Achan took from the spoils, but his family, his community and the entire people had a share in his misdeed. This is not because these others were actively involved or even consciously aware of the crime. In reality, we know that this was not the case. Only Achan's small circle of family and friends were privy to the theft. Rather, responsibility here means the shaping of the social context that allows a person such as Achan to act. What kind of social environment contributes to, and nurtures, behavior such as that displayed by Achan? What kind of social environment promotes and encourages behavior such as that embraced by the miscreants of Giva? If that is the question, then responsibility, albeit in attenuated form, lies with everyone.

Effectively, then, when the tribes of Israel are defeated in battle against Benjamin, it is a sure indication that they too are culpable – not necessarily of crimes of commission but at least of crimes of omission. Like Achan who brought ruin upon those who kept his company, there are many among the tribes who are not blameless. Notwithstanding their grand display of moral indignation now, their exaggerated unity the likes of which have not been seen since the book of Joshua, how many injustices have the tribes of Israel overlooked since our sorry account began? How many vulnerable people have been oppressed, hapless victims abused, and acts of evil countenanced or endorsed to have brought us to this moment? To have handily defeated Benjamin on the first attempt would have implied Israel's ethical superiority; to be mightily defeated twice markedly levels the moral playing field.

THE AFTERMATH

In the end, everyone is a loser in our story: The people of Israel who suffer forty thousand casualties, the tribe of Benjamin that is completely decimated, the Levite who shows no empathy to his abused concubine, and the town of Giva that harbors vicious rapists. Like the account of the idol of Micah that is our text's counterpart, there are no heroes.

The resolution of our story and the concluding chapter of the book of Judges brings us little comfort and fails to assuage our misgivings:

> The people of Israel swore an oath at Mitzpa saying, "Let no man
> among us give his daughter to Benjamin as a wife!" (21:1)

This verse returns us to the eve of the first battle, as the tribes gathered at Mitzpa and prepared to attack Giva. At that moment of
indignation, they swore that any Israelite clan absent from the fray
would pay dearly for their dereliction: "They will surely die!" (21:5).
Additionally, they undertook a harsh pledge to punish the tribe of
Benjamin for their transgression by denying them the possibility of
endogamy with the other Israelites. In a tribal society, nothing is
more powerful than tribal identity and nothing more sacred; tribal
allegiances are forged through intermarriage with allied tribes, and
displeasure is indicated by refusal to intermarry. Effectively, this oath
by the tribes of Israel was calculated to exclude the Benjamites from
the people of Israel.

But in the aftermath of the battles against Benjamin, when it
became apparent that the sole survivors of the tribe were the six hundred
fighters who fled the battlefield to Sela Harimon (20:47), the impetu-
osity of the oath was exposed. With no surviving Benjamite females to
marry, and no possibility of marrying females from the other Israelite
tribes, the six hundred survivors now had no chance of rehabilitation,
and Benjamin would therefore become extinct.

In light of this, the remorseful people of Israel craft a plan: They
carefully ascertain if any clans in Israel were absent from the gathering at Mitzpa, such that they would be liable for death for their non-
participation. When they can find no representatives from the Israelite
town of Yavesh Gilead, located east of the Jordan River opposite Beit
She'an, the Israelites send a force of twelve thousand fighters to massacre the town. Everyone is brutally killed, except four hundred virgin
girls who are now turned over to the surviving Benjamites as wives. As
for the remaining two hundred Benjamites who still remain spouseless,
another creative solution is found:

> They said [to the Benjamites], "Behold, every year there is a festi-
> val to God at Shilo… place yourselves in ambush in the vineyards.
> When the daughters of Shilo come out to dance, then emerge

from the vineyards, seize yourselves wives from the daughters of Shilo and go back to the land of Benjamin." (21:19–21)

Sure enough, the Benjamites lie in wait at the festival and steal wives for themselves from among the merry-makers. When the families of the young women protest the unlawful kidnappings, they are told, on the one hand, to show forbearance for their pitiable Benjamite kin and, on the other hand, not to fear the consequences of the oath, since after all the women were not given in marriage (which the tribes swore not to do) but rather were taken by force.

A REPREHENSIBLE RESOLUTION

The book now concludes with Benjamin restored and the people of Israel satisfied with the outcome:

> The people of Benjamin did so, carrying off women according to their number from the dancers whom they stole. They went and returned to their territory and rebuilt the cities and dwelt in them. The people of Israel left from there at that time, each one returning to his family and tribe, and each one to his tribal territory. In those days there was no king in Israel; every man did what was fit in his own eyes. (21:25)

These final events, offered as the resolution for the whole sorry tale of the concubine at Giva, have the pronounced effect of reinforcing the previous outrages. Violence is heaped upon violence, wrong upon wrong. Motivated by a sincere desire to rehabilitate the Benjamites and to preserve them as a tribe in Israel, the people find a solution that admirably addresses the technical aspects of fulfilling oaths in the name of God but entirely overlooks any concern for human life or dignity. The wholesale slaughter of Yavesh Gilead is no way to compensate for the extirpation of Benjamin; the kidnappings and forced marriages of the female survivors of Yavesh along with the oblivious dancers of Shilo can hardly redeem the killing of the concubine.

A careful reading of the matter yields disturbing parallels with another biblical moment. When the people resolve to punish Yavesh

Gilead, they send a force of twelve thousand men to destroy them; only the young virgins are preserved. This recalls another battle in the Tanakh, against the devious Midianites whose daughters had enticed Israel at Baal Peor (Num. 31:1–20). There, as here, twelve thousand fighters were sent, one thousand from each tribe. There, as here, all of the males and married females were put to death and only the young virgins were preserved as spoils. There, as here, the backdrop for the Israelite attack was licentiousness, in the form of Midianite women who beguiled Israel to embrace idolatry. But there, unlike here, the foe was heathen and non-Israelite, the animosities were ancient, and the hostility was real. Like the battle against Ai, our account consciously reminds us of the battle against Midian, but once again turns the equation on its ugly head: No longer are the people of Israel united against their common foe, be they Canaanites or Midianites. No longer can Israel claim moral superiority over the dissolute heathens. At this awful juncture, Israelites battle other Israelites, the idolaters and killers among them almost indistinguishable from the Canaanite pagans that they were wont to disparage and deride.

The last word on this matter belongs to the prophet Hosea, who was active in the kingdom of Israel in the eighth century BCE, hundreds of years after the events of the concubine at Giva. At that time, the Assyrian empire was ascendant and the kingdom of Israel was in decline. It was only a matter of time before the Assyrian overlords would overrun the kingdom and exile its people to the far-off lands east of the Euphrates and Tigris rivers. Hosea was a social critic who inveighed against the injustices committed by the king and the ruling classes; he protested their harsh oppression of the weak and the vulnerable. He also criticized the people's treachery against God – their religious insincerity, their devotions to false gods and to their immoral cults. Offering a caustic summary of all of their indiscretions, Hosea could think of no better formulation than the following:

> They have grievously corrupted themselves like the days of Giva, but He will remember their iniquity and punish their sins. (Hos. 9:9)

Returning to the subject a chapter later, Hosea exclaimed:

From the days of Giva, you have sinned O Israel; there they stood, at Giva you were not triumphant in battle against the evildoers. (Hos. 10:9)

What is remarkable about these references is that they indicate that the memory of what had happened at Giva was still potent centuries later, such that Hosea could mention it to his listeners and they could understand. Giva was about the unspeakable crime of the Benjamites against the concubine and the less-than-blameless battle of the Israelite tribes against them in turn. The sorry events, colored by dismal failure from beginning to end, hinged in equal measure upon personal depravity as well as national debasement. For Hosea, the downfall of society and Israel's undoing as a people could both be directly traced back to Giva.

A KING IN ISRAEL AT LAST

The book of Judges ends with the refrain that binds our story to the idol of Micah and underlines the lack of inspired leadership that made these outrages possible:

In those days there was no king in Israel; every man did what was fit in his own eyes. (21:25)

While certainly resigned and pessimistic, there is yet a ray of hope in this statement. "*In those days* there was no king in Israel" implies that one day a king will arise in Israel to provide the leadership that the people so sorely need. When that king rules, a man will no longer do what is fit in his own eyes; he will be bound to the righteous laws of the king and held liable for his actions. The story of that king is told in the book of Samuel, which follows breathlessly on the heels of Judges. It takes some time for the era of the judges to finally exhaust itself and conclude, with the demise of Eli the aged high priest and the departure of Samuel the prophet and judge. When that epoch ends, Saul son of Kish is crowned as the first king of Israel.

In a corrective of biblical proportions, Saul hails from the tribe of Benjamin, from a small hamlet by the name of Giva (I Sam. 10:26)! In his first act as king of Israel, he is called upon to rescue his compatriots from the clutches of a cruel Ammonite tyrant. This Nahash of Ammon attacks the people of Yavesh Gilead unprovoked and threatens them with mutilation even as they are prepared to accept him as their overlord. Emissaries are sent to Saul, who must rally troops to fight off the aggressor. In order to impress upon them that no dereliction from the battle will be tolerated, Saul dismembers a pair of oxen and sends the grisly sections throughout the border of Israel with a threatening note: "whosoever does not rally behind Saul and behind Samuel, thus shall be done to their cattle!" The response of the people is stunning: a massive force of three hundred thousand men gather, with the tribe of Judah numbering thirty thousand, and "they go forth as one man" (I Sam. 11:7). Saul marches against the foes, handily routs them, and rescues the grateful people of Yavesh Gilead from imminent harm. His unquestioned rule over Israel is thus established.

While it is not the purpose of our study to consider the narratives of the book of Samuel in depth, it should be eminently clear, even from the cursory outline above, that the debacle of the concubine at Giva is here redressed, in its entirety. Saul the Benjamite is from Giva – the hometown of the scoundrels (who may have been his ancestors!). He must save the people of Yavesh Gilead – the very ones who had been massacred by the Israelites to provide women for the surviving Benjamites. He rallies a huge force to do battle and they go forth as "one man" – just as the tribes of Israel had gathered to fight Benjamin. He dismembers the oxen to persuade them – just as the body of the concubine was dispatched to the borders of Israel to cause outrage.

The mirror effect is stunning. Now it is a Benjamite who *saves* the day; it is Yavesh Gilead that is *rescued* from harm; it is an ox that triggers the necessary reaction; it is all of the tribes of Israel that gather as one to fight off the Ammonite tyrant. A brighter future begins to emerge out of this dynamic, in the figure of an effective and upright leader. Keeping the dismal conclusion of the book of Judges in mind, we might describe this new and wonderful chapter in the history of the people of Israel as follows: "In *these* days there *is* a king in Israel; *no man* does what is fit in his own eyes!"

Conclusion

The book of Judges continues the story of the people of Israel's entry into the land. In the book of Joshua, the Israelite tribes traversed the Jordan River, ascended into the hill country and defeated the powerful Canaanite coalitions that opposed them. But military victories are short-lived unless they are followed by settlement of the land, and settlement takes centuries. When Joshua died and his book ended, the process was only just beginning.

As the book of Judges opens, each tribe labors mightily to secure its own allotment of land. There is no national leader of Joshua's stature to unify or to inspire, and the tribes of Israel have yet to forge a national identity. In tribal societies, one's identity is drawn from the family and the clan; therefore, one's highest loyalties in a tribal society are to one's own. After the great wars against the Canaanite armies are over, there is little to hold the tribes of Israel together. As a result, tribalism rules the day in the book of Judges, with narrow, sectarian interests always prevailing over broader, national goals. It is a rare moment in the book when tribes cooperate with each other, and never do they come together as one unified people.

These social and political trials are exacerbated by the great transformation that the people of Israel had to undergo in the transition from desert nomads to settled farmers. Ancient shepherding traditions had to give way to agriculture if Israel was to prosper in the land. Clearing scrub, dislodging rocks, terracing slopes and securing water are all arduous tasks that tax even seasoned agrarians. For the tribes of Israel, the struggles of the new land were overwhelming.

However, the existent cultural and religious values of the inhabitants of Canaan, more than any other factor, presented the tribes of Israel with their greatest challenge. Many modern westerners easily separate religious beliefs from political loyalties and even from personal ethics; ancient near easterners do not. When the tribes of Israel entered the land, there was already a dominant culture in place, that of the Canaanites. And while Joshua's army opened the door to Israelite settlement of the hill country, most of the Canaanite population was not dislodged. As a result, their polytheistic culture survived intact. It was only a matter of time before the Israelites adopted it as their own.

The God of Israel is a "zealous God" (Deut. 4:24). He brooks no compromise with other gods and their moral laxities. In Canaanite polytheism, no god is transcendent; the Canaanite pantheon can therefore articulate no moral absolutes. The demands of the gods focus on one's worship in the temples and not one's conduct in the street and the marketplace. Ethical behavior in a Canaanite milieu is a personal decision, and an enlightened tyrant who pronounces a virtuous fiat need not himself adhere to it. Therefore, moral calculations can be made as a function of utility and tend to favor the lives and possessions of those with power and wealth. When the Israelites entered the land, the austere directive of Deuteronomy to uproot and destroy idolatry rang shrilly in their ears but it did not take long for it to abate. The Canaanite cults were riotous and pleasurable, the moral and spiritual demands of their gods nonexistent. How could the tribes of Israel not be seduced?

So it was that the tribes of Israel strayed from God. In so doing, they experienced subjugation and failure, falling prey to powerful non-Israelite foes who oppressed them. In their troubles, they cried out to God who inspired a leader – a "judge" – to arise and to throw off the yoke of tyranny. These judges, in the main military leaders, restored stability for a time, but after their demise the people once again drifted and wandered off. This is the foundational cycle of the book of Judges; it numbingly repeats itself no less than six times.

With each repetition of the cycle, however, there is a marked decrease in the caliber of the judge who arose to save them. Otniel, a younger contemporary of Joshua and eventual son-in-law of Caleb, was a righteous man. He was followed by Ehud and then by Deborah, upright judges who led the tribes with confidence and, when the time came, left the scene with grace. But Gideon, who followed them, was a more complicated figure, racked with doubts about his mission and never entirely able to overcome the Baal worship that he was charged with extirpating. His son Abimelech, a ruthless and rapacious leader, succeeded his father by force. The way was now paved for the final judges: Yiftah who immolated his own daughter and almost sparked a civil war, and Samson, who spent more time lusting after Philistine women than fighting the Philistine foe.

The final narratives in the book provide us with a most sobering conclusion. There are no specific judges in these final accounts, only unruly criminals operating within a landscape in which tribal loyalties run wild. All of the earlier challenges in the book – every moral failure and every sociopolitical dysfunction – are amplified tenfold in the final chapters. Finally, and not a moment too soon, the book of Judges gasps to an agonizing close with a harsh indictment of its very name: judges cannot save, and deliverance must therefore be sought by another form of government.

The optimism of the book of Joshua was not sustainable; the book of Judges is its needed counterpoint. Idealism must be tempered by realism if it is to address actual problems in the material world. While we pine for perfect solutions to intractable problems, sometimes we must make do and recognize that there is no ultimate fix. The book of Judges offers us a gaze into leaders that are faulty, followers that are flawed, and societies that are broken. It is a vision that can be disturbing and wretched, but is also a more accurate portrayal of the human condition. This makes the book of Judges and its lessons more relevant for us today than we may have realized.

In the Hebrew Bible, there is never a definitive, last word. Every verse asks us to listen, to ponder, to consider and to question anew. Every story is an opportunity for more analysis, a fresh insight, and a bold comment that can inspire. The book of Judges is full of such moments, even as the overall trajectory of the story is negative and pessimistic. Leaving the book behind, chastened by its sobering stories, cautioned by its solemn message, we anticipate better days. May we have the wisdom and the fortitude to hasten their arrival.

Other books in the Maggid Studies in Tanakh series:

Genesis: From Creation to Covenant
Zvi Grumet

Joshua: The Challenge of the Promised Land
Michael Hattin

I Kings: Torn in Two
Alex Israel

II Kings: In a Whirlwind
Alex Israel

Isaiah: Prophet of Righteousness and Justice
Yoel Bin-Nun and Binyamin Lau

Jeremiah: The Fate of a Prophet
Binyamin Lau

Ezekiel: From Destruction to Restoration
Tova Ganzel

Jonah: The Reluctant Prophet
Erica Brown

Nahum, Habakkuk, and Zephaniah: Lights in the Valley
Yaakov Beasley

Haggai, Zechariah, and Malachi: Prophecy in an Age of Uncertainty
Hayyim Angel

Ruth: From Alienation to Monarchy
Yael Ziegler

Eikha (forthcoming)
Yael Ziegler

Esther: Power, Fate, and Fragility in Exile
Erica Brown

Nehemiah: Statesman and Sage
Dov S. Zakheim

The fonts used in this book are from the Arno family

Maggid Books
The best of contemporary Jewish thought from
Koren Publishers Jerusalem Ltd.